SMALL BUSINESS START-UP:

HOW TO WRITE A
BUSINESS PLAN

by Mike McKeever

Nolo Press • 950 Parker Street • Berkeley, CA 94710

IMPORTANT

Nolo Press is committed to keeping its books up-to-date. Each new printing, whether or not it is called a new edition, has been revised to reflect the latest law changes. This book was printed and updated on the last date indicated below. Before you rely on information in it, you might wish to call Nolo Press (415) 549-1976 to check whether a later printing or edition has been issued.

PRINTING HISTORY

New "**Printing**" means there have been some minor changes, but usually not enough so that people will need to trade in or discard an earlier printing of the same edition. Obviously, this is a judgment call and any change, no matter how minor, might affect you.

New "**Edition**" means one or more major, or a number of minor, law changes since the previous edition.

FIRST EDITION	September 1984
SECOND EDITION	March 1986
Second Printing	October 1986
THIRD EDITION	June 1988
Second Printing	November 1988
Third Printing	July 1989

Production	STEPHANIE HAROLDE
	ANDROMACHE WARNER
Book Design & Layout	KEIJA KIMURA
	JACKIE CLARK

ISBN 0-87337-081-3
Library of Congress Catalog Card No.: 84-61578
Copyright © 1984, 1986 and 1988 by Mike P. McKeever

ACKNOWLEDGMENTS

Useful work is rarely accomplished without a cooperative effort. This book was no exception. I would like to heartily thank the people who helped make it better. First and foremost, I want to thank Ralph "Jake" Warner, of Nolo Press. It was Jake's idea to write such a book in the first place. And it was his patience and tact in translating some of my "shoot from the hip" remarks into English that moved this book from a recreational project to a useful, step-by-step manual. Second, thanks to my wife, Margie, and sons, Michael and John, who understood my absences from the really important things, like Little League games.

And special thanks to a number of generous individuals, each of whom knows a great deal about starting and operating a small business. Peg Moran, author of *Invest In Yourself: A Woman's Guide to Starting Her Own Business*, made several suggestions which improved the book greatly. Terri Hearsh, an Assistant Vice-President of the Bank of America, contributed a number of helpful suggestions from a bank loan officer's point of view. Roger Pritchard, a Berkeley, California small business consultant who has counseled hundreds of small business owners, reminded me that in starting any new endeavor, small is often beautiful. Also, thanks to two people who took the time to read the book carefully and offer suggestions. Their input was extremely useful—but I am responsible for any information that is incorrect: Jason Wallach is a friend and a CPA in Santa Rosa; his input was very helpful. Harry Keller of the Santa Rosa SBA office was kind enough to explain several intricacies of that system to me.

Dan Peters took time from starting his new manufacturing business to read the manuscript and offer several valuable suggestions. Sharyn Simmons kindly allowed me to use her business concept as an example of a service business. Larry Healy let me modify his business plan as an example of a manufacturing business.

Steve Elias, of Nolo Press, designed many of the helpful charts and made a number of editorial suggestions. And I want to extend my appreciation to the rest of the folks at Nolo Press who cooperated to move this manuscript from its initial stages to the final product on your bookstore shelf.

Finally, I want to thank all my clients and students who have shared their hopes and dreams with me over the years. Many of their stories appear here in disguised form. I hope you will profit from their experiences as I have.

Mike McKeever
Santa Rosa, California

CONTENTS

Chapter 3   Potential Sources of Money to Start Your Small Business

Chapter 10 After You Open—Some Things to Consider

Chapter 11 Good Books For Small Businesses

BIOGRAPHY

Mike P. McKeever has twenty years experience in financial management, marketing, project management and entrepreneurship. Since 1974, he has purchased, improved, expanded and sold a number of small businesses, including a manufacturing company, a tune-up shop, a gas station, multiple unit residential dwellings, a retail store and a commercial building.

Currently he acts as a business broker and management consultant in Santa Rosa, California, where he helps small business people start and expand their dreams. He has taught sales, marketing and business management at Santa Rosa Junior College and managed the construction of a $3 million dollar mall in his role as vice-president of a merchant's association. He is currently president of WE CARE, a community group interested in reducing the incidence of drug use among Sonoma County school children. Mike has a B.A. in Economics from Whittier College, and a Master's Degree in Economics from the London (England) School of Economics and Political Science.

INTRODUCTION

"Nine to five ain't taking me where I'm bound."

—Neil Diamond, from Thank the Lord for the Nighttime

Here is a book designed to help you raise the money necessary to start or expand your small business. As such, it provides step-by-step instructions on how to prepare a first-rate business plan and loan application. But this book does more than just provide the paperwork techniques necessary to borrow money. Of far more importance, it helps you decide if your business idea will work. This is because one of my principal concerns is to show you how the same financial tools necessary to convince potential lenders and investors that your business idea is sound, can help you decide whether your business idea is likely to be profitable.

Start-Up Money: How to Finance Your New Small Business contains detailed forms and instructions designed to help you prepare a well-thought-out, well-organized business plan and loan package. It shows you how to apply proven financial and business planning techniques used by traditional lenders and investors to your endeavor. Coupled with your positive energy and will to succeed, this book will show you how to design a business plan and loan package you will be proud to show to the loan officer at your bank, the Small Business Administration, or your Uncle Harry. Specifically, you will learn how to prepare:

1. A resume that will demonstrate your business sense;

2. A detailed personal financial statement;

3. An honest and convincing description of your proposed business;

4. A profit and loss projection and cash flow estimate for your new business in a form understandable to banks and other traditional money sources;

5. A marketing plan that demonstrates to you and others how your business will succeed;

6. A convincing personnel and capital spending plan; and

7. A risk analysis, including a profile of your competition.

In addition to giving you the forms and instructions necessary to design your business plan, this book lists and describes the seven most likely sources of new business financing, together with a longer list of secondary business financing sources. Is it better to raise money from a bank than your family? Do you want to borrow money or sell a share of your business? How can you borrow money from yourself to avoid starting with a heavy burden of debt? All of these issues are discussed in detail, and while the final decision as to how to structure and finance your business is yours, this book will prove an invaluable aid to focus your thinking.

In addition, *Start-Up Money: How To Finance Your New Small Business* helps you understand how to approach each potential source of financial assistance once your plan is complete. Your banker will most surely think about your proposal differently than your wealthy uncle and you need to take these differences into consideration when asking for money.

One major theme of the book may surprise you. It's as simple as it is important. You, as the prospective business owner, are the most important person you must convince of the soundness of your business proposal. Therefore, much of the work you are asked to do here serves a dual purpose. It is designed as much to give you the certainty that your business will make money as it is to convince others to back you. The detailed planning process described here is not infallible—nothing is in a small business—but it will help you uncover and hopefully correct potential flaws in your business concept. And if this analysis

demonstrates that your idea won't work, it will give you the opportunity not to start your business. This is extremely important. It should go without saying that a great many business people owe their ultimate success to an earlier decision not to start a business with built-in problems.

Another major theme of what follows is that once you have convinced yourself that your business will work—that is, you have prepared a thorough business plan that includes financial projections you believe in, and which demonstrates a good profit potential—you will have little trouble getting the money you need to start. You may not believe this now, but it's nevertheless true. There are as many potential lenders and investors as there are prospective business owners. If you have a thoroughly thought-out business and financial plan that demonstrates a good likelihood of success, and you are persistent, you will get the money you need to start.

Now, let me confess to one major bias here at the beginning. I believe that most small business owners and founders are better off starting small and borrowing, or otherwise raising, as little money as possible. Put another way, there is no such thing as "raising plenty of capital to insure success." Unless you, as the prospective business founder, learn to get the most mileage out of every dollar, you may go broke and will surely spend more than you need to. But, that doesn't mean that you should try and save money by selling cheap merchandise or providing marginal services. In today's competitive economy, your customers want the best you can give them at the best price. They will remember the quality of what they get from you long after they have forgotten how much they paid.

In practical terms, that means you must buy only the best goods for your customers—the best equipment, the best tools, the best materials, etc. Anything that affects the image your business has in your customer's mind should be first-rate. It also means that you shouldn't spend money on things which don't affect the customer. For example, your customers probably won't care if you drive an old, beat-up car to an office in a converted broom closet as long as you provide them an honest product or service for an honest price. Save the nice car, fancy office and mobile telephone until after your business is a success.

Although they are broken down into easy-to-understand components, and presented in clear and simple English, the planning tools used in this book are sophisticated. Many, such as the cash flow analysis, competition profile, and profit and loss forecast, are simplified versions of the planning techniques used by successful entrepreneurs worldwide. However, I have excluded discussion of several other financial concepts because I do not feel they are essential to getting start-up money. For example, there is no discussion of balance sheets or sophisticated tax planning techniques. While these concepts will ultimately be important to the growth and success of your business, they are secondary to raising money to begin.

Now a few words about a housekeeping detail. In an effort to make sense out of the thousands of types of small businesses, I have roughly divided them into four main ones; retail (including restaurants), wholesale, service and small manufacturing. All the financial tools I present can be used by all four. However, for the sake of simplicity, I follow one particular retail business—a dress shop—in the text. In so doing,

I illustrate most of the planning concepts and techniques necessary to raise money applicable to any business. In addition, Appendix 1 contains a complete sample business plan for a service business, and Appendix 2 contains a sample plan for a small manufacturing business.

Finally, to avoid always using the pronoun "he" when referring to individuals in general, and to further avoid clumsy neologisms like "s/he," and awkward phraseologies such as "he/she" and "he or she," I have compromised by the random use of "he" in some instances and "she" in others. I hope we have arrived at a fair balance.

And a Few More Words

Writing this book was a lot of fun and a great learning experience. As I write this, the book has been in print for about four years, and many thousands of copies have been sold. As a result, I have met or heard from a number of people who have read the book. I remain friends with some of these people. This is the most gratifying part of the whole experience for me. So, I extend this offer: for the price of a lunch, I will be happy to read and critique your written business plan. My advertising and marketing consulting business keeps me busy, so I ask only that you respect my schedule when you ask. Please call me at 707-538-7590 if you wish to take advantage of my offer.

Chapter 1

DO YOU REALLY WANT TO START A BUSINESS?

ONE

A. Introduction

"Hope springs eternal in the human breast," said English poet and essayist, Alexander Pope, several centuries ago. He wasn't describing the state of mind of people starting a business, but he may as well have been. Everyone who goes into business for themselves hopes to meet or surpass a set of personal goals. While your particular configuration is sure to be unique, perhaps you will agree with some of the ones I have compiled over the years from talking to hundreds of budding entrepreneurs.

Independence: A search for freedom and independence is the driving force behind the positive energy of many new business people. Wasn't it Johnny Paycheck who wrote the song: "Take This Job and Shove It"?

Respect: Successful small business owners are respected (both by themselves and their peers). For many people, owning a business is a genuinely fulfilling experience, one that lifetime employees never know.

Money: You can get rich in a small business, or at least do very well financially. Most entrepreneurs don't get wealthy, but some do. If money is a driving force behind your business plan, admit it.

Power: When it is your business, you can have your employees do it your way. There is a little Ghengis Khan in us all, so don't be surprised if power is one of your goals. If it is, think about how to use this goal in a constructive way.

Right Livelihood: Another way to say this is "a search for immortality." Many of us are happiest when we feel we are doing good. From natural foods to solar power to many types of service businesses, a great many cause-driven small business people have done very well by doing good.

If starting a small business can help a person accomplish all these goals, it's small wonder that so many are started. Unfortunately, while the potential for great success is present, so too are many risks. Running a small business is hard, demanding work that requires a wide variety of skills few people are born with. But even if you do possess (or more likely learn) the skills you need to successfully run a business, you will need one more critical ingredient to get started: money. You need money to start your business, money to keep it running, and money to make it grow. This is not the same thing as saying you can guarantee success in your small business if you begin with a fat wallet. Indeed, as you will see, I believe the opposite is as likely to be true. However, all businesses, no matter how lean your business plan, need some money to begin.

This book is designed to help you raise the money you need to start or expand your small business. Specifically, we provide you with instructions on how to draft a comprehensive business plan and loan application. You will need these documents when you ask other people to invest in your business. However, I would like to make one point loud and clear at the outset: even if you do not need money to start your business, it's a good idea to write a business plan. Why? Because as part of the process of completing your business plan, you will discover a great deal about whether your idea is likely to succeed. If you don't write a plan, you won't know whether your business idea is a good one until after the business is open, and then it's too late to do much about it.

If writing the business plan convinces you that your idea is a loser, you will save a great deal of time and money by dropping it before you invest any cash. On the other hand, if writing your business plan convinces you that your idea has an excellent chance of success, you will have a solid foundation on which to generate the honest enthusiasm necessary to convince others to invest in your idea.

Perhaps you have already started a business or know exactly the sort of business you want to start. If so, you may want to skip ahead to Chapter 2, Section D, and then to Chapter 3, and get to work on your business plan. However, you may still be at a more preliminary stage: You're pretty sure you want to go into business for yourself, but you haven't made the final commitment. This chapter and the next one are for you.

Simply put, I've learned that no business, whether or not it has sound financial backing, is likely to succeed unless you, as the prospective owner, make two decisions correctly.

• First, you must evaluate your own skills and personality honestly and decide correctly that you possess the skills and personality needed to succeed in a small business;

• Assuming your self-assessment is affirmative, you must choose the right business.

Books have been written about these subjects I discuss several good ones in Chapter 11. For now, let me recommend *Honest Business*, by Michael Phillips and Salli Rasberry, and *Small*

Time Operator, by Bernard Kamoroff, if you have doubts about your skills or business personality. The next chapter discusses choosing the right business for you. Before you think about this, however, pay close attention to whether you really have the personality and skills suitable to run your own business successfully.

THE COOKERY

Doreen Cook

417 Indian Rock, Taos, N.M. 87571
(505) 641-8759

Lunch · Dinner · Banquet

B.　Are You Qualified to Run a Small Business?

A small business is a very personal endeavor. And while it should honestly reflect your likes and dislikes as well as your ideals and attitudes toward the world, you must focus on one basic fact—to succeed, you will need to ask people for their money every day and must successfully convince at least a substantial number of them to give it to you. By taking money in exchange for your goods or services, you will create intimate personal relationships with a number of people. It makes no difference whether you refer to people who give you this money as clients, customers, patients, members, students or disciples. It makes a great deal of difference to your chances of ultimate success if you understand that these people (no matter what you call them) are exchanging their money for the conviction that you are giving them their money's worth.

Think of it this way. The shadow your business casts will be your shadow. If you are sloppy, rude, crafty, or naively trusting, your business will mirror these attributes. If your personal characteristics are more positive, those of your business will be more positive, too. To put this concretely, suppose you go out for the Sunday paper and are met by a newsie who is groggy from a hangover and badmouths his girlfriend in front of you. Chances are that next Sunday will find you at a different newsstand.

I'm not saying you need to be psychologically perfect to run a small business. But if you're going to be successful, you need to understand two important truths clearly. First, most people are cautious about spending money. Second, your business personality, as well as your product or service, will have a lot to do with whether people do business with you.

Take a moment to review your personal strengths, weaknesses and attitudes toward life in general. Then, examine how they fit with the type of business you want to start. For example, if you love meeting new people and feel comfortable with strangers, you may be bored in a business with little customer contact. Or, if you are generous to a fault and have difficulty saying "no" to anyone, you are unlikely to succeed in a business that requires you to buy inventory cautiously. That your personality will have a direct bearing on your business success may seem painfully obvious. Unfortunately, it isn't. Every year tens of thousands of people fall in love with being their own boss in one or another business, only to learn the hard way that while the business itself may have been a good idea, their participation in it was a mistake.

An example close to the experience of folks at Nolo Press involves bookstores. In the years since Nolo began publishing, they have seen all sorts of people, from retired librarians to unemployed Ph.D.'s, open bookstores because they like to be around books. A large percentage of these bookstores have failed. Why? Because the skills needed to run a successful bookstore involve more than liking to read.

Let's take a moment now to examine an ideal business owner from a potential lender's point of view. After all, banks and other people and institutions that lend money have plenty of experience in what makes small businesses work. But aren't banks often overly cautious in making loans to small businesses? Sure, and for that very reason it makes sense to study their approach.

An experienced lender will look for all of the following in deciding whether to loan money to a new business:

• A business owner who has a track record of profitably owning and operating the same sort of business;

• An owner with a sound, well-thought-out business plan;

• An owner with a cash reserve sufficient to solve the unexpected problems and fluctuations that affect all businesses.

Why does such a person need a loan, you ask? He or she probably doesn't, which, of course, is the point. People who lend money are most comfortable with people so credit worthy (bankable) that they don't need to borrow. However, to stay in business themselves, banks and other lenders must loan out the money deposited with them. To do this, they must lend to at least some people whose credit worthiness is less than perfect. Who are these ordinary mortals who slip through bankers' fine screens of approval? And more to the point, how can you qualify as one of them?

A good bet is the person who has worked for, or preferably managed, a successful business in the same field as the proposed new business. For example, if you have profitably run a dress shop for an absentee owner for a year or two, a lender may believe you are ready to do it on your own. All you need is a good location, a sound business plan, and a little capital. Then, watch out Neiman-Marcus!

Further away from a lender's ideal is the person who has sound experience managing one type of business, but proposes to start one in a different field. Let's say you ran the most profitable hot dog stand in the Squaw Valley ski resort and now you want to manufacture drill presses in Cleveland, Ohio. Arranging financing for your new venture is going to be tough. In your favor is your experience running a successful business. On the negative side is the fact that drill press manufacturing has no relationship to hot dog selling. In this situation, you might be able to get a loan if you hire people who make up for your lack of experience. At the very least, you would need a partner or employee who has a strong manufacturing background, as well as a person with experience marketing machinery. Naturally, both of those people are most desirable if they have many years of successful experience in the drill press manufacturing business, preferably in Cleveland, Ohio.

In short, bankers and investors look for two qualities in a potential business owner. First, the person needs some sort of demonstrable experience and/or skill in running a small business generally. Second, the borrower should have an intimate understanding of the particular business he proposes to run.

Now it's time to take a good, hard look at yourself in another way. What is it that makes you think you will be one of the minority of small business people who will succeed? Don't just shrug off this question—it's important. Over two-thirds of new businesses fail. The large majority of the survivors do not genuinely prosper. Everyone from your spouse to your

banker knows this and is going to ask why your endeavor will be different.

To orient your thinking about how to answer this question, pay close attention to this truth: business is a post graduate course in goal-oriented behavior. Do you have a clear view of your goals? Or, put another way, what exactly do you expect the business to do for you? If you don't have some specific answers, you are in trouble. After all, it's hard to know when you've arrived in any endeavor—business or otherwise—if you have neither map, compass, nor objectives.

Many people start their own business because they can't stand working for others. They don't have a choice. They must either be boss or bum. They are more than willing to trade security for the chance to call the shots. They meet a good chunk of their goal when they leave their paycheck behind. This is fine as far as it goes, but in my experience, the more successful small business people have other goals as well.

One venture capitalist put it this way: "Find me a man with a sound business plan and a neurotic desire to succeed and I'll give him all the money he wants." That's another way of saying that a burning desire to succeed is necessary and critical, but not enough; a sound business idea is also required. A small distributor we know illustrates the other element of this point. He has a well-thought-out business and a sound business plan for the future. Still, he believes that his own personal commitment is the most important thing he has going for him. He puts it this way: "I break my tail to live up to the commitments I make to my customers. If a supplier doesn't perform for me, I'll still do everything I can to keep my promise to my customer, even if it costs me money." This sort of personal commitment enables this successful business owner to make short-term adjustments to meet his long range goals. Sometimes these adjustments are painful. And while it would be an exaggeration to say he pays this price gladly, he does pay it.

Here is a specific job for you to do now. Make four lists, each on a separate piece of paper. Head the first, "My Strong and Weak Points." Include everything you can think of, whether or not you believe it has any relationship to your potential business. Your strong points may include the mastery of a hobby, your positive personality traits, good looks, sexual charisma, and anything else you can think of. Take your time and be generous.

The second list should be entitled "Things I Believe a Business Owner Must Know." Don't worry about being exhaustive. Just set out the items that come to mind right away. Concentrate on general business skills and attributes. We will worry about the specifics that go into running your particular business in Chapter 2.

Entitle the third list, "Things I Really Like to Do." If you enjoy talking to new people, include that. If you like keeping books or working with computers, be sure to include both, and so on. Take a long time on this list. Put down all the activities that really give you pleasure, including personal ones.

Fourth and finally, list your "Specific Business Goals." Exactly, what do you want your small business to accomplish for you? Freedom from 9 to 5? Money (and if so, how much)? Happiness? An early retirement? Maturity? Close contact with people? Respect? Making the world (or your little part of it) a better place? It's your wish list, so be specific and enjoy the process of writing it.

To provide you with a little help, at the end of this chapter we include the sample lists for Antoinette Gorzak, a personal friend with what she hopes is a good business idea—a slightly different approach to selling women's clothing. You will get to know Antoinette better as we go

along. Her strengths, weaknesses, fantasies and fears are surely different from yours. So too, almost certainly, is the business she wants to start. So be sure you make your own list—don't copy Antoinette's.

After you've completed the four lists, spend some time reading them over. Show them to your family and, if you're brave, to your friends, or some other advisor who you feel knows you well and can be objective. If this is a person who knows the tough realities of running a successful small business, so much the better. Otherwise, find a former teacher, fellow employee, or someone else whose judgment you respect. What do they think? Do they point out any obvious inconsistencies between your personality or skills and what you want to accomplish? If so, pay attention. Treat this exercise seriously and you will know yourself better. Oh, and don't destroy your lists. Assuming you go ahead with your business and write your business plan, they will be valuable later.

You have accomplished several things if you have followed these steps. You have looked inside and asked yourself some basic questions about who you are and what you are realistically qualified to do. As a result, you should now have a better idea of whether you are willing to pay the price required to be successful as a small businessperson. If you are still eager to have a business, you have said "Yes, I am willing to make short-term sacrifices to achieve long-term benefits and to do whatever is necessary—no matter the inconvenience—to reach my goals." Your next step is to compare the skills needed in the business you want to begin to the list of skills you have. We show you how to approach this detail in Chapter 2.

1. Antoinette Gorzak: Four Lists

List One: My Strong and Weak Points

Strong Points (in no particular order)

1. Knowledge of all aspects of women's fashion business;

2. Ability to translate abstract objectives into concrete steps;

3. Good cook;

4. Faithful lover;

5. Kind to animals;

6. The belief that to receive a lot, I must give a lot;

7. The ability to make and keep good business friends. (I have had many repeat customers at other jobs.)

Weak Points

1. Impatience;

2. Dislike of repetitive detail;

3. Romantic (is this a weak point in business?);

4. Tendency to avoid problems;

5. Tendency to suffer fools ingraciously. (Sometimes I carry this too far—especially when I'm tired.)

List Two: Things I Believe a Business Owner Must Know

1. How to motivate employees;

2. How to keep decent records;

3. How to make customers and employees think the business is "special";

4. What the customers want (today and, more important in the clothing business, to keep half-a-step ahead);

5. How to sell.

List Three: Things I Really Like to Do

1. Be independent and make my own decisions which affect my future;

2. Keep things orderly. I am almost compulsive about this;

3. Take skiing trips with Jack;

4. Work with good, intelligent people;

5. Cook with Jack;

6. Care about my work.

List Four: My Specific Business Goals

1. Have my own business that gives me a decent living and financial independence;

2. Work with and sell to my friends and acquaintances;

3. Introduce clothing not now available in my city and provide a real service for working women;

4. Be part of the growing network of successful business women (face it, I have a lot of pride and I want to do well and be respected for my success).

Chapter 2

STARTING THE RIGHT BUSINESS

TWO

A. Introduction

By now you should have a good idea of what business you want to start. If you don't, you have lots of work to do before you even think about writing a business plan. Three good places to get more information include *How to Pick the Right Small Business Opportunity*, by Kenneth J. Albert, McGraw Hill, *In Business*, Box 323 Emmons, PA 18049, and *Entrepreneur Magazine*, available at your newsstand. See Chapter 11 for more small business resources.

When considering which business idea to choose, it is helpful to know which businesses have a higher than average failure rate. Recently, a score of experts were asked to name the ten small businesses most likely to fail. Here is the list:

1. Local laundries and dry cleaners;

2. Used car dealerships;

3. Gas stations;

4. Local trucking firms;

5. Restaurants;

6. Infant clothing stores;

7. Bakeries;

8. Machine shops;

9. Grocery and meat stores; and

10. Car washes.

Unfortunately, the experts didn't list the reasons why these businesses fail so often. If your business idea is on the list, it doesn't mean you should abandon it. However, it should be a good reminder to be extra careful to make sure your business plan will work. I've known successful business-people in every category listed, just as I have known people who have failed in all of them.

My task here is to encourage you to match your desires and skills with a business concept you know, like, will work hard for, and which makes economic sense. As part of doing this, I ask that you place your business idea under a critical microscope. Your first job is to honestly acknowledge one great danger that threatens almost every potential entrepreneur. Precisely because your business idea is yours, you have an emotional attachment to its brilliance. You should. Your belief in your business idea will help you wade through all the unavoidable muck and mire that lies between a good idea and a profitable business. However, your ego involvement can also have negative effects. One of these is likely to be a loss of perspective. I've seen people start hopeless endeavors and lose small fortunes because they were so enamored with their "brilliant idea" that they were never willing to honestly examine some very obvious negative factors which doomed their venture from the beginning.

Deciding whether your potential business has **a reasonable chance to succeed is a two-step** process. The first of these steps is to do a preliminary analysis along the lines set out in this chapter. If your idea survives this process, the second step involves writing a detailed business plan.

Ideally, you will use this plan as part of your loan package to raise some of the money you need to begin. However, regardless of whether you get money from others or finance your business yourself, this two-step process will be important to your own decision-making. It should serve as a reality check to your enthusiasm. Or, to restate the central premise of this book, it's at least as important to convince *yourself* that your business has solid financial prospects as it is to convince your potential financial backers.

B. Know Your Potential Business

Sadly, many people enter businesses they know little or nothing about. I did it once myself. I opened an automobile tune-up shop at a time when, seemingly, they couldn't miss. I knew a good deal about running a small business, had a personality well-suited for it, and could borrow enough money to begin. The end of what turned out to be a very sad story is that it took me two years and $30,000 to get rid of the business. Why? Because in my hurry to make a profit, I overlooked several crucial facts. The most important of these was that I knew nothing about either cars in particular or machines in general, and I didn't really want to learn. Not only was I unable to roll up my sleeves and pitch in when it was needed, I didn't even know enough to properly hire and supervise mechanics. In short, I made a classic mistake—I started a business in a "hot" field because someone was foolish enough to lend me the money.

How can you apply my lesson to your situation? Let's say you've heard pasta shops make lots of money and you want to start one. First, if at all possible, get a job working in one. Learn everything you can about every aspect of the business. Pump the owner for details on how she is doing financially and why she isn't doing better. After a few months, you should be an expert in every aspect of pasta making, from mixing eggs and flour, flattening the dough, and then slicing it into strips. Ask yourself whether you enjoy the work and whether you are good at it. If you answer "yes," go on to the second important question: Is the business a potential money maker? You should have a pretty good answer to this question after working in the field for a few months.

If you're unable to find employment in the pasta business, at least make a tour of delicatessens and shops which make their own pasta. Interview the owners. To get reliable answers, it's best to do this in a different area from the one in which you plan to locate your business. Small business owners are often quite willing to share their knowledge once they are sure you will not compete with them.

In short, don't start your small business until you know it from the ground up. I mean this literally. If you're opening a hamburger stand, you need to be able to fry 25 hamburgers at once. If you're opening a gourmet deli, you need to be able to cook everything on the menu. If you're opening a print shop, you should be able to run the presses, do paste-up and layout, as well as keep a coherent set of books. I remember reading a management philosophy some time ago which said that a good manager doesn't have to know every job, only how to get other people to do them. For a small business, that's dangerously naive. When it's your tune-up shop, and your mechanic is sick or drunk, you lose money if you can't do tune-ups. If it's your elegant little restaurant and the food isn't perfect, you're the one who either improves it in a hurry or goes out of business. If you don't like getting your hands dirty, choose a clean business.

C. Be Sure You Like Your Potential Business

Does the business you want to start require skills and talents you possess and/or enjoy? Think about this for a good long time. The average small business owner spends more time with his business than with his family. This being so, it makes sense to be as careful about choosing your business as you were about picking your mate. A few of us are sufficiently blessed that we can meet someone on a blind date, settle down a week later, and have it work out wonderfully. However, in relationships, as in business, most of us make better decisions if we approach them with a little more care.

Oh, and one final thing. Be sure you aren't so blinded by one part of a small business that you overlook all others. For example, suppose you love music and making musical instruments. Running your own guitar shop sounds like it would be great fun. Maybe it would be, but if you only see yourself contentedly making guitars in a cozy little workroom, you'd better think again. Who is going to meet the customers, keep the books, answer the phone and let potential customers know you are in business? If you hate all these activities, you either have to work with someone who can handle them, or do something else.

D. Describe Your Potential Business

What is your good idea? What business do you want to be in? It's time to look at the specifics. Let's say you want to open a restaurant. What will you serve? What will your sample menu look like? What equipment will you need? Note that including french fries means you have to install french fryers, grease traps in the sewer line, and hoods and fire extinguishing systems. On the other hand, by not serving fried foods you will save a lot of money in the kitchen, but maybe you'll go broke when all the grease addicts go next door.

Or suppose you want to sell stereos, video games or sophisticated camera equipment. If so, will you offer a delivery service? Do you plan to have a service department? If so, will you require that people who need repairs come to you, or will you make house calls? What sort of security system will you install to protect your inventory? What about selling records and tapes? What about competition from nearby video equipment retailers? Answers to these questions and dozens more will be crucial to the success of your business.

Now let's get to work. Here is where you write a complete description of how you see your business operating—including both what you will do and what you will avoid doing, or job out. Some of you will say, "Why bother to write it down? I know how I want to operate. And besides, I'm in a hurry to prepare my loan application." Let me tell you from hard, personal experience that you need a foundation document to refer to. If you don't have one, you are all too likely to forget your good plans and resolutions in the heat of getting your business underway. This isn't to say that you won't need to make changes in your original business description as you go along. Of course you will. However, the advantage of having a well-thought-out description of your business to refer back to is that any changes you make will be made both consciously and with consideration. And, as you will see in Chapter 7, much of this preliminary work will also be recycled into your business plan and loan application.

Your business description will also be of help after you start the business because it will help you see if you are really meeting your objectives. It's all too easy to delude yourself into keeping a business going that will never meet its goals if you approach things with a "Just another month or two and I'll be there" attitude, rather than comparing your results to your goals. The black and white of your written business description will help you face facts if things don't work out as expected. For example, if you planned to be making a living three months after start-up, and six months later you're going into the hole at the rate of $100 per day, your business description should help you see that changes are necessary.

Enough said. How do you write a complete description of your proposed business? It's not difficult if you follow the suggestions on the next few pages. For the purposes of this exercise, I divide businesses very broadly into wholesale, retail, service and manufacturing. Here are definitions of the four basic types of business:

Retail: A retail business buys merchandise from wholesalers and manufacturers and sells it to end users without changing the goods in any significant manner. Some retailers provide service and repair facilities, while most do not.

Wholesalers: Wholesalers buy merchandise from manufacturers or jobbers. Normally, a wholesaler maintains an inventory of a number of lines. A wholesaler sells to retail businesses only and does not sell to end users, to avoid competing with his retailer customers. Wholesalers normally offer delivery service and credit to customers. This type of business is

characterized by low gross profit margins and high inventory investment.

Service: People with a particular skill sell it to end users. Occasionally, a service business sells products as an ancillary function. Service people are either expert in their chosen field or they usually don't last long. Service business customers normally come from repeats and referrals. It's common to have to meet state licensing requirements.

Manufacturing: Manufacturing businesses assemble components or process raw materials into products usable by consumers. This type of business ranges from an artisan making craft items to General Motors. All manufacturers face long lists of challenges. Larger manufacturers can afford to hire well-qualified people to assist them, while small entrepreneurs must do an incredible array of tasks for themselves.

Warning! If your small business idea will involve you in several of these basic types of business, it may be too complicated for you to run efficiently. As a general rule, new business start-ups work best when their owners know exactly what they are about and strive for simplicity.

To design your business description, answer the following questions, depending on the type of business you plan to enter. Once you reduce your answers to writing, turn them into a narrative. Take your time and do a thorough job. It's very likely that the first time you attempt this task, questions will occur to you that you have never considered previously. If so, figure out a good answer and rewrite your description. The important thing is not how long it takes to do this, but that you end up with a realistic, well-thought-out business plan. After all, it's cheaper to answer questions and solve problems on paper than it is with real money, which is what will happen if you don't plan carefully.

DO-RITE
TYPESETTING

MORT A. DELLA

2110 Murray St., Rohwer, Ark. 71666   (501) 549-1911

1. Retail Business Owners

• Describe my typical customer. What will his or her age, income, taste, place of residence, place of employment, family status be?

• What is the image of my shop? How will it be different from my competition?

• What is the competition's location, size, strengths, weaknesses?

• What merchandise will I sell? Where will I buy it? How much will I charge? What does the competition charge?

• How big a building do I need? Where should it be located? How much rent will I have to pay? Will I have to make any alterations to the building? How much will that cost?

• How many employees will I need? What qualifications will they need? What will I have to pay them?

• What days and hours will I be open? Will my location affect my hours of operation? (It will if you locate in a shopping center.)

• How will I contact my potential customers? What's my marketing plan? Does it include advertising? Or better yet, have you figured out creative (and less expensive) ways to reach potential customers without buying ads?

2. Wholesale Business Owners

• What product lines will I carry in inventory? Which will I sell, but order from other suppliers as needed? Where will I buy each item I sell?

• What product or service can I offer potential customers that is better than what they get now?

• Are there exclusive distributorships available to me?

• How will my prices compare to prices my potential customers are paying now?

• How much profit can I expect on each sale? What credit terms can I obtain? How quickly must I pay for the goods?

• Who are my potential customers and what do they need?

• How big a building do I need? Where should it be? How much rent will I have to pay? Will I have to make any alterations to the building?

• How many employees will I need? What qualifications must they have? What will I pay them?

• Will I deliver the merchandise? If so, how?

• Do I need a catalogue? What types of advertising or networking will I do?

3. Service Business Owners

• What is my service and who will use it?

• How will my service save clients time and/or money or provide them a better quality of service than they get now?

• Who is my competition? How will I be different or better?

• Who are my potential clients? How do they purchase or use the service I will offer now?

• How do my qualifications fit with the requirements of the service? Am I the best person my potential clients can find?

• How do I contact my clients? Advertising? Membership in voluntary organizations? Lectures and workshops? Referrals? If referrals, how will I get them?

• How much will I charge? Will I charge by the hour or by the job? What about speculative work? Will I take jobs on commission or will I demand a fee for all service?

• Will I hire assistants? When? How will I pay them?

• What's my image? Do I need high price office space or can I work just as well from my home? If I plan to rent space, where will I locate and how much will I pay? Is it important to be near my customers?

• Do I have a client or clients to start? Or, will I start cold?

• Are there people offering services similar to mine who I can cooperate with to get my business established?

4. Manufacturing Business Owners

• What is my product and how is it different from others? What other products most closely compare with it?

• What is the sales history of the most closely competitive products?

• What is the market profile of the most closely competitive products? Who buys them? (Income, age, location, etc.)

• What are the trends, fashions, and new developments in the product line I want to manufacture?

• Are similar products made by small, local companies, or will I be competing with large, national or international outfits?

• How will I market my products? Will I use sales representatives? Salaried salesmen? Direct mail? What are my costs and benefits of each type of selling? How do my competitors sell?

• What other products do I plan to develop and sell? If I am successful on a small scale, do I plan to sell out to a larger company, or try to compete nationally?

• Does my process create toxic or polluting materials? If so, what regulatory agencies will I have to deal with?

• Can I buy some pre-assembled parts or do I have to make everything from scratch?

• What facilities do I need? Equipment? Raw materials? Access to transportation? Plant? And so forth. Where can I find them? How much will it cost? What skilled labor do I need? Where can I find it and how much will it cost? Are there unions involved? If so, is it better to move to a place where non-union labor is available?

• What do my abilities and time allow me to handle personally? Who will do the other jobs? What about accounting and marketing? If my proposed business involves engineering, research and development, labor relations and purchasing, as well as actual manufacturing (even if this is only baking cookies in the kitchen), who will do each task and how will they be paid?

5. Project Developers

• Am I confident of the price I can sell the project for when it is complete? What do similar projects sell for, and how long does it take to sell a typical project?

• Am I sure that I have accurately estimated all the costs it will take to complete the project? Do I have the cost history of similar projects to verify my cost projections? What will be the effect of having costs come in 10%-20% higher than estimated?

• How long will it take to complete the project and then sell it? Am I sure of the time factors? What will I do if the project is late?

• How much cost will be needed to complete the project and hold it for a reasonable selling period? Where will the cash come from? If I plan to borrow, has the lender seen and approved my plans for the project?

• How will I pay the loan back? What happens to the project and to my profit if the economic climate changes for the worse between the time I start the project and the time I am ready to sell it?

Here is one sample business description, again using Antoinette Gorzak's preliminary description of her clothing store as a model. You will find three additional business descriptions in Appendix 1-3 at the back of the book.

PRELIMINARY BUSINESS DESCRIPTION: ANTOINETTE'S DRESS SHOP

by Antoinette Gorzak

Antoinette's Dress Shop will be a women's clothing store designed to serve the growing market of women under 40 years of age. Antoinette's will specialize in fashionable, reasonably-priced clothing suitable to this city's working environment. Antoinette's will specialize in business suits, pants suits and dresses for daytime wear, together with normal accessories like purses and belts. We will publish clothing tips for working women and schedule regular fashion shows. We will make prompt minor alterations at no charge. We offer a relaxed atmosphere with personalized attention and unlimited fitting room time. Antoinette's will be open Monday through Friday from 11:00 a.m. until 9:00 p.m. and on Saturdays from 10:00 a.m. until 6:00 p.m.

E. Does Your Business Fit Into the Overall Scheme of Things?

Let's now assume you have a good description of your proposed business, and the business is an extension of something you like to do and know how to do well. Perhaps you have been a chef for ten years and have always dreamed of opening your own restaurant. So far so good—but you aren't home free yet. There is another fundamental question that needs answering. Does the world need, and is it willing to pay for, the product or service you want to sell? For example, do the people in the small town where you live really want an Indonesian restaurant? If your answer is "yes," because times are good and people have extra money to experiment on new things, ask yourself what is likely to happen if the economy goes into a slump ten minutes before you open your doors.

To make this point more broadly, let's use a railroad train as a metaphor for our economic society. And let's have you, as a potential new business person, stand by the tracks. How do you deal with the train when it arrives? You have three choices. You can get on and ride. You can continue to stand by the tracks and watch the train disappear in the distance. Or you can stand in the middle of the tracks and get run over. To continue this metaphor, let's now assume the economic train has three engines: taste, trends and technology. Together they pull the heavy steel cars which can give you a comfortable ride or flatten you. Let's take a moment to think more about each of these engines.

• **Taste:** People's taste drives many of the changes our society speeds through. For example, in the 1970's, many of us changed our taste in automobiles from large gas guzzlers to small, well-built cars. American manufacturers didn't recognize this change in taste until they almost went broke. The Japanese were in the right place with small, reliable cars and realized great prosperity.

To take another example, recently many groups in society have rejected double knits, polyester fabrics, etc. and have returned to wearing clothes made out of natural fibers. As a result, many people have succeeded with import businesses bringing in fabric from places like Bali, India, and Guatemala, where good quality natural fabrics are still produced. What does this mean to you? Look at your business idea again. How does it fit with today's tastes? Is your business idea part of a six-month fad? Are you going into something that was more popular five years ago than it is now and is declining rapidly? If so, you are likely to go broke no

matter how good a manager you are and how much you love your business?

• **Trends:** It's one thing to understand that people's taste has changed and will undoubtedly change again and again, but it's a lot harder to accurately predict exactly what will be popular in a few years. Nevertheless, a little research can do wonders. Read everything you can about your field of interest. The *Readers' Guide to Periodicals* at the library is a good place to find a general range of material. Talk to people in similar businesses. Contact trade associations, attend trade shows, and read back issues of magazines aimed at your proposed field. Your goal is to know enough about your proposed business to spot the trends that will continue into the next decade. For example, if you're interested in opening a piano bar serving alcoholic beverages, you should know that the consumption of hard liquor is down sharply in recent years and that certain types of wine and imported beer are doing very well. Putting this information together with other facts about where you want to locate and who you think your customers will be, etc., should give you a pretty good idea of what drinks you should offer. For example, you might decide to serve a number of varieties of fine wine and imported beer, and forget about a hard liquor license altogether.

• **Technology:** This is a fancy name for the new items just coming out on the market. Technology is your innovative kitchen appliance, your home computer, NASA's new space craft, and even the proverbial better mousetrap. For example, lots and lots of people are working feverishly to come up with better video games, laser tooth brushes, wrist watches, TV's, and the like. Sometimes it takes years to perfect an item. That can be good news for small business people, as there is plenty of time to prepare to profit. Perhaps you've heard of Digital Audio Tape (DAT). This is the new sound technology perfected in Japan that is so good, and reproduces sound so clearly, that American tape and record producers have convinced Congress not to let the tape be imported until a foolproof method of preventing home duplication has been invented. Record and tape makers are terrified that the sales will drop precipitously if people can borrow a record or tape from a friend and easily duplicate it using this new technology. At this writing, it is not clear what opportunities for entrepreneurs may develop in the DAT area; but one thing seems to be sure—before long many clever people will surely profit handsomely from the opportunities that arise.

Of course, there is a down side to new technology too. It often involves high risk. There's no guarantee of success just because the product is new. In fact, something like 80% of the new products introduced into the marketplace die a quick death. Remember 3-D movies, the Edsel, and pet rocks?

What should you do to take advantage of new technologies? First, recognize that large scale, new technology ventures require vast amounts of money and will be beyond your reach unless you plan to have your small business grow in a hurry. For example, most genetic engineering companies will lose money for years before developing a big hit. However, there are often ways creative small business people can find to participate in new technological trends. For example, many computer software companies started with little more than a good idea and an Apple II computer. Or to think even smaller—but not necessarily less profitably—lots of carpenters have done very well making custom computer work stations.

Pay attention to new developments in your chosen field and think about how you can take advantage of them. With all the small computers being sold, many people will make a good living

repairing them. Maybe that's a good business for you. Or, if you plan to open a television repair shop, you should know that in the next few years many, if not most, televisions will have stereo sound. If you are the first TV shop to specialize in stereo in your area, you may do very well.

In short, new technology is a mighty engine which can pull the economy in new directions at terrific speed. Be sure you are riding on the train and not picking daisies on the tracks in front of it.

With this discussion of taste, trends and technology, I have attempted to focus your attention on the broad movements in the greater national and world economy which can affect your business idea. You must pay attention to them. But, remember that there are similar trends in your local community. It's at least as important that you pay attention to these. For example, perhaps you live in a farming community with no manufacturing industries and many migrant workers. It is unlikely that a high fashion clothing store would do well there, but you might do very well selling a new lighter, stronger, cheaper work boot, or chain saw, or stump puller.

F. Will Your Business Make Money?

How can you tell if your business idea will be profitable before you do it? The honest answer is, you can't. This essential fact makes business scary. It also makes it fun. Just because you can't be sure you will make money, however, doesn't mean you should throw up your hands and ignore the whole problem. You can and should make some educated guesses. I like to call them SWAGS ("Scientific," Wild Ass Guesses). The fun part is making your profit estimate SWAGS as realistic as possible and then making them come true.

Some people have a bigger problem than others when opening a new business. These are folks who are positively enamored with their business concept and are desperately eager to begin. They are so smitten and eager to start, they have no patience with the economic realities involved in their business. If you recognize this tendency in yourself, it's really important that you prepare the financial forecast carefully and pay attention to what it tells you.

The best way to make a SWAG about your business profitability is to divide it into three separate components. These are your:

- Sales volume component,
- Variable costs component, and
- Fixed cost component.

I know this sounds suspiciously like business planners' gobbledygook, but stick with me for a minute and you will quickly see the sense of these planning tools. We discuss them briefly here and more fully in Chapter 5, Sections C, D, and E.

For a detailed discussion and example of how these cost factors apply to the project development business, please turn to Appendix 3 for the development example.

1. Sales Volume Component

First, estimate your monthly sales volume for your first two years of operation. This is both the hardest thing and the most important. Much of your hope for success rides on how accurately you estimate sales volume. While there are whole libraries written on how to control and forecast costs, there are no such libraries on how to forecast sales volume. If there were, business book authors wouldn't have to write another

word. They could simply sit back and cash in on their rare skill. Most business books I have read take sales volume as a given and go from there. Your job is to make a pretty good SWAG about sales.

How can you do it? About the best way I know is to compare your business and market to already existing businesses and then allow for the factors that will make you different. This can work pretty well in the retail or wholesale business. It's bound to be more iffy if you plan to begin a service or manufacturing enterprise. The important thing to remember is that you're honestly trying to decide if your business will be profitable. That means basing your sales forecast on the volume of business you really expect, not on how much you need to take in to make a good profit. Be sure to make your sales volume forecast without regard to your cost structure.

Example: Let's look at how our new friend Antoinette Gorzak accomplished this task. Assume Antoinette is still considering whether to open a 2,000 square foot dress store in a downtown shopping mall. She has looked at all the competition and decided her city really needs a dress shop for younger, upwardly-mobile working women.[1] The Chamber of Commerce says the average retailer in the mall does annual sales of $100 for every square foot of floor area.

After checking with other clothing retailers, reading trade magazines, visiting several similar stores in other cities, and integrating this with her own experience in the business, Antoinette decides this estimate is slightly on the conservative side of reasonable and adopts it. This means her annual sales should be $200,000.

---

[1]As you read through this book, you will see that Antoinette has invested a great deal of time and effort in deciding she is selling the right product in the right market and she has the experience to know she can run a tight shop. For now, just take this on faith.

(2,000 square feet x $100). A simple way to arrive at her estimated monthly sales volume would be for Antoinette to divide this $200,000 by twelve months and get $16,666 per month. In the dress business, Antoinette knows, this is overly simplistic. In retail selling, there are generally two peak times: Christmas and Spring. The clothing business, especially the kind of shop Antoinette plans to open, is slow in the summer and in January and February. Also, Antoinette figures that sales will probably be a little lower than the average for the first few months, until her advertising campaign catches on and people know she is open. Accordingly, she projects that if she opens March 1, her first year sales plan would look like this:

March	20% off average because of just opening, $13,320
April	10% off average because of just opening, $15,000
May	20% over average because of cumulative effects of grand opening & seasonal peak, $20,000
June	An average month, $16,666
July	10% below average due to seasonal slow-down, $15,000
August	10% off due to summer slow-down, $15,000
September	10% above average due to back to school, $18,330
October	10% above average due to fall season, $18,330
November	20% over average due to fall season, $20,000
December	40% over average due to Christmas, $23,330
January	30% off average because everybody's broke after Christmas, $11,666
February	20% off average, $13,330

All those monthly sales add up to $199,972 for the first year.

That's one way to estimate sales for a retail store, and it's a good one. Chain supermarkets and drug stores have refined the art of estimating sales to a science. Of course, they have the advantage of learning from their experience with their other stores. Even so, they occasionally make bad estimates. Nevertheless, here's how some of them do it. Supermarket executives first gather statistics on how much the average person living in the town in which they plan to build a new store spends every week in grocery stores. These numbers are available by obtaining total sales volume of grocery stores from the state sales tax agency; normally that data is broken down by county.

Next, they make a current estimate of how many people live in the county, or other area for which sales volume statistics are gathered. Dividing the sales volume data by the number of people in the area gives them the average sales per person from grocery stores. Then they compare that number with state averages. If it's higher, it might mean that the area has a higher than average income per person. They can verify that by referring to the United States Census, which lists average income per family and per person for every census tract in the country. If the income per person is average, or below average, and sales per person are higher than average, it probably means that people come from surrounding areas to do their shopping. If the sales per person are lower than average in your area, it might mean that income is below average or that people leave the area to do their shopping. Both of those assumptions can be verified as discussed above. On the basis of this sort of data, together with an analysis of how many people live in the area, what the competition is, etc., supermarket executives can develop an accurate estimate of sales volume for a new store.

Estimating volume for a service business is a different matter entirely. Here's how one professional personnel recruiter sees her business:

(This discussion refers to the Central Personnel Agency business plan in Appendix 1.)

If you plan to be in a service business, you'll need to go through similar arithmetic to develop your sales volume forecast. Of course, service businesses vary greatly. You should know what makes yours tick and use that information to construct a business that will run like a good watch.

If you plan to be in the manufacturing or wholesale business, you'll need to combine some of the concepts discussed above to estimate your sales volume SWAG. Detailed discussions of that process are beyond the scope of this book. For now, just know that sales volume forecasting is both very difficult and very important. If your business has a trade association, they may be asked to provide some comparison factors. Refer to the manufacturing business plan in Appendix 2 to see how one company did it.

CENTRAL
PERSONNEL
AGENCY

71 wooster st., new york city 10012 (212) 966-1300

SALES VOLUME ESTIMATE FOR
CENTRAL PERSONNEL AGENCY

"The key to my employment agency is this: I know from my experience in the field that it's harder to find qualified people than it is to find job openings. I estimate I can find about ten job openings per week starting from scratch. So, when I start, I will allow myself two weeks to find twenty job openings. After the first twenty, I'll get plenty of openings by referrals and repeats. I also know from experi-ence that I can fill about two-thirds of the job openings I get. Since my income goal is to gross $3,000 to $4,000 per month, and since I know that the average job order filled is worth $500 to $600 in gross fees, I needed twenty openings to be sure of meeting my monthly sales volume goal

"Finding good people is the hard part. It takes me up to twenty interviews to find one excellent person. Some of these interviews are done over the phone, but just the same, I allow one hour per interview. Also, I know that it takes an average of three good people sent out on interviews to fill one job. Of course, once I have a good person, I send that person out on every interview I can. This means that to fill six to eight job orders per month and meet my gross income goal, I need 25 to 30 good people on file. Since it takes an average of one hour per person and twenty interviews to get one good person, I have a lot of interviewing to do. I can average eight per day and it will take me about 60 days of interviewing to build a base of qualified people. This means I anticipate three months of fairly low income before I begin to reach my income goals."

2. Break Even Analysis

Now that you've made an estimate of the sales volume you really expect, ask yourself this question: "What sales volume will I need each month or year to break even just to pay the bills?" If you can answer this question with confidence, you will be able to make preliminary decisions about whether or not to go further with the business plan at an early stage.

Think of it this way: if the sales you really expect to make will not pay you enough profits so that you can pay your bills, your business will not last very long. On the other hand, if the sales you really expect to make will pay you a lot more than enough to just pay the bills, then the business idea may be a good one. This question is one experienced entrepreneurs often ask as part of deciding whether or not to look at a venture closely. Of course, you can use it as a "quick and dirty" profit analysis as well, but don't forget to complete the full profit and loss forecast as presented in Chapters 5 and 6, or you may find yourself in a bad situation simply because you didn't take the time to do a full analysis. Remember, "quick and dirty" means just that: it is a great screening tool, but you need a more complete analysis before spending any money.

Step 1:   Fixed Costs[2]

The first step in estimating the sales volume you need to just pay your bills is to estimate your fixed costs. Here's how. Make a list of the monthly costs of the business which will stay about the same each month. This list will include cost items such as rent, utilities, salaries of

---

[2]Another name given to the fixed costs is Operating Expenses; most profit and loss statements show Operating Expenses as the last deduction from sales before showing the profits.

employees, perhaps your own personal draw from the business, insurance payments and so forth.

Your fixed cost list should also include some costs which may change from time to time, as long as the changes are the result of a conscious decision you make about the particular cost item. For example, your promotion budget may show changes occasionally as you increase or decrease advertising to take advantage of slow or busy times. However, if you decide in advance that you will regularly spend money to promote your business, this expenditure should be included in the fixed costs.

Your objective in making this list is to develop a dollar amount of expense that you are committed to pay every month. This is your "nut" or the dollar figure you must be able to pay in order to keep the business viable.

To illustrate, let's go back to Antoinette's Dress Shop and see how Antoinette estimates her fixed costs on a monthly basis:

Rent	$ 2,000 per month
Wages	
(average including fringe	3,300 per month
Utilities	200 per month
Advertising	500 per month
Telephone	100 per month
Supplies	350 per month
Insurance	200 per month
Freight	350 per month
Accounting/Legal	150 per month
Bad Debts	100 per month
Misc.	100 per month
TOTAL	$ 7,350 per month

Having completed this simple exercise, Antoinette has gained important information—she now knows she must sell enough every month so that she has at least $7,350 left after paying for the merchandise. If she doesn't, she obviously won't avoid bankruptcy for long. Also, note that Antoinette has not shown any salary or draw for herself in the costs. To prosper, she obviously must not only cover fixed costs, but must take in enough to pay herself a decent salary as well.

A note about freight: Freight expenses are often included in Cost of Sales as a variable cost instead of in the Fixed Expenses portion of the income statement. Whether they should go there or here depends on your business. Antoinette included them here because she pays no freight for shipments to customers and because the freight for the shipments she receives from the manufacturers and wholesalers tends to be about the same each month.

Step 2.   Incremental Costs

After you have made an estimate of your fixed costs, the next step is to figure out how much you will pay for the merchandise for every sale. To oversimplify a bit, assume Antoinette sells dresses for $250 and pays $125 for each. Obviously, her incremental cost, or cost of the next sale, is $125, which is also the amount she has left over to pay for her fixed costs and profits after paying for the dresses.

The next question you will want to ask is: How many dresses must Antoinette sell for $250 in order pay her fixed costs of $7,350. The answer is 58.8 dresses ($7,350 divided by $125 profit on each dress.) This seems simple enough, but in the real world, it isn't. To illustrate why, remember that Antoinette sells many different types of dresses, suits, handbags and so forth, and they all have different prices and different

costs. In other words, no simple division of profit per sale into fixed costs will work. Fortunately, there is a much more useful way to use this information to estimate the sales revenue needed to pay fixed costs as set out in Step 4 below.

Step 3.   Developing Average Profit Per Sale

Before you can estimate the sales volume needed to break even, you first need to know the gross profit per average sale. Remember, gross profit is the profit remaining after subtracting the cost of the mechandise, or incremental costs, from the selling price.

There are two ways to get this average number. If you have a profit and loss statement from your business from prior months, simply subtract the total incremental costs, or cost of sales, from the total revenue or gross sales to get the average gross profit for the period.

If you don't have a history, you'll have to work a little harder. Don't despair—it's worth it. Make up a chart that shows each product category you will be selling. After the category name, put the gross profit for the category, expressed in percentage terms. Next, take a guess as to how much, in dollars, of each category you'll sell in an average month; then multiply the sales dollars in each category by the gross profit percentage to get the gross profit dollars per category per month. Last, add up the gross profit dollars and divide by the total sales dollars, to get the average expected gross profit percentage for your business.

Here's how it will look:

AVERAGE GROSS PROFIT ESTIMATION:
ANTOINETTE'S DRESS SHOP

Category	Gross Profit %	Sales Dollars	G.P. $
Dresses	49.0	10,000	4,900
Accessories	64.1	3,122	2,000
Mark down sales	30.0	3,000	1,000
Total	49.0	16,122	7,900

When making up this chart, the total gross profit percentage number is the last number to write in the chart; that's obvious because you will know all the other numbers first.

Note: Sharp-eyed readers will note that this exercise is similar to the average cost of sales chart shown on page FIVE/5. This chart focuses on the gross profits, while that chart has a different focus.

Step 4. Estimating the Sales Revenue Needed to Pay the Fixed Costs

The easiest way to find the dollar sales amount that Antoinette needs to have enough profits available to pay the fixed costs is to take the profits per sale or average gross profits and express them as a percentage of the selling price. Using the average gross profit of 49% from the above chart to find out how much Antoinette must sell each month in order to pay her fixed costs, simply divide the 49% profit per average sale into the $7,350 fixed costs. Here's how that works:

1. $7,350 fixed costs divided by profit per sale expressed as percentage (49%) equals sales needed to break even.

2. $7,350 divided by 49% = $7,350 divided by 0.49 = $15,000.

By the way, don't forget to convert the percentage to a decimal before you divide; otherwise you will get a funny number. To make sure you have done it right, multiply the sales answer you get by the percentage of profit per sale to see if you get the same number as the fixed costs. If you don't get the same number, you have done something wrong. If you have trouble with percentages, relax. You have lots of company. Ask someone who knows percentages to give you a hand.

In this example, Antoinette needs $15,000 in sales each month in order to pay her fixed costs. After she sells the $15,000, she gets to keep 49 cents of every dollar that comes in the store over and above the $15,000.

Here, then, is the break-even formula: divide the estimated fixed costs, expressed in dollars, by the gross profit from sales, expressed as a percentage (decimal), to get the forecast amount of sales required to pay the fixed costs.

STARTING THE RIGHT BUSINESS

Please refer to Chapters 5 and 6 for a complete discussion of how to create a thorough analysis of your expected profit picture.

3. Fixed (Operating) Costs Component

To help decide if your business is a good idea, make a SWAG for all your sales revenue and your fixed and variable costs for two years. For the first step in that process, write your sales estimate each month for two years. From that, subtract the variable cost (cost of sales) necessary to achieve this amount.[3] The remainder, your gross profit, is available to pay fixed (or operating) costs and profit. Next, subtract your monthly overhead or fixed (operating) costs from your gross profit. The remaining number will be your profit. If it's a minus number, it's a loss.

To illustrate this idea, let's go back to Antoinette's Dress Shop. Assume Antoinette doubles the cost of everything that comes into the store and plans no special sales for the first year. She allows one percent for packaging and other minor costs attributable to each sale. This means her variable cost is 51%[4] of her sales dollar. If Antoinette's first year sales are $200,000, her cost of sales will be 51% of $200,000, or $102,000, leaving $98,000 to pay for

rent, wages, electricity, advertising and so forth. Let's look at how Antoinette itemizes her fixed costs on a monthly basis:

Rent	$2,000	per month
Wages (average, including fringe)	3,300	per month
Utilities	200	per month
Advertising	500	per month
Telephone	100	per month
Supplies	350	per month
Insurance	200	per month
Freight	350	per month
Accounting/Legal	150	per month
Bad Debts	100	per month
Misc.	100	per month

These fixed costs add up to $7,350 per month, or $88,200 for the year. Subtracting the fixed (operating) costs expenses of $88,200 from the gross profit of $98,000 leaves Antoinette an annual salary of $9,800, assuming she hasn't borrowed money to get started and thus has no debts to repay. This is a fairly low overall profit, even for the first year. Antoinette needs to ask herself what she will do in those slow months (January, February and March), when the fixed (operating expenses) costs total more than the gross profit. And what about those other months (April, July and August) when she can cover her fixed costs, but can't pay herself a full salary? She also needs to ask herself what she can do to improve her profit prospects both immediately and in the future.

Here's the way this information looks in profit and loss (P & L) or financial forecast format, as summarized for the entire year:

---

[3]You should know what this is by now. For example, if you're in a service business and the service consists mostly of your time, your variable costs will probably be mostly what you want to pay yourself for your own time. If you plan to make cookies though, it will include the ingredients, fuel, and packaging, as well as your time.

[4]For now, I am making this example simple to illustrate the concepts involved. In fact, Antoinette will very likely not be able to move all her merchandise at full price, but will have to get rid of a portion of it at sale prices. I discuss this in detail in Chapter 5 when I show you how to make your profit and loss forecast.

ANTOINETTE'S DRESS SHOP PROFIT AND LOSS FORECAST, 198_

	$	%
Sales Volume	$200,000	100%
Less: Cost of Sales (Variable)	102,000	51%
Equals: Gross Profit	98,000	49%
Less: Operating (Fixed) Expenses		
Rent	24,000	
Wages	39,600	
Utilities	2,400	
Advertising	6,000	
Telephone	1,200	
Supplies	4,200	
Insurance	2,400	
Freight	4,200	
Accounting/legal	1,800	
Bad debts	1,200	
Miscellaneous	1,200	
Total Operating Expense	$88,200	44%
PROFIT	$9,800	5%

Note: Additional examples of how to do this exercise for service, manufacturing and project development businesses are set out in Appendices 1, 2, and 3, respectively. You will find that the profit and loss forecast for a service business looks very similar to the one shown above, except there is only one sale, and the cost categories are somewhat different.

Now let's assume you have done this sort of projection and show a profit on the sales volume you honestly expect to generate. Now, compare this profit to the money, time and effort you invested to make it. Allow for repayment to yourself of any money you invested from your savings, plus the reasonable interest it would have earned had you left it there. If you borrowed money, you will have to do this. If you still see a profit after allowing for the repayment of the money you invested and you think the profit is a reasonable return for your time and effort, you're ready to begin your business!

Note: If you show a loss, or too small a profit, you may want to redo your numbers. Remember though, your SWAG will lose all meaning if you simply inflate your profit potential with no real justification. At this stage, you are convincing only yourself whether the business will work. Later on, you may want to allow yourself a greater degree of optimism when dealing with skeptical lenders. Now, if you err, let it be on the conservative side. We shall complete this exercise in more detail in Chapters 5 and 6. For now, it's enough to introduce you to these concepts.

Chapter 3

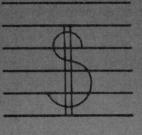

POTENTIAL SOURCES OF MONEY TO START YOUR SMALL BUSINESS

THREE

A. Introduction

This chapter is concerned with the many places where you may be able to get money to help start your small business. Some of these sources are more tedious to deal with than others, but they all share one common attribute—they will lend to, or invest in, a sound small business that will provide a good return with little risk. If you have a good business idea and are patient and persevering, you will be able to find money to get started from at least one of these places. I think it was Calvin Coolidge who, sometime in the 1920's, said, "The business of America is business." It's no less true today.

The many potential sources of funding for your business present an obvious danger which you probably haven't worried much about: You may be able to get money for a dumb idea. Or, to make this important point in another way, just because you find someone to lend you money or invest in your business, it's no guarantee your business idea is sound. At bottom, it's your business and you must take responsibility for it, even if a lot of people want a piece of your action.

Many people and institutions are looking for sound investments. From their side of the fence, it can often seem extremely difficult to find a good one. Take a moment and think about how the world looks from an investor's point of view. Many potential investors have been frightened by news stories about small business financial problems, con men selling phony tax shelters, business bankruptcies, and so on. Quite sensibly, they view anyone who asks for their hard-earned cash with suspicion. What does this mean to you? Simply that your job is not only to create a sound business plan, but to present it, and yourself, in a way which appeals to lenders' and investors' needs for both security and profit. And, as with most everything else, once you can demonstrate good fundamentals, it doesn't hurt to add a dash of charm.

B. Security and Profit: The Reasons People Invest

People put large sums of money in banks, government securities and the conservatively-managed money market funds because they offer security. Banks and savings and loan organizations guarantee safety because they are backed by the United States Federal Deposit Insurance Corporation (FDIC). Other conservative investments, such as top-rated bonds, or money market funds with conservative portfolio policies, don't have this guarantee, but are nevertheless thought to be extremely safe. To an investor, this means any money he puts into a bank or other blue chip investment is sure to come back with at least some interest.

The formula that normally confronts people with money to invest goes something like this:

The more conservative the investment, the more modest the return and the less the risk. Correspondingly, for a risky investment, there is usually a relatively high return to make up for the fact that the investor has a much greater chance of losing his money.

Your new business proposal will be far less safe than a bank deposit. This means that to attract money, you must offer investors the possibility of fairly high returns. Investors will not classify your proposal as quite so risky as casino gambling, but the smart ones will know that, statistically, putting money into a new small business isn't a whole lot safer. In addition to the possibility of a big gain, the investor will want to minimize his risks by looking for any security-enhancing feature your investment proposal offers. We will discuss some common ones, such as putting up valuable property as security for your loan, or having the loan co-signed by someone with solid assets, later. For now, let's just make a general point. One of the best ways to convince a potential investor that his money is secure is to convince him that you are an honest, sincere person. At least as many businesses fail to get financed because potential investors don't like the person making the sales pitch or fail because they don't like the pitch itself.

In sum, since you are competing with all sorts of people wanting money, you need to make your project seem desirable. To do this, you will need to offer the possibility of a good financial return, a sense of security, and, if possible, a little more. Often, this something more is a sense of excitement, and sometimes it is a vision of engaging in a business designed to enhance some particularly worthwhile objective (e.g., health, education, environmental concerns, etc.). After all, since you're probably in love with your idea, there is nothing wrong with trying to get others to share your enthusiasm. Even if you're not a terrific talker, don't despair. If you're sure your project is good, if you believe in it, and if you're persistent, you'll get the money you need.

1. Return on Investments: What's Fair

Several people have requested a formula for offering investors a fair return on their money. Of course, every investor has her personal requirements and every deal is different, but here are some suggestions that have worked well for others in arms length situations. Obviously, if your investors are family members, close friends or people who wish to support your business for political or personal reasons, they may be willing to accept a lower rate of return than those suggested here.

Before having the first conversation with an investor, you need to decide whether you will pay the return to the investor regardless of the project's profitability. If you answer this question in the affirmative, it means you will pay the investor's return, even if the deal goes sour. Doing this is great if the project makes the profit you think it will. But, of course, it also means you'll have to get the money to pay off the investor from some other source if the project goes sour.

If you are willing to guarantee the repayment, you may be able to get an investor to accept the return of her investment, plus a 30% profit, within a year or two time frame. This can be a good deal for you, as once you pay back the investment, plus the additional 30%, they are out of the picture. Of course, every deal is different and you may find you have to pay a higher percentage to get someone to invest in yours. Surely the investor will want to know how you will repay the investment if the business goes poorly. As discussed earlier, one way to do this is to provide security, such as a second mortgage on real estate.

In instances when you are not willing to guarantee the return of the investment should the business fail, you'll almost always need to offer the investors the possibility of a higher return if it succeeds. One rule of thumb says that the people who put up all the money for a business should get 75% of the profits, and you, the promoter, should get 25% of the profits for your work to make the project go. Of course, it is rare that a person who starts a business doesn't invest at least some of his own money, so the investors' percentage would normally be adjusted downward.

Another alternative where the investor bears the entire risk of loss is for the person who begins the business and works in it on a daily basis to receive a small wage as a project expense. After this, the first profits are used to pay back all the money advanced. Finally, profits are split on an agreed percentage. If the investor puts up all the money, this might be 50/50; if the investor puts up less, his share should also be less.

These are some suggestion for a place to begin the discussions with your investors. The important thing is that both parties understand the risks and think it is a good deal.

C.   Types of Investments

Before you can sensibly plan to raise money, you need to know something about the various common ways it's done. If you already understand the difference between a loan and an equity investment and have decided on the type of business organization you will adopt (e.g., a limited partnership as opposed to a small corporation), you may want to skim the next few sections and concentrate on the material in Part E, below, which discusses where the money you need is likely to come from. Most readers will benefit from a review of these basics, however.

1. Debt Investments

Debt investments are loans. At bottom, a loan is a simple concept—someone gives you money in exchange for your promise to pay it back. Often the lender will also want you to pay interest, and commonly will want you to put up security (known as "collateral") in case you fail to repay the loan. While these basic concepts are simple, not everyone seems to clearly understand them. For example, some borrowers put a great deal of energy into arranging to borrow money, but think very little about the hard work that goes into repaying it. The important thing to understand is that the lender expects you to pay the money back. It's only fair that you honor your promise if you possibly can.

As for the manner and methods in which loans are repaid, there are about as many variations as there are loans. You and the lender may agree that you will pay back the entire loan (the "principal"), in one lump sum, one year (or three months, or two years, or six years, etc.) from the time you receive the money. Or, you may agree to pay off the loan in equal installments over some pre-established time period. Or you may come up with some other repayment schedule. But no matter how you agree to repay the money, you will normally also agree to pay a fee for its use. This is called "interest," and compensates the lender for the risk he takes that you will be unable or unwilling to pay back the money as you agreed. Usually the lender has you sign some papers (called a "note and loan agreement") spelling out the details of your agreement to repay the money.

A common way for a lender to protect himself against the possibility you won't repay is to take a security interest in something valuable that you own. Usually, this is your house or other real property. The principle behind taking a security interest is simple. If you don't repay the loan, the lender sells the asset you put up as security and pockets the unpaid balance of your note, plus any costs of sale. Not surprisingly, if you have valuable property (or a co-signer who is financially solid) to secure a loan, a lender will be much more willing to advance you money.

Note on Co-Signing: In some circumstances, a banker may ask you to find someone with good credit to co-sign your loan. Bankers will do this if you have insufficient collateral, or they otherwise feel the risk of lending you money is too great. Occasionally, it's easier to find a co-signer than it is to get someone to lend you money. Perhaps one of the people who likes your idea and has a lot of property, but who is short of cash, will co-sign for a bank loan. But remember, legally a co-signer agrees to make any and all payments you can't make. That's a big obligation, even though a co-signer's obligation is limited to the amount of your loan. You might want to consider rewarding your angel for taking this risk.

From my own experience, I co-signed a car loan for an employee once, and I'll think twice before I do it again. The employee made all the payments, and I didn't lose any money, but the bank called me every time a payment was 24 hours late, and a couple of times I thought I might have to pay. I didn't like that feeling.

One of the most common methods of loan repayment is to provide for principal and interest to be paid off in equal monthly payments for a certain number of months. Once all the payments have been made, the loan is

paid off. That is called a "fully amortized loan." You may be familiar with the little books of numerical tables which tell how to figure out monthly payments for different amounts of loans over different numbers of months at different interest rates. For example, if you borrow $10,000 for five years at 10% interest, you will agree to make sixty monthly payments of $212.48. Multiplying the monthly payments times sixty gives you a total repayment of $12,748.80 ($212.48 x 60). That means you will pay $2,748.80 in interest over five years. Let's say you borrow $10,000 for five years, but have to pay 20% interest; your monthly payments will be $264.92, and you will end up paying a total of $15,895.00 ($264.92 x 60). You can buy one of those little books, which are called "Mortgage Loan Tables." Or, ask at your bank; they will have a copy you can examine.

The most popular alternative to the fully amortized loan is a loan in which you pay smaller amounts, sometimes interest only, for some pre-established period of time and then pay the entire remaining amount off at once. This last large payment is called a "balloon payment," because it's so much larger than the others. A typical loan of this type works like this. Let's say you borrow $10,000 and agree to make interest-only payments for two years and then pay back the full principal amount at the end of the twenty-fourth month. Your monthly payment at 10% interest will be $83.33 ($10,000 x 10% = $1,000/12 = $83.33), and your balloon payment will be $10,000 at the end of two years.

If you borrow money, you'll have to allow for loan payments in your fixed expense forecast [see Chapter 2, Section F(3)]. Also, as I have said, you will very likely have to offer some kind of security or collateral to the lender. Again, this is your valuable property which the lender takes title to and probably sells if you can't pay back the loan. Many borrowers find it hard to believe that they are expected to give the lender a second mortgage on their house as well as paying interest. From a lender's point of view, however, interest at anything like conventional rates doesn't sufficiently compensate her for the risk of loss she takes lending to a new, small enterprise. Given the history of many small businesses, this isn't an unreasonable view.

Let's say that Mary needs $75,000 to open a take-out bagel shop. She has $25,000 in her savings account and wants to borrow the rest. She owns a house worth $200,000 and has a first mortgage with a remaining balance of $100,000. Uncle Albert has offered to lend Mary the amount she needs at a favorable interest rate, taking a second mortgage on Mary's house as collateral for the loan. Mary agrees and borrows $50,000, obligating herself to repay in five years with interest at 10%, by making sixty payments of $1062.50. If Mary can't make all the payments, the second mortgage gives Uncle Albert the right to foreclose on Mary's home and sell it to recover the money he loaned her. Uncle Albert feels secure, since he is confident the house will sell for at least $150,000, and the only other loan against the house is the $100,000 first mortgage. If a foreclosure did occur, Mary would, of course, collect the difference between the selling price and the balance of the two mortgages.

But is this a wise loan for Mary to become involved in? What if the business goes bad and she loses her house? There is no one answer to this question. Obviously, if Mary can get a loan without putting up her house as security, even if she would have to pay a little more interest to do so, she would be better off.

Lenders like collateral, but it never substitutes for a sound business plan. They don't want to be selling houses, cars, jewelry or whatever, especially if they belong to family members. All lenders really want is for you to pay back the loan, plus interest. If they have to foreclose on your house, it makes them look, and probably feel, bad. Depending on the lender, a

sound business plan may even substitute for collateral for a loan. However, convincing a lender to make an unsecured loan for a new business can be difficult unless he has some personal reason to want to help you. Remember, the lender's maximum profit from the loan will be the interest he charges you. If you make super profits, he still only gets his money back, with interest. Since he won't participate in the profits, no matter how big, naturally he is going to be more concerned with security. That's where the collateral comes in.

From your point of view, the advantage of a loan, compared to an investment, is that you don't have to give up any of your business (see Section D, below). A lender doesn't become your partner. As long as you make the payments, a lender won't interfere with the way you run your business. If your business does as well as you think it will, you simply pay off the loan and whistle a happy tune. If you have the collateral to offer, or can otherwise qualify for a loan, this approach has many advantages. The big disadvantages are that loan payments normally increase your fixed costs, just when you are trying to start your business and want to keep costs as low as possible. The other major downside risk is that you may lose your collateral if your business fails.

2. Equity Investments

An equity investor becomes a part owner of your business. Her return on the money she advances comes from that ownership share. The equity investor shares in your profits when you succeed. Normally, she only shares in your losses up to the amount of her initial investment. Put another way, most equity investors' risk is limited to the money they put up.

Typically, an equity investor chooses among three options in sharing ownership in your small business. She may become your general partner, your limited partner, or a shareholder in your small corporation. A general partner joins you in owning the business. She shares in your profits and losses in proportion to her partnership share. General partnerships work best when all the partners plan to work full-time in the business. Equity investors normally prefer not to become general partners because most investors don't want to work in your business day-to-day and because, by law, a general partner has a downside risk in addition to the initial investment. This means that if the partnership loses money, the investing general partner must make good at least a portion of the losses. If you've no resources yourself, she may even be legally obligated to satisfy all partnership debts.[1] Everybody has heard stories of partnerships that went sour with dire consequence. These were usually general partnerships.

Investors normally prefer a "limited partnership." This is a legal form of business organization under which one or more person(s), usually the business founder(s), serve as a general partner or partners. A general partner has the legal responsibility of managing the business, and also has personal responsibility for making good all business losses. Under this scheme, a passive investor becomes a limited partner. By law, a limited partner has no say in the day-to-day operation of the business. In exchange, her risk is limited to the initial investment.[2]

---

[1]We only touch on partnership law here. If you are interested in forming a partnership, or learning more about them, see *The Partnership Book: How to Write Your Own Small Business Partnership Agreement*, Clifford and Warner, Nolo Press.

[2]Limited partnerships raise a number of issues beyond the scope of this book. For example, one common one involves how much return a limited partner gets if the business does well and how this is calculated. See *The Partnership Book: How to Write Your*

Example: Jerry Rivers needed a tax write-off because he had some other absentee investments that produced a good cash flow for him in addition to his comfortable salary. He is one of the fortunate people able to take advantage of the tax laws under the 1987 tax reform act. For $10,000, he was promised an ownership share in a $1,000,000 apartment house in town. Upon examination, it turned out that by investing, Jerry would become a limited partner in the building, with a 5% interest or share. As a limited partner, he was to receive 5% of the cash flow from the building and 5% of any profits when the building was sold. His liability was limited to his $10,000; if there were problems, he was not required to put up more cash. That was the general partner's job. Under the agreement, however, if there were financial problems and Jerry didn't put up more cash, his ownership share of 5% could be reduced.

As you probably noticed, $10,000 isn't 5% of $1,000,000. So why would Jerry be offered a 5% share? Because the partnership planned to borrow 80% of the $1,000,000 purchase price from a bank, which means that Jerry put up 5% of the $200,000 down payment. The tax advantage of his ownership of the apartment building came from the fact that the interest expense on the $800,000 loan the partnership borrowed to buy the building together with the depreciation expense on the building exceeded the income from the rental units (see Chapter 5, Section E for a discussion of depreciation). Thus, Jerry got some income from the building on which he did not have to pay taxes and some extra write-offs by which he could reduce some of his other tax obligations. His CPA cautioned him to be very careful with these write-offs, since the new tax law put some stringent limits on the tax benefits of passive investments.

Own Small Business Partnership Agreement, Clifford and Warner, Nolo Press.

One of the most popular methods of selling equity investments is to form a corporation and sell shares of stock. State and federal laws place a number of restrictions on stock sales. Among the most burdensome of these are exhaustive reports and disclosure statements. However, in most states, small businesses are exempt from most of these restrictions and requirements. Also, in most states, if you sell stock to 35 or fewer knowledgeable investors, your sale requires little red tape. How much people are willing to pay for your stock depends mostly on what they think of your prospects. If you have a firm, exclusive contract to sell a hot, new type of computer peripheral and only need money to build a showroom, potential buyers will probably find you. However, if you're trying to build a factory to mass produce a new and relatively untried type of pooper-scooper, you will almost certainly have more difficulty.

Example: Michael needs $100,000 to finance kitchen equipment and the necessary remodeling to open The Dream Cafe. To do this, he creates a profit corporation and sells 49% of the shares to five friends, while retaining the other 51% for himself. Each friend gets slightly less than 10% of the stock for $20,000.

The cafe has a terrible first year, but prospects seem better for the second. However, Michael needs another $20,000 to pay bills and see him through to the hoped-for better times. The original five investors are somewhat disillusioned and refuse to invest more. So Michael decides to find another investor and sells him additional corporate stock. To do this, Michael can either sell some of his own stock and lose his majority position, or increase the total stock of the corporation and retain his majority share. The latter action would likely involve a stormy meeting with the five original

investors, who will not be happy that their share is reduced.[3]

Assuming more stock is issued and sold, the new investor is now in an ownership position. The original investors' shares are reduced. Michael retains his 51% ownership. If the second year is better, and the corporation pays a dividend to all the stockholders, things will look up. If the saga of The Dream Cafe continues to resemble a nightmare, it will either be sold, in which case the investors may recover some portion of their investment, or it will go out of business, and chances are there will be nothing left for anyone. However, because corporate shareholders have "limited liability" status, they will not have to put up more than their initial investment.[4]

Equity investors will commonly ask for a bigger share of ownership than you are willing to give. It's not uncommon for people with money to ask for as much as 60% of a venture. They want a controlling share so they, not you, can call the financial shots. People trying to raise money to begin a business routinely hope to offer a 30% to 40% share to get needed money. This may sound like a great deal for an investor, but from the point of view of many, it isn't. Why? Because relatively high interest rates have produced a number of very safe investments

---

[3]Normally they can't object, unless they have voting control of the corporation, or there was a shareholder's agreement preventing Michael from selling more.

[4]If you are interested in forming a corporation, I recommend *How to Form Your Own California [Texas, New York or Florida] Corporation,* by Anthony Mancuso, (Nolo Press). These books show you how to set up your own small profit corporation and also go into considerable detail on limited liability, electing Subchapter S tax status, issuing shares, holding your first Board of Directors meeting, etc. Nolo/Legisoft, Inc. also publishes *California Incorporator,* a software package which does the paperwork for you.

that produce excellent returns. The result is that potential investors interested in buying shares in small new corporations look for considerably higher returns.

Warning! Be sure you examine your motives carefully before you sell more than 49% of your new incorporated business. In essence, if you sell 51% or more, you're working for the investor, not yourself.

D. Debt and Equity Investments Compared

One of your first decisions in raising money for your new business is to decide whether you prefer to borrow money or sell a piece of your project to an equity investor. Often, you may not end up controlling this choice. The person with money to invest—especially the sophisticated investor—will obviously have a lot to say about it. But you should know the general characteristics of each form of financing, as well as the general trade-offs you normally make by preferring one to the other. The material set out in the previous two sections of this chapter should give you a start, but if you're new to business finance, you will want to do some more research. If you don't already know an accountant specializing in small business affairs, you will be wise to find one. Your personal tax situation, the tax situation of the people who may invest, and the tax status of the type of business you plan to open are all likely to influence your choice.

E. Getting the Money to Start Your Business

Most small businesses are started with money from one of seven readily available sources. They are:

1. The savings of the person starting the business;

2. Money from close friends and relatives (we make this a separate category because even though you will still end up with some sort of debt or equity financing, the motive for advancing you the money and the interest rates charged, as well as other factors, will not be primarily, or at least completely, based on commercial considerations);

3. Scaling back your cash requirements and substituting dollar-stretching equity for financial equity;

4. Selling equity in other property;

5. Money from supporters or others who care about what you are doing. As with Category 2 just above, we treat this source of funds separately because people who are cause-oriented will often provide financial help on better terms than are available commercially;

6. Bank loans;

7. Venture capital.

These sources are listed in order of frequency. In other words, more small businesses are started with owner's savings and money from family and friends than are started with bank loans. This list is not exhaustive; there are many more theoretical sources of business start-up money. I limit it because you are more likely to get money from the sources listed than you are from secondary sources. Some of the more visible secondary sources of start-up financing, like the Small Business Administration, the Farmers' Home Administration and others, are discussed briefly toward the end of this chapter, but experience convinces me that most small businesses start with the seven sources listed above.

Remember, this discussion is primarily oriented to funding small business start-ups; if your business is already established, funds for expansion can come from a larger list of lenders and investors. Information on expansion financing can be found in Small Business Administration Self-Instructional Booklets 1003 and 1004, entitled "Understanding Money Sources," and "Evaluating Money Sources," and in the book *How to Negotiate a Business Loan*, by Richard C. Belew, Van Nostrand Reinholt. See Chapter 11 for details.

Now let's look at each of the most likely funding sources for new businesses in more depth.

1. Raising Money From Personal Savings

Most businesses are started, at least in part, with personal savings. Sure, it's hard to save money, but this form of financing has so many advantages, it's worth an effort. Incidentally, savings don't necessarily come from a bank account or piggy bank. Lots of businesses get their original financing when the entrepreneur sells or refinances a house or some other valuable property. The recent increase in housing prices has provided capital for many new enterprises. This subject is covered in more detail below in Section E(4).

Starting a business with your savings is the quintessence of the capitalist idea. As the entrepreneur with capital, you hire labor, equipment, buildings, etc., and create profits (hopefully) from your efforts. It's a long and honored tradition. Henry Ford, John D. Rockefeller, and more recently, Stephen Jobs of Apple Computer, all started with at least some money from their own pockets and ended up creating industrial empires.[5] While chances are

your goals are more modest, the idea is pretty much the same.

If you start a business with your own money, you won't have to worry about making loan payments or keeping investors happy. Think of it this way—the more you borrow, the more you increase your fixed operating costs and make it more difficult to survive the slow periods and mistakes almost every new business faces. I recommend never starting a business with 100% borrowed money, even if it's possible. My rule of thumb is that you should never borrow more than 50% of the money you need to begin your business, and ideally, less. In other words, it's usually more dangerous to borrow too much than too little. One great benefit of this approach is that it allows you to make your inevitable start-up mistakes cheaply and survive to borrow money later, when you know better how to use it.

Another reason to try to start a business with savings is that you enhance your borrowing capacity for the future. The inventory, fixtures, and equipment you purchase with your cash investment are treated as assets should you later apply for a loan. To these assets you can add your business experience. The potential investor now has the advantage of looking at a going business.

Of course, not everybody is lucky enough to be able to start a business entirely from savings. But there are several ways you may be able to augment the money you have put aside.

a. Living Expense Deferral

We put this heading under savings, although it doesn't precisely belong here. It might more appropriately be called "Borrowing from the Future," as it involves deliberately falling behind in your monthly living expenses. This way of

---

[5]Of course, as their business expanded they learned to skillfully employ other types of debt and equity financing.

getting extra money involves risk, and it's not for everybody.

If you have a good payment record with the telephone company, gas and electric company, landlord, bank and so forth, you will be able to skip several months' payments without seriously damaging your credit rating. Of course, you'll have to catch up again fast. In the meantime, you can use the money for some other purpose, such as helping get your business going.

This scheme should be tried only when you're sure you'll be able to come up with the money when you need it. As with everything else, common sense should be applied to living expense deferral plans. Otherwise, you may find yourself trying to read a foreclosure notice in a dark room. For example, if you own your house, you can simply not pay your property taxes for quite a while before the county will grab your property (they will charge interest and penalties, but these are bearable in most places). However, if your house is financed and you don't pay your taxes, the lending institution may have the right to take quick punitive action. Check on this thoroughly before you try it.

b.   Trade Credit

We put this heading under savings also, since it is similar to living expense deferral. Arranging for trade credit involves borrowing from the companies from whom you will buy your merchandise or raw materials. This form of borrowing rarely works for service businesses because salaries are the biggest expense and employees are usually not interested in lending you their salaries, although I do know of a number of new businesses where friends and family members pitched in for free in the early days. It never hurts to ask.

If you're in the retail, wholesale or manufacturing business, arranging for trade

credit can help considerably. In most businesses, you will normally order supplies and pay for them 30 to 60 days after you receive them. That's routine practice and causes no problems as long as you pay promptly when the appointed day arrives. The problem for new businesses is that it's also standard practice for suppliers to demand cash on the line from start-ups. This policy isn't immutable, however. Usually, if you present your business plan and loan package materials to potential suppliers, you will be able to arrange to order at least some supplies and merchandise on credit. After all, your supplier has an interest in helping you succeed so that you will buy his merchandise for many years to come.

The key to maintaining good relations with suppliers while borrowing their money is to keep them informed of what you're doing and why. Make sure you keep any agreements you make with the credit department. Many small business people fall behind on payments without any communication. This is almost guaranteed to make a supplier paranoid. Most suppliers will work with you up to a point as long as you keep communication lines open. This rule is particularly important for new businesses. If you do arrange credit and then can only pay a part of your first bill in thirty days, pay that amount and ask the supplier for a short extension.

Some suppliers may offer extended payment terms to get your business. Occasionally a supplier will ship you the merchandise in a slow part of the season and let you pay for it three or six months later, in the busy season. Before you try any of this, check with your suppliers' sales reps about company policies. Your suppliers are among your most valuable business assets and you want to keep them on your side.

2. Close Friends and Relatives

Lots of small business people get financial help from a parent or other relative or friend. The help may be either a gift, a loan, or an equity investment. You, of course, have the responsibility to be sure that taking money will not damage your friend or relative's financial security if you can't pay it back. In addition, think about what a business reversal could do to your personal relationship, even if your relative or friend says they don't need the money. I know families which have been literally torn apart because a borrower didn't meet the agreements she made with a lender.

The type of financing provided by close friends and relatives does not normally vary much from that provided by strangers, except that where loans are involved, interest rates are often lower than bank rates. The basic idea is generally the same. You get the money and eventually you have to provide a fair return. The big difference is the availability of the money in the first place.

With friend- or relative-provided financing, however, the commercial model isn't the only one. A common alternative is the loan-gift hybrid. Here a relative or friend with considerable assets lends you money at either a low interest rate, or with no interest at all, telling you to pay it back when you can and to treat it as a gift if you can't.

Obviously, this type of help is invaluable if it's available. It gives you time to get your business established with a minimum of pressure. It's important that the person extending this sort of generous offer can really afford to do so, however. If you learn later that they really do need the money back and you don't have it, you will truly be in a mess. If you've any doubt, make sure they consult their banker, attorney, or financial adviser before they advance you the money.

Also, make sure you check with a CPA on the tax ramifications of a gift before you proceed with this concept. And be sure that all terms of the loan or transaction are thoroughly understood by both parties and written down. After all, you want to feel like you can go to family reunions even if your business fails.

One advantage of dealing with your relatives and friends is they already know your strengths and weaknesses. Consequently, they are likely to be more understanding than a banker if you have start-up problems and make a few late loan payments. Nevertheless, you'll be wise to treat people close to you in a businesslike manner. Ask for the loan by pointing out what a sound business idea you have, and avoid asking for money just because you're a relative or friend and need some help. Pay attention to criticism and suggestions, especially if they come from people with business experience. If they don't wish to invest, accept their reasons at face value—you might not like their hidden reasons.

Some people looking for financing for a new business will write a business plan and loan package and then show it only to the bank, assuming relatives or friends don't need to see it. This is a mistake. Make sure those people close to you get the benefit of all your hard work. A good business plan may even help them see you in a new light and encourage them to make a financial commitment.

Note: In Chapter 9, I discuss selling your business plan in some detail. Obviously, this involves tailoring your presentation to your audience. For example, if you stop by your brother's place early Saturday morning wearing a necktie with your new pant suit, he will probably laugh you out of the kitchen. Still, the point is that your brother will be as interested in seeing that you have prepared a well-thought-out business plan as will your banker.

3. Dollar-Stretching Equity

Although not really a funding source, it's important to realize that one of the most effective ways to finance a small business is to figure out ways to begin with less. If your initial business proposal calls for $50,000 to get started, think about how you can reach the same goal for half as much. Perhaps family members will work in your restaurant or shop for a few months at no charge. Perhaps you can begin your consulting business in your home, or perhaps you can work out a way to share expensive equipment with an established business rather than buying it, etc.

I like to think about this concept as borrowing from your own business plan. When you think about all the interest (and future borrowing capacity) you save, it's clearly the best potential source of funds. Of course, there will be many situations where you will need a fair amount of money to get started (it's hard to cook without a stove, paint without a ladder, or compute without a calculator). The important principle is not that you should never raise outside money, but that you should borrow or raise equity capital only if you absolutely can't do without it. For more on this concept, I again recommend *Honest Business,* by Michael Phillips and Salli Rasberry, Random House.

4. Equity in Other Assets

You can also raise money by selling your existing assets or by pledging your equity in them as collateral for a loan. Basically, equity is the difference between the market value of property you own and what you owe against it, plus any costs necessary to turn the asset into cash. For example, let's say you own a car with a blue book value of $6,000 and you owe the bank $3,000. Your equity in the car is $3,000, less your costs to sell it. To convert the equity to cash, you could either try to sell the car for $6,000 cash and pay off the bank loan, or try to borrow another $3,000 against the car. (Normally you would get less.)

5. Supporters

Many types of businesses tend to have loyal and devoted followers—in many ways their customers care about the business as much as the owners do. Examples are as myriad and varied as the likes, loves and desires of the human community. A health food restaurant, an exercise facility, a motorcycle shop, a family mediation facility, a solar heating business, a religious book store, or a kayak manufacturing shop all qualify, assuming you can find your audience.

As with the discussion about family members just above, people who care about what you propose to do may well be willing to support you on better terms than would a commercial investor. No matter what your business idea, think about who you know, or can get to know, who really cares about what you plan to do. Share your idea with these people and be ready to listen to their ideas. You may be surprised at how easy it is to raise money for what people perceive as an honest and needed endeavor.

You can probably make a pretty good horseback estimate of your net equity. Check your conclusion by making a personal financial statement (see Chapter 4). After you do this, you'll know whether you have any assets which might qualify as collateral for a loan.[6] Normally,

---

[6]Remember, collateral is something you own which you give your lender title to until you pay back

lenders only accept things on the order of real property, stocks and bonds, and vehicles as collateral. Other items of personal property, such as jewelry, furniture, artwork, collections, etc., usually don't qualify. You'll have to sell them yourself to raise cash. Also, remember, if you want to borrow against equity in an asset, you will not realize the entire amount. Just as you have to make a down payment on a house or car, a lender will expect you to maintain some ownership stake in the asset. This will normally be 10% to 30%, depending on the type of asset and the type of lender.

6. Banks

When asked why he robbed banks, Willie Sutton said, "Because that's where the money is." For the same reason, banks are high on the list of sources for business start-up funding. Unfortunately, as far as budding entrepreneurs are concerned, banks act cautiously when lending out money. This makes sense when you remember it isn't their money.

Banks are financial intermediaries. They pay interest to savers to attract deposits which they lend out to people like you. When lending, they charge enough interest on loans to pay for their cost of funds and produce a profit. Any transaction you have with a bank will be a loan and will come with a repayment schedule. The important thing to understand is that banks don't invest in businesses. As I discussed earlier in this chapter, there is a big difference between a loan and an investment. Investors will take risks in the hope of getting a large return. Banks try to minimize risks by making sure you have enough assets to pay them back, even if your business does badly.

---

all the money you borrowed, plus interest. If you fail to repay the loan, the lender keeps the collateral.

Banks will sometimes lend to a start-up business. When they do, however, they almost always ask you to pledge good collateral to secure the loan. They also ask that you invest at least as much as they lend you. In other words, the most a bank will lend in a start-up venture is half the cash needed. In addition, they usually require that you do not raise your portion by borrowing all or most of it from someone else. In other words, in addition to pledging solid collateral, they want you to have as much to lose as they do.

The bank will always want to see a written business plan along with your loan application. In Chapters 4, 5, 6 and 7, we show you how to create both. As part of your personal financial statement, which is one part of these documents, you will be asked to list your assets available to pledge as collateral. You may want to do so now; if so, turn to Chapter 4.

The good news about banks is that money generally costs less from banks than from other professional lenders, such as mortgage loan brokers. If the bank lending officer likes your business plan and loan application, and you have sufficient collateral, she may give you an interest-only loan for a short time, with the option of converting it to an amortized loan later, which means that instead of making heavy loan payments at the start, you can delay principal payments until your business has a chance to generate a positive cash flow.

Example 1: Let's say you have saved $20,000 to start the Rack-a-Frax Fastener Company, but need an additional $10,000. After careful study of your business plan, a banker makes you an interest-only loan with payments to be made quarterly for one year and takes a second mortgage on your home as collateral. At the end of the year, you must repay the entire principal. Your interest rate will probably be something like the prime rate charged large institutional borrowers, plus 3%. If the prime interest is 12%, this means you'll be paying about 15% interest. Fifteen percent of $10,000 is $1,500, so your quarterly interest payment will be $375. At the end of the year, you will be obligated to repay the $10,000, in one lump sum.

Example 2: To continue this story, now let's assume you ask the bank to convert the loan to a three-year payment schedule, including principal and interest, rather than have to pay back the $10,000 at the end of the first year. Based on your favorable first year results, the bank agrees to amortize the loan rather than demanding immediate repayment. You would now have to make 36 equal monthly payments of $341.75. After you make those 36 payments, the loan would be paid off completely.

Example 3: Now let's forget about Rack-a-Frax and switch to the story of a friend of mine. Mickey wanted to start a garage specializing in Italian cars in Santa Fe, New Mexico. He estimated that he needed a total of $50,000 to get his business started. He had $25,000 cash saved from his job as chief mechanic at an independent Ferrari garage in Los Angeles and $30,000 equity in his home. He thought he was home free and confidently walked into a local bank and asked for a $25,000 loan.

An hour later he walked back out with his head spinning. The banker asked him a number of questions about monthly sales projections, cash flow, financing a parts inventory, etc. Mickey hemmed and hawed. It came down to this. The banker didn't want to talk to Mickey seriously until he produced a written business plan demonstrating that he understood how his business would work. After the initial shock of his bank interview wore off, Mickey went to work. Putting his plan down on paper and doing a budget encouraged him to deal with a number of details he never thought about before. When he did, he changed his plan considerably.

After having his work reviewed by a knowledgeable business advisor and making several changes based on the consultant's suggestions, Mickey presented the plan to the bank loan committee. This time they agreed to lend him $20,000, provided he put up the other $25,000 and give the bank a second trust deed on his house and title to all equipment purchased for the shop. The bank also required that Mickey buy a life insurance policy for $25,000, naming the bank as beneficiary. He agreed and the loan was made, subject to being repaid in 36 monthly payments, at an interest rate that was calculated at the prime rate (interest rate charged the bank's favored customers) plus 3%.

By this time, Mickey and the banker, whose name was Fred, had established a good relationship. When the business got off to a slow start, Mickey kept Fred informed of the problems and his plans to deal with them. Fred let Mickey delay three payments in a row with no penalty. Eventually, when the business began to do well and Mickey wanted to expand, Fred worked out a financing package, this time taking as collateral Mickey's accounts receivable and inventory.

7. Venture Capitalists

This book is designed for new small businesses. Most readers will be interested in starting service, retail, wholesale, or low technology manufacturing operations. Large scale venture capitalists traditionally do not invest in these areas, preferring instead the emerging technological fields where a lot of money is needed to get started and where it's possible to achieve enormous returns. Computers, genetic engineering, and medical technology are familiar examples. Nevertheless, venture capital is also available on a smaller scale. Relatives, friends and local business people with a little money to invest can all be pint-sized venture capitalists. Many do very well at it.

Example: Jack Boots loved to ride dirt bikes on the weekends. He was frustrated that no retailer in his county carried either a good selection of off-road bikes or the right accessories. He sometimes had to drive 200 miles to buy supplies, and noticed that his friends had the same problem.

Eventually, it occurred to Jack to quit his job and open a local cycle store. He talked to several manufacturers and was encouraged. The only problem was, he would need $50,000 to swing it. As he only had $20,000, he was about to give up the idea when some of his biker buddies offered to help raise the cash. Jack found six people willing to invest $5,000 each in a limited partnership. Each of these friends was, in reality, a small-scale venture capitalist, betting a portion of his savings on the notion that Jack would succeed and they would participate in his financial success.

Would-be entrepreneurs like Jack need to remember that the shares they sell, whether they are called limited partnership interests or shares in a closely-held or other type of corporation, are legally classified as securities and must be registered with the State. Care must be taken that the applicable regulations are followed. An alternative to a limited partnership would be to form a closely-held corporation. In this situation, Jack would probably want to hold onto at least 51% of the stock, dividing the rest among his investors [see Section C(2) above].

Jack's Cycles opened for business and is doing well. All the limited partners were paid back their initial investments plus the agreed-upon return set out in their limited partnership agreement, and Jack is now the sole owner. The only sad part of it is that Jack is too busy to ride much anymore.

When thinking about raising money by selling a share in your business, as opposed to getting a loan, it's important that you have a hardheaded picture of what you're getting into. Equity investors gamble on your idea. They invest money hoping that you'll make them rich, or at least richer. If you intend to look for equity investors, your business plan needs enough economic and marketing research to show investors that your idea has the potential of making a substantial profit.

Also, you'll need to show potential investors exactly how they'll profit and how much they'll make if everything goes according to plan. For example, Jack Boots told his limited partners that they would receive 50% of the profits paid monthly according to their relative share of investment after he paid himself a nominal, agreed-upon salary for running the store. In addition, of course, they qualified to buy merchandise at a substantial discount and owned a share of the assets of the business. Jack estimated that a $10,000 investor would receive a monthly cash flow of $200 for an annual return of 24%. When added to the partner's investment share in the inventory of the shop, this would make a $10,000 investment worth $20,000 in three years.

The equity investor will want to be a part-owner of the business, normally either through the device of owning stock in a small corporation or a share in a limited partnership [see Section C(2) above]. She may also want to help in the management. This can be a great help if she has skills you lack. It can be a big drain if the person doesn't know what she is doing or doesn't have a personality compatible with yours.

How do you find investors willing to invest in your new venture? One good way is by networking all your past business acquaintances and relatives. For example, you might call your attorney or accountant or someone you know who owns a small business and say, "I've got a great business proposal in the retail clothing business. I need about $40,000 and the investor will get a 25% annual return on the money they invest, paid monthly. Do you know anybody who might be interested?"

She might reply, "Well, I'm not interested myself, but why don't you try Joe Spats? He just retired from the men's wear business and has been a little restless lately." Obviously, the next step is to call Joe, mention your mutual friend's name and set up a meeting. If he's not interested, ask if he knows anyone who might be. If you strike out with your accountant, attorney, or business friend, try your uncle, the owner of the local hardware store who you trade jokes with, or the investor who put money into the bakery where you trade. If all else fails, you can run an ad in the paper, unless you're selling stock in a corporation. If so, consult an attorney before placing any ads.

A Warning About Equity Financing: Selling equity investments requires care. If your business succeeds as well as you hope it will, you are likely to be extremely unhappy about giving 30% to 60% of your profits to your passive investors. In addition, when you sell an interest in the business to equity investors, you have an obligation to keep them informed and happy. If you're like most of us, one of the major reasons you go into business for yourself is to get some freedom. Simply put, your freedom is limited when you take money from someone else. If you're worried about this, try to negotiate the terms under which you can buy back your investor's interest in the business.

Religious Record Roundtable
Ronnie Ryann
212 R St., Rye, N.Y. 10580   (914) 873-4102

F. If No One Will Finance Your Business, Try Again

Let's say that you've been unsuccessful in your attempts to raise money for your business from the primary sources listed above, or, you have raised some money, but still need more. What do you do next? The first step is to go back to the people who initially seemed interested but ultimately turned you down to find out why. This is not a waste of time. You need to know what turned people off. If you get the same answer from several people, you will know what you have to work on. And then there is also the possibility that someone's circumstances have changed and they have more funds now. Remember, it took the man who invented dry paper copying twenty-one years to raise the money to get the first photocopier made. Finding money can often be at least 75% persistence.

If a bank lending officer, or even two or three, turned you down but you still think borrowing is a good way to start your business, try other lending officers at other banks. A friend once got a $15,000 unsecured loan to improve some agricultural property just by going to five different banks. The first banker laughed him out of the office, the second banker listened to his story for five minutes, and the third for ten minutes. By the time he got to the fifth bank, he knew what questions the banker was going to ask and was ready with some solid answers. The banker was impressed and he got the loan. In fact, for this very reason, it's not a bad idea to try a long shot bank first and the most likely one last. See Chapter 9 for notes on how to present your business plan to bankers.

Example: Sue Lester tried all the usual sources to get the $10,000 she needed to open a piano school. One person she talked to was her Aunt Hillary, who had loaned her money to go to school several years before. This time Hillary said, "Sorry, but no." One afternoon a few months later Sue ran into Hillary at her niece's birthday party. Hillary asked how she was doing with plans for the school. Sue told her she was short $10,000 and was going to try the Small Business Administration as soon as she made one or two changes in the plan. Aunt Hillary asked about the changes. Sue told her that an experienced teacher had suggested she charge slightly more per hour and start with a good second-hand piano instead of a new one and try to work out a referral arrangement with a local piano store. This way she could pay herself more salary and wouldn't need to take another job to make ends meet. Hillary asked to see the changes when they were complete.

After Sue showed the revised plan to her Aunt Hillary, she offered to lend her the money. Sue was both delighted and curious. When she asked, Aunt Hillary said there were two reasons for her change of heart. First, she was pleased that the more realistic sales projections left Sue enough money to live on so she would be able to keep her enthusiasm for the hard job of creating a new business. Second, she had sold a small piece of land for more than expected and now had the money to invest.

G. Secondary Sources of Financing

Let's assume you have followed these suggestions, trying all of the primary sources of financing small businesses at least twice, and have been turned down each time. Is it time to head for the showers? Not if you really want to start your business. If everyone turns you down, you have no choice but to get creative. Remember Knute Rockne's exhortation, "Winners never quit and quitters never win." Here are some suggestions.

1. Small Business Administration

Many years ago Congress recognized both that small businesses provide most of the employment and growth in the country and that they have a great deal of trouble borrowing money because large corporations tend to hog too much of the money banks have available to lend. As a result, Congress created the Small Business Administration (SBA) and several other government organizations specifically to help small businesses compete for funds with larger corporations.

The SBA can make direct loans to small businesses. However, it is much more common for them to guarantee loans from commercial banks. The SBA will guarantee 90% of a bank loan up to $500,000 if the loan meets the SBA criteria. Bankers are interested in working with loans guaranteed by the SBA since these loans are easy to sell at a profit shortly after the loan is funded. In other words, the originating bank retains a commission but doesn't have to worry about future problems. Since the bank's fee is based on the size of the loan, the bank will be more interested in processing loan requests for more than $50,000 than it will for smaller ones, which require almost as much work, but produce a smaller return.

Loan approvals for guaranteed loans can be processed reasonably quickly, usually within two to four months from the time that all the paperwork is accepted for processing. At the time this was written, the SBA is aggressively interested in making loans and will help the applicant wherever possible.

The key to working successfully with the SBA is to have your application prepared by a professional loan packager familiar with the rules and requirements of the SBA. These are people who prepare a loan request to conform with SBA requirements and charge a reasonable fee which is contingent on loan approval; that is, the fee is not payable unless the loan is approved. Since these people prepare a large number of applications, they are familiar with the requirements. Your likelihood of success is fairly high if an experienced loan packager agrees to prepare your application. Call the nearest office of the SBA or loan officers of banks which work with the SBA to obtain the names of people in your area who do this work.

Using a professional loan packager is also a good idea if you apply for a direct loan from the SBA. Your chances of receiving a direct loan in a reasonable time from the SBA will be greatly enhanced if you qualify for a preference category. For example, if you are handicapped, or a Vietnam veteran, requirements are slightly less restrictive.

There are also small business lending concerns which act like a bank in assisting small businesses obtain SBA financing. To obtain the names and addresses of these organizations in your area, write the SBA, Financial Assistance Division, Office of Lender Relations, Non Bank Lender Section, Washington, D.C. 20416.

2. Small Business Investment Companies (SBIC's)

A Small Business Investment Company (SBIC) is a corporation established with the assistance of the SBA to lend money to small businesses. A SBIC can borrow up to four times its invested capital from the SBA. It then lends out these funds to other businesses. It aims to make a profit on each loan transaction. There are some 400 of these across the country and they each have different investment goals and objectives. To obtain a list of their addresses and their areas of investment specialty, contact your nearest SBA office. Some of the SBIC's aim specifically at minority enterprises, and are called Minority Small Business Investment Companies (MSBIC's).

3. Farmers' Home Administration (FmHA), U.S. Department of Agriculture

Goals of this loan program include having or creating jobs in rural America. Business loans through the FmHA are guaranteed in towns with a population of 50,000 or less or in suburban areas where the population density is no more than 100 per square mile. Loans have been made to enable a grocery clerk to buy the store he worked in and for $150,000 for a McDonald's fast food franchise. The loans will normally be made through a local bank. To start the process, look under U.S. Government, Department of Agriculture, Farmers' Home Administration, in the local phone book and make an appointment with the FmHA county supervisor. Loans under this program can take months to complete, so allow plenty of lead time.

4. Economic Development Administration (EDA), Department of Commerce

The EDA makes or guarantees loans to businesses in redevelopment areas. These are usually in cities with high unemployment. Eligible areas are listed in a publication available quarterly from the regional EDA director. If you're in one of the designated redevelopment areas, this program bears looking into.

5. Federal Directory

Other federal assistance programs are published in the Catalog of Federal Domestic Assistance, available from the U.S. Government Printing Office, Washington, D.C. 20402 for $20, or at your library.

6. State and Local Government Agencies

Every state and many local governments have aid programs, normally called Development Agencies or Development Administrations, available to help businesses create local jobs. These programs are too numerous to list here. You can find out about them by contacting your local Chamber of Commerce or by asking a banker. Remember, whenever dealing with governmental agencies, it helps to have elected officials on your side. If you plan to create several jobs by applying for a government guaranteed loan of any type, make sure your local politicians know of your plans. They may well be able to offer invaluable assistance. After all, creating jobs helps create votes.

7. Leasing Companies

If your new business needs expensive equipment, leasing it may be a good idea. Leasing works like this. Normally you deal with a leasing company which buys the equipment you want for cash from the manufacturer and then rents it to you. Some leasing companies will also repair and service the equipment. In the long run, you normally pay more for equipment you get in this way. However, it can be a relatively inexpensive way to get started, especially if you can't borrow the money to buy the equipment. Leasing companies vary a great deal. Some specialize in short-term arrangements, while others require that you rent the equipment for longer periods of time. When dealing with start-ups, it's not uncommon for the leasing company to ask you to pledge your own collateral, in addition to the equipment, to qualify for the lease.

Leasing can offer significant tax advantages. All of the lease payments can be considered an operating expense with an equipment lease, whereas only the interest portion of the loan payment can be considered an operating expense with a purchase contract. If your business plan forecasts large profits and a need for lots of equipment, it's a good idea to explore the tax implications of an equipment lease with your CPA. The chances are, however, that most readers of this book will be more interested in obtaining a positive cash flow than obtaining tax savings.

8. Insurance Companies and Pension Funds

You may have heard about the possibility of borrowing money from insurance companies or pension funds. Normally, neither is a viable lending source for small new businesses. Both have money for investments, but they are tightly regulated and very cautious. Some insurance companies have a small fund they can invest in businesses, especially if you can offer a combination of equity and debt. However, most small businesses will find money from less restrictive sources long before they r‾ ke an application to an insurance company.

9. Selling Stock to the Public and Raising Outside Capital

Selling stock to the general public through a major public underwriting effort is an expensive, time-consuming process. It can cost $200,000 minimum just to meet the government filing costs, attorney and accountant fees, printing expenses, and the underwriter's commission associated with a public offering of shares.

However, less expensive alternatives exist when going public. For example, the SEC has promulgated a simplified Form S-18 to allow smaller business access to public capital markets. Form S-18 is available, generally, to companies offering up to $7,500,000 worth of shares to the public for cash. Although S-18 filings have become a popular, if not preferred, means for smaller corporations to seek public capital, another, less burdensome, procedure is available under SEC Regulation A. This procedure is available to corporations making public offerings of up to $1,500,000. Note that even these less cumbersome public offering procedures require considerable time and money to implement.

In addition, other avenues are open to smaller businesses for obtaining capital from outside investors under much simpler and inexpensive "limited offering" procedures contained in federal and state securities laws (briefly discussed in Section C2). For example, SEC Regulation D contains three rules which provide exemptions from federal registration for

the offering and issuance of securities (stock) which simply require the filing of a Notice of Sales form with the SEC. While two of these rules include a ceiling on the total value of the securities which may be sold ($500,000 and $5,000,000 respectively), one rule does not impose any upper limit on sales. With some simplification, sales of securities under Regulation D may be made to an unlimited number of "accredited investors" (defined to include principals of the business, such as directors, executive officers and general partners, as well as outside investors who meet certain minimum investment, net worth, or individual net income requirements) and to 35 or fewer persons non-accredited investors.

The federal Regulation D exemption rules can provide an extremely cost- and time-effective alternative to corporations and other businesses, allowing them to raise considerable sums of capital from a number of outside investors without subjecting them to the costs and procedural hurdles associated with a decision to go public. Other more traditional and less defined federal statutory exemptions, such as the federal private offering and intrastate offering exemptions allow many small businesses the opportunity to raise capital from investors in the context of small private or local offerings. For further information on Regulation D (and other federal and state securities laws), consult a lawyer.

H.   Conclusion

There you have it—the primary, and some of the secondary, sources of finding money to start your business. If you really believe in your idea, go on and complete the business plan as outlined in the rest of this book. Then, contact all the sources listed above. If you have a good plan and refuse to take "no" for an answer, you will find the money you need. The Chinese say the longest journey begins with a single step. Let's get started.

Chapter 4

YOUR BUSINESS PLAN AND LOAN APPLICATION, PART 1

FOUR

A. Beginning Steps

Your real work begins here. The next four chapters and Appendix 3 contain all the sample work sheets and instructions you need to produce a first class loan proposal and business plan. Because it helps to understand the whole process before you try to deal with any specific aspect, I suggest you read them carefully before writing anything. Appendix 3 contains all the blank tear-out forms you will need.

When you are ready to put words on paper, you will need:

• a good supply of 8 1/2" x 11" typing paper;

• a typewriter (or word processor);

• a columnar pad with at least 13 columns across and 30 rows vertically;

• access to a photocopy machine;

• a calculator;

• several pencils and a good eraser.

Note: If you can't type, do your work neatly in longhand and take it to a typing service. Make sure you provide them with the proper format for each document. Probably the simplest way to do this is to give the typist a copy of this book and ask him to refer to the sample plans in the Appendix 3.

Step 1. Draft Your Resume

Refer to the worksheets listing your personal strong and weak points which you prepared in Chapter 1. Gathering this information helped you decide both whether to go into business for yourself and what kind of business to enter. Now you will use this same material in a different way, to help convince the person you will ask for money that you are a good risk.

As you review this material, remember that lending money is a very personal activity. Investors and lenders want to be certain that you have the experience, education and desire to make your business a success. In this regard, they need to know what you can do. But, don't fool yourself into thinking that just because you have good credentials you will necessarily get a loan. When it comes right down to it, few people will part with their money unless they also have a positive feeling about you as a person. In short, they want to like you and feel that they can trust you.

What happens if you have had a bankruptcy or other credit problems, such as a lawsuit for a delinquent student loan? Don't try to camouflage them. The banker or investor will probably find out this sort of information from a credit-reporting agency anyway, so if anything, it will help you to be up-front with the negatives. However, you do need to come up with a plausible explanation for your past credit problems. Your explanation should be true. It should also reflect your determination to meet your obligations in the future. For example, here's the wrong sort of explanation for a student loan lawsuit:

"Yes, I acknowledge that I took a student loan and didn't pay it back. I didn't pay it back because the militaristic system we live under is shameful. It's my firmly held conviction that students have an obligation to take what they can to partially balance the scales."

Here's a better one:

"Yes, I did have a student loan and wasn't able to pay it back. I had a rough time adjusting to the working world for several years after I graduated and simply never was able to come up with the money in time. Since then, I have discovered work I like to do and am good at, as evidenced by my recent work history. I have contacted the organization collecting my loan and have arranged a sensible monthly payment schedule. I am honoring this schedule."

The second explanation shows that you will play by conventional credit rules. It also tugs at the heartstrings a little, something that never hurts a good cause.

Potential lenders are used to getting information about you in the form of a resume. As with anything else, there are some tricks to writing a resume that is likely to interest a potential investor. Here's how to do it.

First, make a list of every job you ever had. You may be able to do this by cutting up old resumes. If this isn't realistic, start from scratch. Under each former job, list the functional areas of business you have worked in; for example, sales, management, delivery, credit, and so on. Include all experience where you learned job-related skills, even if you were a volunteer or working for yourself.

When your list is complete, put each heading (i.e., employer and functional area of

responsibility) on a separate sheet of paper. Now, set out the specific things you accomplished for that organization while carrying out your responsibilities. For example, perhaps you reduced costs for your employer by redesigning a delivery route. Perhaps you designed a better canoe. Or maybe you came up with a new marketing strategy that increased sales of tortilla chips, or you figured out how to improve the efficiency of a computer system, or revised a recipe to make brownies taste better. Recall all the positive things you've accomplished. List them. And remember, this isn't the place to be humble. Getting a new business off the ground is no project for the meek.

Here's an example of the wrong kind of resume entry for a credit manager's job:

1979-1984 Credit Manager XYZ Company
Supervised two clerks and the accounts receivable and billing sections; promoted to credit manager after six months.

Why is this a poor entry for purposes of raising money? Because the description doesn't give a potential investor any information as to whether you can run a business. Here is a much better version, detailing what you accomplished for the company while you were credit manager:

1979-1984 Credit Manager XYZ Company

I managed a credit department consisting of ten people. This consisted of an account's receivable section, a billing section, and two people who worked primarily on collecting delinquent accounts. During my tenure, I reorganized both our collection department and our credit granting process to accomplish the following:

1. Keep in closer contact with customers. As a result, we collected $200,000 in delinquent accounts which had previously been consigned to the "unlikely to ever collect" category. As part of this, we successfully prosecuted 15 lawsuits with no new staff.

2. Reduced bad debt losses from 4% of sales to 0.5% of sales between 1982 and 1983 by streamlining the credit application process and credit checking procedures and requiring our sales reps to personally vouch for customers' credit worthiness. Maintained the 0.5% loss percentage in the following years.

3. Reduced accounts receivable from an average of 90 days to an average of 38 days, considerably below the industry norm, again primarily by getting to know our customers better.

4. Through sales conferences, newsletters and frequent phone contact, we worked closely with sales force to insure cooperation in making sure new accounts were credit worthy. During this time, XYZ sales grew from $3 million to $7 million.

The second version of the resume gives an investor or lender something to sink her teeth into. It shows you understand and can improve critical business factors. To borrow money, you needn't prove you can walk on water, but you should show a good understanding of business realities.

Prepare this type of information about all your past activities on the appropriate sheet. Whether you do it from memory, past resumes, or by referring to the exercise in Chapter 1, take your time and do it carefully. When you are done, read it all through carefully. Ask yourself which items are likely to impress a lender the most. This is the material you will want to include in your resume. Discard the rest.

Here are a couple of resumes which inform a potential lender that the writer has good business sense. The first profiles an educated, ambitious, achievement-oriented person who likes to make things grow. He wants to borrow money to open a computer store and seems to have the skills to do it.

RESUME

NAME: James 'Jim' T. Phillips
ADDRESS: 1234 Foxborough Drive, San Jose, CA 94444
TELEPHONE: (408) 555-1212
MARITAL STATUS: Married, two children ages 12 and 16

WORK EXPERIENCE:

1982 to date   MANAGER, THE COMPUTER STORE, San Jose
Manager of retail computer and electronic store with annual sales of
three million dollars and ten employees. During my tenure I:
—Hired sales and support staff to meet sales goals established by chain
management
—Developed promotional plans and merchandising strategy which resulted in
the store exceeding sales and profitability goals by at least 10% each
year
—Developed a computerized inventory plan used by all stores in the
"Computer Store" chain. Received "Manager of the Month" award seven
times. This award is given to the store manager whose store exceeds
monthly sales projections by the largest amount. There are currently 62
stores in "The Computer Store" network.
—Started a newsletter (Compufacts) to maintain close contact with
customers.

1977 to 1982   SELF-EMPLOYED SOFTWARE SALESMAN
Acted as independent sales representative for various software developers
on straight commission basis.
—As a result of my efforts, sales of all three software developers
increased and they were able to expand into new areas and hire an
increased staff of programmers. The principal companies I represented
were: Softy, Inc. of Cupertino, CA; Biosoft of Colorado Springs, COLO;
and Playtime of San Jose, CA.
—During this selling effort, I developed a comprehensive knowledge of the
software marketing process and helped develop a money back-no questions
asked warranty program.

1973 to 1977   COMPUTER PROGRAMMER, SOUTHERN ATLANTIC RAILROAD COMPANY

I worked in FORTRAN, COBOL and BASIC languages on IBM main frame computer
doing real time applications on freight car locations as well as
miscellaneous business programming
—Saved S.A. millions of dollars by designing a better program to handle
both automatic banking and collection of receivables.
—Helped design a new freight car location computer program which provided
better information as to where empty freight cars were stored and
resulted in an increase in car utilization from 60% to 65%.
1972 to 1973 I had several part time jobs doing bookkeeping while
attending programming school.

EDUCATIONAL BACKGROUND: Bachelor of Arts Degree: History. San Jose State
College, 1965 Master of Arts Degree: History. University of California,
Berkeley, 1968 Certified Programmer, ACME Programming School, 1973

HOBBIES: Active in Boy Scouts and United Way; handicap golfer.

REFERENCES: Furnished on request.

The next resume is typical of people who see their potential business as offering them a chance for self-expression as well as profit. Commonly, an individual in an art or craft field wants to begin a business primarily to work in an area they love. Normally this sort of business starts and stays small because of the business owners' desire to keep their hands on a cherished activity, as opposed to trying to achieve big profits or learning the business skills needed to handle fast growth.

Sally Baldwin, whose resume we set out below, is typical. Sally loves to work with fabric and color and has become expert at helping people create a pleasant living and work environment. She wants to open her own small interior decorating design business and will need to borrow some money to do this. She prepares the following resume:

RESUME

NAME: Sally Baldwin
ADDRESS: 725 Harrison Street, Apartment 2G, New Brunswick, New Jersey 03372
TELEPHONE: (619) 555-7653
MARITAL STATUS: Single, no dependents

1981 to date   COMMISSION SALES, MARTHA'S INTERIOR DESIGN STUDIO
I do commission sales work for a full line interior design studio. I locate people who wish to redecorate, establish my credibility with them, prepare a design plan for their house, apartment or office, purchase the supplies and materials necessary, hire the workers to install the design and collect payment from the customers.
—My sales volume last year was just over $500,000. This included a number of small projects and seven complete remodelling jobs, including three offices, one house, two apartments and a small pet hospital.
—In my field, a good design sense is essential, as is keeping up with new trends, materials, suppliers, etc. To make sure I am on top of all of this, I take continuing education courses two nights a week, six months a year at the Design Institute, in New York City, as well as attending at least a dozen textile, furniture and appliance trade shows per year.
—Developed a substantial list of contacts in the design field, including potential customers, contractors, suppliers, etc. [References available on request]

1978 to 1981   COMMISSION SALES, J.C. DOLLAR INTERIOR DESIGN COMPANY
Sold drapes and furniture for J.C. Dollar on commission. Leads came from company advertising, but design, installation, purchase of non-company products and account collection were my responsibility.
—Sold nearly one million dollars worth of company merchandise in 1980 and won *Salesperson of the Year* award.
—My sales normally required several visits to the customer's home or place of work and I became expert at dealing with all sorts of people.

1975 to 1978 HOUSEWIFE

EDUCATION: Graduated high school in 1973, followed by one year at Mount McKinley Junior College

REFERENCES: Available on request

HOBBIES: Decorating on a low budget; collecting Raggedy Ann Dolls

---

These two resumes share one important attribute. They both show a knowledge of the particular business the individual wants to start. In this respect, they are somewhat different from many typical job application resumes. For example, a lender will not be as interested as a potential employer might be in whether you have the social skills to fit in well in an employment environment. Again, the area you should emphasize is your knowledge of how your potential business works and your knowledge of and respect for business (i.e., profit and loss) realities.

The following resume is typical of a person with good general business experience but no work history in the particular business in question. Our subject is an attorney who wants to start a gourmet hot dog stand in a building he owns in Chicago. As far as the lender is concerned, risk is reduced because the attorney owns the building, has another source of income, and because it doesn't take a huge amount of money to start a hot dog stand. Just the same, Mr. Brinkle needs to convince a lender that his general business experience substitutes, at least in part, for his lack of frankfurter finesse. He accomplishes this by demonstrating that he knows enough to hire a manager with enough experience to squeeze the mustard and shake the ketchup.

RESUME

NAME: STEPHEN BRINKLE
ADDRESS: 123 Smith Street, Chicago, ILL.
TELEPHONE: (312) 555-1212
MARITAL STATUS: Married, three children living at home

1972 to date   ATTORNEY IN PRIVATE PRACTICE
I am in private practice, specializing in business law matters, along with some general civil law concerns. During that time I have successfully invested in a variety of small businesses, including an auto tune-up shop, and a sporting goods store.

In some of my small business investments, I have had to take an active role in management. For example, in the tune-up shop, I had to fire the manager and locate additional, more qualified mechanics. After doing that, the business became profitable and I sold it for more than I paid. In the sporting goods store, I spent some considerable time working with the manager in keeping inventory investment limited to fast moving items. He had a tendency to carry too many types of goods.

After several months of work, during which we agreed to concentrate on tennis and running equipment, he became a better inventory manager and the store became considerably more profitable. I still own this store (Bill's Track and Court, 11 Van Renseller Blvd., Chicago).

EDUCATION   B.A. Northwestern University, History, 1962
                   Graduate Northwestern Law School 1964
                   Passed Illinois bar exam 1965

REFERENCES Available on request

HOBBIES: Squash.

COMMUNITY   I am very active in various charitable organizations specializing in relieving worldwide
INVOLVEMENT: hunger.

Because Stephen Brinkle doesn't have experience in selling food, he includes a resume for his key employee. This particular resume is for the individual he has selected to manage his hot dog stand, who happens to be his nephew. If you find yourself in a similar situation, follow a similar strategy. Again, the point of doing this is to show potential financial backers that you have good sense in picking people who complement your background.

RESUME

```
NAME: JONATHAN 'JOHNNY' BRINKLE
ADDRESS: 5678 Palatine Boulevard, West Chicago, ILL.
TELEPHONE: (312) 556-1314
MARITAL STATUS: Single, no dependents


1981 to date MANAGER, BURGER CHEF RESTAURANT

Manager of fast food restaurant. I supervised three shifts (twenty
employees in all). Before I took over, Unit 211 had sales of less than
two-thirds the Burger King national averages. During my managership, I
brought unit 211 up to surpass the national averages. My main strategy to
accomplish this was to maintain tight quality control, and to improve the
cleanliness and general appearance of the unit. Within six months after I
took over, we began getting top ratings for general appearance and
cleanliness from Burger King and many compliments from customers.


1978 to 1981 MANAGER TRAINEE JACK IN THE BOX RESTAURANTS

I was trained in fast food management at a number of Jack in the Box
locations. The principal method of training was to have me rotate through
every job in the operation. I learned a lot about adjusting cooking to
demand so that customers always received freshly cooked food. I also
learned that the cleaner the restaurant the more food you sell.


EDUCATION: Graduate Northside High School, 1977

REFERENCES: Available on request

HOBBIES: Restoring a 1932 Ford; playing softball
```

Step 2. Draft Your Personal Financial Statement

Now it's time to write your personal financial statement. Simply put, this means listing everything you own and everything you owe. However, doing this in a form lenders are used to seeing involves several sub-steps, such as setting out your assets, liabilities, net worth, etc. We will treat each part separately. To best accomplish this, I recommend that you do a rough draft of each of these parts on a separate sheet before transferring all the information to the tear-out "Personal Financial Statement" in Appendix 3. Incidentally, this is the same form we referred to in Chapter 3, when we discussed raising cash by selling or borrowing against your assets, so you may already be familiar with it.

Please pay attention to one more thing. Drawing up a good personal financial statement isn't difficult, but it does involve attention to detail. So, please take your time and make sure you review your work several times before you put it into final form.

B. Determine Your Assets

Turn to the Appendix of this book and take out the form entitled "Personal Financial Statement—Assets." Your task is to briefly describe and estimate the current market value of everything you own, whether paid for or not. This means you should put down the total market value of the asset, even if you owe money against it. Market value means the total price for which you could sell the particular piece of property today. If you're not sure how much a particular item is worth, make an estimate now and verify it later.

Listed below are short descriptions of the possible types of assets you may own, and examples of each:

PERSONAL FINANCIAL STATEMENT—ASSETS

I. CASH

List the cash balance of each of your checking and savings accounts, identifying each by bank and account number. Also, list any cash on hand, in your safe deposit box, or buried in the back yard.

	Amount
Cash on Hand	
Cash in Banks—Savings	

Bank Name	Account #	Date	Balance
1. Thrift Savings Co.	556472	1-25-8_	$3,000
TOTAL SAVINGS $3,000			
Cash in Banks—Checking			
1. Bank of Centerville	1114443231	1-25-8_	$1,876
Money Market Accounts			
1. Charles Chubb Co.		1-25-8_	$2,000
Miscellaneous Cash (Drawers, Safety Deposit Box)		1-25-8_	500
TOTAL CASH AT 1-25-8_			$7,376

II. STOCKS AND BONDS

List any stocks and bonds you own. This list should show the number of shares, whether they are listed and on which exchange, to whom they are issued, the manner in which title is held (joint tenants, etc.), and the market value.

STOCKS (Including Mutual Funds)

Name of Stock	No. of Shares	Exchange	Market Price	Date	Market Value
1. General Computer	50		$65/share	1-25-8_	$3,250
2. Consolidated Radio	100		$12/share	1-25-8_	$1,200
TOTAL MARKET VALUE OF STOCKS AT 1-25-8_					$4,450

BONDS

Name of Bond	No. of Bonds	Market Price	Date	Market Value
1. IMB	50	$250	1-25-8_	$6,250
TOTAL MARKET VALUE OF BONDS AT 1-25-8_				$6,250

III. REAL ESTATE PROPERTY

Describe each piece of property you own and show its estimated market value. Note whether it is unimproved, a personal residence, investment property, or whatever. Include the street address or parcel number of each property. For significant properties other than your house, you should also include a written appraisal.

Description	Date	Market Value
1. Personal residence, three bedrm, two bath frame/stucco house, 33324 Being St., Modesto, CA (Approx. 15 yrs. old)	1-25-8_	$140,000
2. Unimproved lot, one acre	1-25-8_	15,000

TOTAL MARKET VALUE OF REAL PROPERTY AT 1-25-8_ $155,000

IV. TRUST DEEDS AND MORTGAGES

This section is for notes which people owe you. Loans against property you own will be listed under the "Liabilities" section of this form. Itemize any mortgages (deeds of trust) or notes secured by real property which you own. Show the street address of the property, type of improvements (i.e, house, duplex, etc.), name of payer, payment terms, and the current unpaid balance.

Note Description	Monthly Payments	Current Balance
1. Second deed of trust on former personal residence, 4445 Karma Street, Modesto, CA.	$95/mo.	$9,786
2. First mortgage on unimproved lot Brooklyn, NY	$50/mo.	2,098

TOTAL CURRENT BALANCES ON TRUST DEEDS AND MORTGAGES $11,884

V. CASH VALUE OF YOUR LIFE INSURANCE

If you own whole life insurance policies, they may include a cash surrender value. Obtain the value from your insurance agent. If you own term insurance, there will be no cash value, so you needn't bother to list these policies.

Policy Description	Cash Surrender Value
1. Reliable Life Company	$2,457

TOTAL CASH VALUE $2,457

VI. ACCOUNTS AND NOTES RECEIVABLE

List each note (loan) people owe you and show the unpaid balance and payment schedule, as well as a description of any property securing the note. It is also a good idea to briefly state your relationship to the payer and whether or not the payment of the loan is questionable. Remember, you can add a second sheet if you wish to include more information than will fit here.

Note/Account Description	Monthly Payments	Currently Owed
1. Jack Sprat, nephew; unsecured note	$106.25/mo.	$2,356
TOTAL NOTES/ACCOUNTS RECEIVABLE		$2,356

VII. OTHER PERSONAL PROPERTY

List all your valuable belongings. Itemize the larger items like cars, boats, and collections, describing item in as much detail as possible. Don't forget household items and valuable clothing.

Description	Date	Value
1. 1958 Buick Century Hardtop, good condition	1-25-8_	$2,500
2. 198_ Honda Accord	1-25-8_	4,000
3. Household Furniture	1-25-8_	2,000
4. Stamp collection (inherited from my father)	1-25-8_	3,500
TOTAL PERSONAL PROPERTY		$12,000

COMPUTE YOUR TOTAL ASSETS

Now add up the market values of all your property. The result is your total assets.

TOTAL ASSETS $ _____

C. Determine Your Liabilities and Net Worth

Now, take form entitled "PERSONAL FINANCIAL STATEMENT—LIABILITIES AND NET WORTH." This is where you write down everything you owe to others. Again, you will probably want to do a rough draft on a blank sheet of paper before you transfer the information to the form. To a considerable degree, it will be the flip side of what you just did. That is, if you showed the market value of a house as an asset, you will now list the mortgage or deed of trust on that same house as a liability. Here are examples of some of your likely liabilities.

PERSONAL FINANCIAL STATEMENT—LIABILITIES AND NET WORTH

I. PERSONAL NOTES PAYABLE TO BANKS

List any non real estate notes to banks, showing the bank, the unpaid amount, terms of payment, when the loan is due in full (if it is not a term loan), and any security for the loan, etc.

Bank	Terms	Payment	Monthly Amount Owed
1. Merchant's Bank	Unsecured personal note; interest-only quarterly at prime + 2%, all due 9/1/8_	$180	$5,000
2. Bank of Centerville	Personal note (secured by 1958 Buick): 10 equal payments including interest	$100	1,000
TOTAL NOTES TO BANKS			$6,000

II. REAL ESTATE LOANS

List each note and deed of trust showing the property by which it is secured, the unpaid balance, the terms of payment (including any balloon payment), and the time the note will be paid in full.

Bank (or other lender)	Terms	Payment	Owed
1. Bank of Centerville First Trust Deed & Note on Personal Residence	Fixed rate (10%) 30 years ending in 2009	$850	$87,583
2. William Sandusky (former owner) Second mortgage on personal residence	Interest only at 18%, all due January 1, 198_	$150	$10,000
TOTAL REAL ESTATE LOANS			$97,583

III. PERSONAL PROPERTY LOANS

List the same information for any loans against equipment, business vehicles, business inventory or whatever, showing the payee, unpaid balance, security, term of payment and the time the note will be paid in full.

Description	Terms	Payment	Owed
1. Merchant's Bank car loan on 198_ Honda	48 mos; will all be paid off Sept., 198_	$220	$1,000

TOTAL OTHER ASSETS $1,000

IV. LOANS AGAINST LIFE INSURANCE POLICIES

List details. Whole life insurance normally has a cash value (your cash which the insurance company holds for you to pay when you die). You can borrow at least a substantial portion of that money from the insurance company. If the insurance dates back a number of years, the interest rate may be very reasonable.

Insurance Co.	Terms	Monthly Payment	Amount Owed
1. Reliable Life	Borrowed $5,000 against my life insurance policy for 60 mos. at 6% interest	$97	$3,987
TOTAL INSURANCE POLICY LOANS			$3,987

V. CREDIT CARD AND REVOLVING ACCOUNT BALANCES

Write the amount you owe on any credit card accounts. Include bank cards, revolving accounts at stores and gasoline companies. If you don't pay in full every month, show minimum monthly payments.

Name of Creditor	Average Monthly Payment	Amount Owed
1. VISA (Bank of Centerville)	$500	$800
2. American Local	200	0
3. J.T. Henney	60	0
TOTAL CREDIT CARD & REVOLVING CREDIT		$800

VI. ANY OTHER LIABILITIES

This is where you list whatever else you owe. List past due tax liabilities, loans from relatives, loans to bookies, etc.

Name of Creditor	Terms	Monthly Payment	Amount Owed
1. Mother-in-law	When I can repay— no worry.	-0-	$1,000
TOTAL OTHER LIABILITIES			$1,000

COMPUTE YOU TOTAL LIABILITIES

Add up all the loans and amounts you owe others.

TOTAL LIABILITIES $_____

Caution! Before you go on, carefully compare the information on your assets and liabilities lists. Make sure they are consistent, i.e., make sure that you show assets for which you show liabilities, and vice versa. If any of your liabilities need further explanation, append a sheet of typing paper to your financial statement and set out the details. You might want to do this, for example, if you plan to pay off your mother-in-law by building her a deck next summer, or you are well along with a plan to refinance your house which will lower your monthly payments, etc. Simply put, repeat the relevant heading from your financial statement on a blank sheet and write "continued."

PERSONAL PROPERTY LOANS (CONTINUED)

I list a car loan to Merchant's Bank for $1,000. I am in the process of selling my old Buick and will replace it with a car my Uncle Fred is giving me. I expect to sell the Buick for about $3,000, leaving me with $2,000 once the bank is paid.

D. Determine Your Net Worth

To arrive at your net worth, first, add up all your liabilities. Here you include the total amount you owe, not the monthly payments. For example, our mythical person showed a total of $97,583 in outstanding real estate loans (i.e., the principal amount he still owes). Use this figure in determining your total liabilities and enter it on the "Total Liabilities" line. Next, subtract your total liabilities (what you owe) from your total assets (what you own). Do that now. When you transfer your information to the financial statement form, you will enter this amount. For example, if your total assets are $35,000 and your total liabilities are $12,500, your net worth will be $22,500. If your total liabilities are more than your total assets, your net worth will be a negative figure. It should go almost without saying that people with a negative net worth have difficulty borrowing money.

TOTAL LIABILITIES $_____

NET WORTH $_____

TOTAL ASSETS & LIABILITIES $_____

E. Determine Your Income

The next part of the personal financial statement requires a listing of your income. This should reflect your current situation. You should show your present salary, even if you'll quit your job to start the new business. Again, start with a blank piece of paper. Here's a list of possible income sources you may identify.

**PERSONAL FINANCIAL STATEMENT
ANNUAL FAMILY INCOME AND EXPENSES**

My Annual Income

I. SALARY AND WAGES
List all the sources of your wage income. Do the same thing for your spouse.

Source	Annual Amount
1. Consolidated Console, Inc.	$35,000
2. Primavera Community College District	4,500
3. Pine Tree Unified School District	20,000
TOTAL SALARY AND WAGES	$59,500

II. PEOPLE WHO OWE ME MONEY
If anyone owes you money, list it here. If the circumstances are at all unusual or would benefit by further explanation, attach a blank sheet, type this heading, and elaborate.

Person Owing	Terms	Amount Owed	Annual Payment
1.			
2.			
TOTAL ANNUAL PAYMENT			$_____

III. INCOME FROM RENTAL PROPERTY
If you own real property or valuable personal property for which you receive regular rental payments, list them here.

Source	Annual Amount
1. 27 Fruitvale St., New City, IL	$3,600
TOTAL ANNUAL INCOME FROM RENTAL PROPERTY	$3,600

Again, if there are details you want a lender to know, include them on an attached sheet. For example, if you are planning to raise the rent in six months, that would be interesting information.

IV. DIVIDENDS AND INTEREST

List the amount you expect to receive and the source. Again, make sure that the information shown here corresponds to information you have shown in the "Assets" section. For example, if you list dividend income from several stocks, those stocks should also be listed in the "Assets" section.

Source	Annual Amount
1. General computer (50 shares)	$890
2. Thrift Savings (interest on savings account—$3,000 at 6%)	40
TOTAL DIVIDENDS AND INTEREST	$930

V. INCOME FROM BUSINESS OR PROFESSION

List any income you receive from any businesses. For example, if you have already started the business you want to borrow money to expand, list the income you receive here.

Description	Amount
1.	

TOTAL INCOME FROM BUSINESS OR PROFESSION $_____

VI. OTHER INCOME

List and describe any other source of income. (It's generally a good idea to list alimony and child support payments you receive, as they make your income larger.)

Description	Amount
Child Support (former husband) [If there are payments or other problems here, attach an explanation.]	$2,500
TOTAL OTHER INCOME	$2.500

TOTAL YOUR ANNUAL INCOME

Here we want you to add up all the income you receive from all sources and write in the total.

TOTAL ANNUAL INCOME $ _____

F. Determine Your Annual Living Expenses

Here you list your annual living costs, including loan payments you have already identified. Do this carefully, again using a

separate page, and transferring information to the tear-out form at the back of the book. Information about living expenses is properly included on the bottom half of the form entitled, "Annual Income and Expenses."

Annual Living Expenses

I. REAL ESTATE LOAN PAYMENTS

List the annual total of all your real estate loan payments, including principal and interest. If you rent, show your rent here, making sure it's clearly defined as such.

Creditor	Monthly Payment	Annual Amount
1. Bank of Centerville 1st Mortgage on residence	$895	$19,740
2. Abner Small, mortgage on unimproved lot	190	2,280
TOTAL REAL ESTATE LOAN PAYMENTS OR RENT		$22,020

II. PROPERTY TAXES AND ASSESSMENTS

List your yearly liabilities if you own property.

Property Taxes	Annual Amount
1. Winchester County	$1,250
TOTAL PROPERTY TAXES	$1,250

III. FEDERAL AND STATE INCOME TAXES

Show your totals from last year's income tax forms.

Description	Amount
1. IRS	$3,100
2. State of _____	898
TOTAL TAX PAYMENTS	$3,998

IV. OTHER LOAN PAYMENTS (Amount Paid in 198_)

List all the payments for the non-real estate loans, notes, charge accounts and credit cards you listed in the "Liabilities" section; use last year's numbers. If these have changed substantially, append sheet and explain.

Creditor	Monthly Payment	Annual Amount
1. Visa (Bank of Centerville)	$500	$6,000
2. American Local	200	2,400
3. J.T. Henney	60	720
TOTAL OTHER LOAN PAYMENTS		$9,120

V. INSURANCE PREMIUMS

List everything you expect to pay for the year—life, health (unless covered through your job), property, auto, etc.

Insurance Companies	Type Policy	Annual Payment
1. Reliable Insurance	term	$1,164
TOTAL INSURANCE PREMIUMS		$1,164

VI. LIVING EXPENSES

Here is where you put all your other expenses—food, clothing, entertainment, travel, etc.

Description	Annual Total
Annual family living expenses (food, clothing, entertainment, etc.)	$12,000
TOTAL LIVING EXPENSES	$12,000

VII. OTHER EXPENSES

List child and/or spousal support obligations, and any other regular expense not listed above. If you belong to professional associations, have continuing education expenses, belong to clubs, etc., list them here.

Description	Annual Expenses
1. Child support payments per year	$3,600
TOTAL OTHER EXPENSES	$3,600

COMPUTE YOUR ANNUAL EXPENSES

Now add up all your expenses. Your total should be less than your annual income total above. If it's not, you will have some explaining to do.

TOTAL ANNUAL EXPENSES $ _____

Now, if you have not already done so, it's time to transfer the information on your four sheets of paper to the blank financial statement which you will find in Appendix 3. As noted above, many financial institutions will prefer their own form, which they will supply you, although they'll usually accept yours if it's neat,

up-to-date and signed. Here's a personal financial statement (in a slightly different form than we have used thus far) for a person with fairly healthy assets. We introduce a different type of financial statement here to emphasize the fact that no matter the form, the information is the same.

PERSONAL FINANCIAL STATEMENT: JOAN RICE

December 15, 198_

	$
ASSETS listed at market value this date:	
Cash on hand and in bank	21,000
Accounts Receivable, consulting work (due by Jan. 1, 198_)	5,000
Antiques and jewelry on hand, see attached schedule*	50,000
Notes receivable:	
1. First trust deed on 777 Lucky Street, in Centerville single family residence, market value as estimated by Johnson Realtors last year of $100,000, payments $600/month, interest at 10%, will be all paid in about 9 years at current rate, current balance	56,768
2. Unsecured note, term 5 years at 10% payment $164 per month, will be paid in about three years at current rate, current balance**	5,789
Real Estate:	
My residence at 4444 Easy Street, 2,400 sq.ft. market value based on estimate from Smith Realty last year	175,000
Autos:	
1987 BMW	14,000
1985 Buick	4,000
TOTAL ASSETS	331,557

LIABILITIES	
First trust deed on residence payable at $400 per month, including interest at 10% will be paid off in about twelve years	60,000
Home improvement loan on residence, $200 month including interest at 13% will be paid off in about ten years	20,000
Note to Bank of Centerville secured by first trust deed on Lucky Street, payable at $500 per month will be paid off at same time as Lucky Street note	35,000
Note to Bank of Centerville on BMW payable at $220 per month, including interest at 15% will be paid off in 4 years	9,000
Credit cards (MasterCard, Visa), revolving credit, total	3,000
TOTAL LIABILITIES	127,000

TOTAL ASSETS	331,557
NET WORTH	204,557

ANNUAL INCOME

Consulting (Net income after business expenses of self employment)	60,000
Real Estate Loan (777 Lucky St., Centerville) (to my brother)	7,200
Unsecured note	1,968
TOTAL INCOME	69,168

ANNUAL EXPENSES

Real Estate Loan Payments	7,200
Property Taxes	1,500
Income Taxes (returns attached)	4,500
Insurance premiums	5,000
Living Expenses	30,000
TOTAL EXPENSES	$ 48,200

*A schedule is no more than a detailed list of the particular objects which make up the total for a general category. In this situation, you would list all your valuable antiques and jewelry and how much they could be sold for (their market value).

**A potential lender will be interested in the details of this sort of note. Explain on a separate sheet, emphasizing why you think you will be repaid.

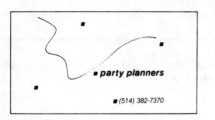

■ *party planners*

■ *(514) 382-7370*

G. Verifying the Accuracy of Your Financial Statement

Of course, potential lenders will want to verify your statements. Tax returns for the last two or three years are normally adequate to back-up your income and expense statements. Have them ready. Most credit granting agencies accept income tax returns as proof on the theory that very few people pay taxes on more income than they make. In addition, they will usually obtain a personal credit check from a credit information agency on your track record in making payments. That shows them the bills you pay and when you pay them as well as any bills you haven't paid.

Most of the time they will accept your signature on your Net Worth statement, the one you filled out in Section D, since it is a crime to knowingly make false financial statements. Banks will also verify the cash deposits you claim by contacting the relevant institution and using the account number you provide. Also, any lender will want evidence of your title to any property they take as security for a loan. Other than that, your income tax returns and your personally signed financial statements, together with the verification they do through credit agencies, will be enough proof.

Occasionally, your actual income will be somewhat greater than your tax returns show. If this is your situation, be ready to verify your "Assets" statement in some other way. Don't worry too much about this sort of disparity unless it is large. In an age of overly high taxation, your lender will not be surprised if your actual income is a shade higher than your reported income. His probably is too.

Now you've completed your resume and personal financial statement and you're ready for the next step in writing your business plan and loan application. Set these two documents aside for now and go on to the next chapter.

Chapter 5

YOUR BUSINESS PLAN AND LOAN APPLICATION, PART 2

FIVE

A. Introduction

Now you've finished the easy part of your financial statement, the part where you talk about yourself. Next, we deal with financial information about your projected business. This is a little trickier, as it involves "guestimates" about the future. But don't let this discourage you. Most likely, you've been thinking about the financial side of your business for some time. Your job now is to write down your financial projections in an organized way so that a potential lender can clearly see how your proposed business will work. We can help you do this.

As you begin dealing with all the details inherent in any financial statement, it is easy to lose perspective and forget the larger picture— that is, what all your work is supposed to prove. If this happens, pause for a moment and remember that, at bottom, the point of what you are doing amounts to informing your potential funding source of the following:

- How much money you need;

- What you will spend it on;

- How you will pay it back.

We will show you how to develop the numbers necessary to produce good answers to all three questions in this chapter. In Chapter 6, we will help you deepen your understanding of what the numbers mean and how you can best use them to achieve your goal.

In order to arrive at how much money you need to get started, and how much it will cost to get your business underway, you will have to make a number of decisions about how your business will operate. In other words, you can't make realistic financial projections in a vacuum. They must be integrated into a completely thought through business plan. As part of doing this, you will inevitably make some assumptions, and even a guess or two. You simply won't have hard information on everything. Just the same, your projections should be as accurate as possible. Shoot for an accuracy rate of plus or minus 10%. Base all your estimates on a two-year period, unless your business absolutely dictates a shorter or longer time frame, as it might if you were starting a beer stand for the county fair, or a vineyard with a five-year growing cycle. In these instances, you need to adopt a time frame that makes sense in the circumstances. If you are going to sell more than one product, or provide several services, make a projection for each product or service separately.

B. What is a Profit and Loss Forecast?

Let's begin with your projected profit and loss forecast (called a "P & L," or an income statement forecast, in the money business). This is a necessary part of any business plan. It gives you and the people who you want to borrow money from the basic information necessary to decide whether your business will succeed. Basically, a profit and loss forecast forces you to estimate how many dollars you will take in and how many dollars you will spend to do it for some future period. While there are other extremely important factors, such as your cash flow (see Chapter 6), your business will be in good shape if you can confidently predict that the money coming in will exceed the money going out by a healthy margin. You will find a blank profit and loss forecast in Appendix 4.

Note: If you plan to do a project development, skip to Chapter 6 concerning cash flow, and to Appendix 3, where you will find a project development example.

2710 Cabrillo Ave.
Columbus, Ohio 43215
(614) 386-1397

JEFFER'S ASSOCIATES

C. Determine Your Average Cost of Sale

Before you can begin to fill in your profit and loss forecast, you need to determine your average cost of sale. Pretend you're Antoinette Gorzak, the potential dress shop owner we introduced in Chapter 2. Let's say you plan to sell dresses for an average price of $45 and your research tells you they will cost $22.50 each. Your cost of each sale before you allow for labor and other overhead will be 50% of the selling price. If you plan to give your customers anything with the purchase, say a specially-printed shopping bag and an imprinted dress box, don't forget to include the cost of these

items as part of your gross sales cost. Maybe this will make your cost of each sale 51% or 52% instead of 50%.

Now develop separate figures to deal with the proportion of your sales you expect in accessories and other lower cost of sales items. Assuming you plan to sell mostly dresses, with only a few other small items, such as belts and scarves, you can include all your accessories in one entry. If, however, you plan several important secondary merchandise lines, make a separate detailed profit & loss forecast for each.

Finally, whether you make one P & L forecast or six, don't forget about the inevitable percentage of merchandise you will have to move at sale prices. In other words, don't assume you will sell all your merchandise at the standard discount. Whether you're in the book business, bake cookies or are a child psychologist, chances are you will commonly sell your product or services for less. This may be because you need to move out last year's styles or because you need to move broken cookies or because you provide your services cheaper to low-income groups. Whatever the reason, be sure you take this into consideration in making your profit and loss forecast.

If you have trouble developing the numbers for any of this, review Chapter 2, Section F. Basically, your own personal experience, coupled with the information available from trade sources, should make this sort of projection fairly routine.[1] If you do not find this to be the case, it is probably an indication that you plan to enter a new field, or you need more knowledge about and experience in an established business before you begin.

---

[1]A couple of good resources for business operation ratios are *Expenses in Retail Business*, published by the NCR Corporation, and *Key Business Ratios*, published by Dun & Bradstreet, Inc. (see Chapter 11).

A chart for Antoinette's Dress Shop might look like this:

AVERAGE COST OF SALES CHART: ANTOINETTE'S DRESS SHOP

ITEM	EXPECTED SALES REVENUE	COST PER SALE	TOTAL COST OF SALES
Dresses	$125,000	50%	$ 62,500
Accessories	10,000	35%	3,500
Sale Items	65,000	80%	52,000
TOTAL	$200,000	59%	$118,000

The total cost per sale figure (59% in Antoinette's example) is not an average of the cost per sale percentages. Instead, it is weighted according to the amount of expected sales revenue and is derived by dividing the total cost of sales by the expected sales revenue ($118,000/$200,000).

An average cost of sales of 58% to 60% is typical for a profitable dress shop. But it is wise to be a little conservative and use 60% as your cost of sales when forecasting profits. This would mean your gross profit would be 40%.

Here's a similar Cost of Sales Chart for a bar and restaurant. Not surprisingly, it doesn't look much like Antoinette's.

AVERAGE ANNUAL COST OF SALES CHART: BAR AND RESTAURANT

ITEM	SALES REVENUE	COST PER SALE	TOTAL COST OF SALES
Food	$300,000	38%	$114,000
Liquor	60,000	29%	17,400
Beer/Wine	40,000	75%	30,000
TOTAL	$400,000	40%	$161,400

Service Business Note: By definition, service businesses sell services or labor and do not sell merchandise. As such, service businesses commonly have mostly fixed costs, or operating expenses. The cost of sales, or variable cost, portion of a service business' total costs will be small. For example, a consulting firm may incur outside typing, photocopying and report binding expenses which will vary somewhat with every sale, but by and large, most expenses, such as salaries and rent, will be fixed.

Here is a cost of sales chart for a consulting firm:

AVERAGE ANNUAL COST OF SALES CHART: CONSULTING FIRM

ITEM	SALES REVENUE	COST PER SALE	TOTAL COST OF SALES
Publications, phone, travel	$100,000	20%	$20,000
Contract services (Typing, photocopying, etc.)	50,000	75%	37,500
TOTAL	$150,000	38%	$57,500

D. Complete Your Profit and Loss Forecast

You should now have a handle on your average cost of sales. If so, you are ready to fill out the first three lines of your profit and loss forecast (see sample that follows). If not, read Chapter 2, Section F and do some more research.

Line 1. Your Sales Estimate

Put your sales estimates by month for the first two years here. This is simply an estimate of how many dollars you will take in for what you sell.

Line 2. Your Monthly Cost of Sales

To arrive at your monthly cost of sales, multiply your sales estimate by the cost of sales percentage you developed in the cost of sales chart just above. Returning to our dress shop example, Antoinette would multiply her monthly sales figure estimate by 60% (0.6)[2] and write that number in the cost of sales line. For example, if January sales are forecast at $12,000, then cost of sales for January would be 60% of $12,000 (0.6 x 12,000 = 7,200), or $7,200. See the sample profit forecast for her dress shop on the next two pages.

Service Business Note: The consulting firm discussed above could use 10% rather than 38% as its cost of sales if it chose to consider labor as a fixed expense, making labor costs independent of sales.

Line 3. Your Gross Profit

Again, gross profit is simply the difference between total sales dollars and the direct cost (in dollars) of making those sales. Or in other words, it is what is left to pay the rent, other overhead, and hopefully, a few extra dollars so you can go to the grocery store. For example, looking at the dress shop example for January, to arrive at gross profit just subtract the cost of sales of $7,200 from the sales, $12,000, and enter the result of $4,800. Do the same thing for each subsequent month.

---

[2]Antoinette actually came out with a 59% figure, but as I've said, it's wise to be a little conservative.

E. Determine Your Operating Expenses (Fixed Costs)

Unfortunately, every business has lots of costs in addition to what it spends for merchandise. Indeed, for most small businesses, the difference between success and failure often has to do with keeping these fixed operating expenses low. For this reason, the world is full of savvy people who started successful businesses in a garage, a spare room in their house, the corner of a warehouse, or store front in an undesirable neighborhood and put most of their money into the product. Unfortunately, there are lots of others who sank too much of their original capital into essentially cosmetic aspects of their business. Many of these people enjoyed their fancy offices, stores and restaurants for a very short time and then they went broke.

Fixed and Variable Cost Note: In Chapter 2, Section F, I pointed out that "operating costs" can generally also be called "fixed costs" (costs you're stuck with every month, no matter how much you sell). I summarize this discussion below and caution you that if you don't know the difference between a fixed and variable cost (also called a "cost of sale") and don't have a pretty clear idea of why it's better to keep your fixed costs low, you should reread Chapter 2, Section F in addition to the following discussion.

Costs other than those for merchandise and its direct packaging (lines 1-3, above) should all be set out under "Operating Expenses"—that is, below your gross profit line. One useful way of thinking about what should be put into the direct (variable) cost of sales category as opposed to what should be treated as a fixed operating expense, is to think about whether the particular cost in question is incurred only if you make a sale (a variable cost of sale), or exists whether or not a particular transaction is made (an operating, or fixed, expense). Clearly, what you pay for your merchandise is a cost of the sale under this theory. Just as clearly, things like utilities and rent, which do not normally fluctuate with sales, should be listed as fixed operating expenses, that is, below the gross profit line.

What about wages and salaries? Most small businesses keep their employees on a fixed weekly or monthly work schedule regardless of how business fluctuates. If this is your situation, put wages into the fixed operating expense category. Some small manufacturing businesses pay workers on a piece-rate basis or hire employees when orders are high and lay them off when business is slow. Others don't pay a salary at all, but compensate workers with a commission for each sale. In all of these situations, a portion, if not all, of money paid workers should be considered a variable cost of sale.

Example: Ronnie Ryann runs the Religious Record Round Table in Rye, New York. It's a small business, but she loves it dearly. The gross profit on the records and tapes she sells is 50%. This is the same as saying that after adding up the cost of the records, packaging and postage (all variable costs), Ronnie is able to sell at double this amount. Ronnie rents 1,000 square feet for $400 per month, pays her part-time clerk $500 per month, and budgets $300 per month for utilities, taxes and so forth. This means her operating expenses (all fixed costs) are $1,200 per month. Therefore, Ronnie has to sell $2,400 of records per month to break even. Her salary comes out of the money she takes in over the $2,400. Fortunately, it will cost Ronnie very little in extra overhead to sell up to $5,000 of records per month, so if she can achieve this volume, she will get to keep close to half of it.

Line 4. Operating Expenses

Lines 5 & 6. Wages and Salaries

Decide how many employees you'll need to handle the level of business you expect. For example, assume Antoinette Gorzak decides that her dress shop will need two people on the floor at peak times (lunch and after work), but one clerk can normally handle business at other times. Antoinette decides she can open the store at 11:00 a.m. and can usually be available to fill in if the store suddenly gets busy at an unexpected time in the afternoon as well as doing the books, ordering, etc., when the store is not crowded. Therefore, she plans to hire only one full-time clerk, with the title of assistant manager, to work 40 hours a week and a part-time clerk for the 8 busiest hours. That's a total of 48 hours per week of labor. The assistant manager will work from 12:00 p.m. to 8:00 p.m., Tuesday through Friday and from opening to closing on Saturday. The part-time clerk will work evenings for two hours Wednesday and Thursday, and Saturday from 10:00 a.m. - 4:00 p.m.

In checking with the state employment agency and several private employment agencies, Antoinette learns that part-time clerks make minimum wage, even with one or more year's experience, and that there are lots of qualified people looking for clerk positions. Assistant managers with several year's experience make minimum wage plus 30% to 50%. In each case, Antoinette plans to pay slightly above minimum figures to assure herself of competent people and to minimize problems with turnover.

Accordingly, Antoinette plans to pay her part-time clerk $3.75 per hour. This translates to a weekly wage cost of ($3.75 x 8 = $30). Although she could probably get an assistant manager for $5.00 per hour, she decides to pay

$5.75 (40 x $5.75 = $230) because she knows an excellent person who she really likes and trusts. Multiplying these weekly figures times 4.3 results in an average monthly wage cost of $1,118. Extra costs for mandatory employers' contributions to Social Security, Unemployment Insurance and so forth will average out to about 12% of each person's salary. She uses this 12% figure since she plans no extra benefits, like health insurance or vacations, until the business is a success and can afford them. This means Antoinette will use a figure of $1,120 for monthly wage costs and $135 for employee benefits. When you work out these numbers for your business, enter them on Lines 5 and 6 of the profit and loss forecast.

Don't worry about withholding of taxes from employee wages for now; stick with the gross amount the employee makes.

Line 7 ▪ Rent

Rent is the next major item to consider, unless you plan to operate out of your home or some other space which will not result in additional out-of-pocket costs. If you don't already have a spot in mind, check building availability and costs by talking to a commercial real estate broker and people who occupy space similar to the one you have in mind. You should know what kind of location you want by now (whether you need high visibility or whether an obscure, low-cost location is just as good). You should also know how large a space you need, what plumbing, electrical and lighting you want, and how much storage you need. Sometimes cheap rent doesn't turn out to be such a bargain if you have to build walls, a bathroom, a loading area and install a kitchen sink, or, if a poor location means you get few customers. At any rate, if you don't already have a firm cost estimate for rent, develop one.

Leasehold Improvements Note: Any time you build something like a wall or a bathroom, it is considered a capital expense. That means you should treat the expenditure in the same way you treat the purchase of equipment. Do not show the expenditure as a current operating expense. Only the depreciation is an operating expense. You can write off or depreciate leasehold improvements over the term of the lease in most cases. Check with your CPA to be sure. See the heading "Line 12" later in this chapter for a discussion of how to treat capital items.

Lease Note: Normally you will want to sign a lease for a business space rather than to accept a month-to-month tenancy. This is because, generally, business leases protect the tenant more than the landlord, although it may not seem so if you read all those fine print clauses. The advantage of a lease is that you know what your rental costs will be with some certainty for at least a period of time and you are sure that you will be able to stay at the location long enough to build your business around it. But what happens if your business fails or you discover the location is poor? Aren't you legally on the hook for the rent until the end of the lease term? Not necessarily. Under the legal doctrine called "mitigation of damages," in most states the landlord must rent to another suitable tenant if you leave. Assuming someone else will pay as much or more than you do, you have no further obligation.

Be sure you know exactly what your rent will include. Commercial leases often require the tenant to pay for a number of things that a landlord commonly pays for in residential rentals. For example, some shopping center leases require you to pay a pro-rata share of your property taxes, building maintenance, fire insurance on the building, as well as a pro-rata share of the parking and common area charges, in addition to the base rent. A friend of mine who rented a small building for a retail nursery business put it this way: "That blankety-blank landlord sold me the building; he just kept the title." So, as part of making your financial projection, be sure you know exactly what charges, if any, the realtor or landlord expects you to pay in addition to the rent. And no matter what you determine the rent to be, expect to put up the first and last month's rent and often a security deposit when you sign the lease.

Many leases that last longer than a year contain a method to protect the landlord from inflation. Some are tied to a cost-of-living index, which means your rent goes up each year at the same amount as the inflation rate. Others contain a percentage of sales clause. In these leases, you pay a set rent or a percentage of your gross sales, whichever is higher.

Example: Bob Smith signed a shopping center lease for his optometry office which called for a base rent of $1,200, or 6% of monthly sales plus a set charge of $200 for taxes, maintenance and insurance. In Bob's case, if sales exceeded $20,000 per month ($1,200 divided by .06), he would be obligated to pay the landlord more rent. Bob was pleased to sign the lease, however, because his sales projections ($16,000 per month) indicated he would be making a healthy profit if his sales volume reached $20,000 a month, and so would not mind paying a higher rent. Of course, this sort of lease is not a good idea if the amount of sales needed to trigger a substantially higher rent is too low. In Bob's situation, for example, if he was required to pay more rent if monthly sales reached $14,000, he probably would have looked elsewhere. Similarly, Bob would not have been happy with this lease proposal if he projected sales of $30,000 per month. In this situation, he probably would be better off to offer the landlord a slightly higher base rent in exchange for being able to sell more contact lenses before having to pay a percentage of gross sales.

When you have figured out your total monthly rent, including any rent-related expenses, write that amount on Line 7 of your profit and loss forecast.

Line 8. Compute Your Advertising Costs

Here's a story about advertising.

Back in the early 1930's, John Axelrod opened a hot dog stand on the main road into Pine Valley. Business was fair. When he put up a small sign, business got a little better. Then he added several more signs and things got a lot better. Finally, he put up a dozen big signs. Business became so good, he had to expand his seating area and hire more cooks. He was feeling pretty good about life when his son, whom he thought was a positive wizard, came home from college. The son, who was an economics major, was appalled at all the new signs and seating.

"Dad, what are you doing spending so much on advertising? Don't you know there's a depression going on and everybody's going broke? If you don't pull in your horns a bit, you will never make it."

"No kidding," John replied, and took down the signs and stopped the construction program.

Soon business dwindled away to nothing and John went broke.[3]

---

[3]Incidentally, the son went on to get his degree and opened his own business consulting firm.

The moral of this fable is obvious. When the signs went up, business improved. When they came down, there wasn't enough income to buy ketchup. One way or another, successful businesses get the word out.

There are small libraries full of books about how to do this. They used to focus on "advertising." More recently, the broader concept of "networking" has come into prominence. Networking involves getting the word out to the people and groups who are most apt to need your goods or services, rather than advertising your product or service to the community as a whole. Many good advertising people did this all along. Just the same, the concept of networking, or marketing without advertising, is a good one. If you get creative, there are all sorts of ways you can inform people in your network of your existence, for little or no cost.

For example, if you invent a better milking machine (or develop a consulting business based on improving dairy production), you could advertise on the radio, or you could network by going to a meeting of dairy farmers and demonstrating your product or talking about your ideas. Your next step might be to get someone to write about your business for a 4-H Club magazine. Similar opportunities exist in every business. If you open an oboe repair shop, for example, one of the first jobs is to figure out ways, at the lowest cost possible, to let every oboeist within a hundred-mile radius know of your existence. One way to do this might be to contact every orchestra in the area and supply them with free information on oboe cleaning.

Many successful businesses allow 3% to 5% of their gross sales for promotion. They budget half that amount for a continuing, low-level effort to let people know about their product or service and schedule the other half to advertise sales and special events.

Think about what you will need to do to tell people about your business. Will your business need cards? Flyers? Newspaper ads? A good-sized box in the yellow pages? Sample merchandise sent to media outlets so they can review your product? Window displays? Mailings? A part-time marketing expert to help you pull this together? When you make your plans and budget, however, think about this. A great deal of money spent on conventional advertising is wasted. New businesses especially are prone to spend too much in the wrong places. So use your common sense. Check with friends in business. Check with trade associations to see what they suggest as a good budget number for telling potential customers about your business. When you get your estimate, write that amount in the profit and loss forecast on your chart on Line 8.

Marketing Hint: Avoid expensive promotions that you haven't tried before. For example, if you get an idea that involves mailing out 100,000 flyers, test it by mailing only 5,000. If it works, go for the rest. If not, use the money you saved for something else.

Line 9■ Insurance

You need at least some insurance in this litigation-happy society. If you have a place of business where the public comes, public liability and property damage insurance is a necessity. This will protect you from the person who slips and falls on your floor mat. You also need workers' compensation insurance, since you are absolutely liable if one of your employees injures herself while at work. You will probably also want to carry insurance on your inventory and fixtures if they have any substantial value. Also, your lease may require you to keep fire insurance on the building. And if you manufacture any product that would possibly harm any one, such as food or machinery, you will want to consider product liability insurance.

Talk to an independent insurance broker who specializes in business insurance to get an idea of what coverage you'll need and how much it will cost. Then shop around warily. Lots of over-enthusiastic insurance people will try to sell you far more insurance than you need. Although you need some insurance to protect you against obvious risks, you don't need so much that your main risk is starving to death trying to raise enough to pay your premiums.

Warning: Some people try to avoid the responsibility of paying workers' compensation by calling their employees "independent contractors." Aside from the problems this can cause with other government agencies, such as the Internal Revenue Service and the Unemployment Insurance people, you should realize that if the independent contractor is hurt, the Unemployment Appeals Board will almost always rule in favor of the employee and against independent contractor status, unless your worker genuinely has her own business. This means you may end up paying huge sums if one of your workers becomes disabled while you don't have insurance. In other words, trying to save a few pennies on this insurance is just not worth the risk.

Once you arrive at a good estimate for your total insurance bill, inquire as to the existence of deferred payment programs. Most companies which offer these often require that you pay 20 percent of the total premium up front and the balance in ten payments. For purposes of your profit and loss forecast, divide the total annual insurance payment by twelve and use that number. Enter this figure on Line 9 of your profit and loss forecast.

VACATION SPECIALIST■

tommy tucker■

↑↑↑↑↑↑↑↑↑↑↑↑↑↑↑↑↑↑↑↑↑↑↑↑↑↑↑↑↑↑■ *(808) 647-1478*

Line 10■   Bookkeeping and Accounting Expenses

You can do your own books if you like working with numbers. Chances are, however, you'll be so busy with the business, you won't have time. One good approach is to budget for a CPA to set up your books to start with. Then hire a part-time bookkeeper to do day-to-day upkeep. If you are starting small, your initial cost should only be $200-$500, with a monthly cost of $100-$200 to keep the records up-to-date and prepare routine employee withholding tax returns, statements, etc. Once a year you will pay the CPA another few hundred dollars to review this work and help you prepare your yearly returns. If your business is going to be fairly good-sized from the start, this figure will be larger. Make as good an estimate as you can and enter this figure on Line 10 of your profit and loss forecast.

Line 11■   Interest

This line of your profit and loss forecast concerns the interest portion of the payments you make on any money you borrow. For example, let's assume Joanie Ricardo borrowed $25,000 from the bank to open a Gelato's Ice Cream store in Providence, Rhode Island and agreed to repay it in 36 equal monthly installments of $830.40, including 12% interest on the unpaid balance. While Joanie's monthly payments remain equal, the portion of the payment which is credited to principal increases every month, while the portion of her payment going toward interest decreases monthly.

Here is how you figure this out. Start with the interest total for the total amount borrowed for a year. In this situation, interest on $25,000 for one year at 12% is $3,000 ($25,000 x 12). This figure allows you to arrive at the interest portion of the first month's payment by simply dividing by twelve. One-twelfth of $3,000 is $250, leaving $580.40 credited to repaying the principal (the original $25,000 loan). For the second month, things get a little trickier. This is because the principal amount is now $24,419.60 ($25,000 minus $580.40). You now figure annual interest on this figure at 12%. Do this just the same way as we did above. Divide the total owed for the year ($2,930.35) by 12. Interest is now $244.20 for the month, with principal (interest subtracted from the total monthly payment of $830.40) of $586.20. This reduces the amount of principal due in the third month to $23,833.40 ($24,419.60 less $586.20). You then take 12% of this amount and divide it by 12, and so on for each month. Finally, add the total of payments credited to interest and enter this amount on Line 11 of your profit and loss forecast.

Note of Sanity: You don't need to be perfect in forecasting your interest costs. Just make your best informed guess. Be sure that the interest expense line from the profit and loss forecast and the principal repayment line from your cash flow forecast (see Chapter 6, Section C, Step 3), add up to the total monthly payment.

Line 12. Depreciation

Depreciation is a gift to the business person from Uncle Sam. Ask not what your country can do for you—this is it. Depreciation is an amount you can subtract from your gross income when you pay your taxes for the fact that your business equipment and buildings are wearing out. The government allows you to assume that your fixed assets wear out over some period of years, depending on the asset. This means that for tax purposes, your equipment is worthless at the end of that period. Your depreciation allowance simply lets you show a percentage of this wear as an expense on your tax return each year. In a sense, it is a sinking fund for equipment replacement, or would be if you put the depreciation amount in the bank.

Often, equipment is depreciated over five years and buildings over 30 years for tax purposes. In actuality, the stuff usually lasts a lot longer than this, which is why depreciation can be seen as a friendly federal gesture. You can depreciate all fixed assets. These are things you buy for use in the business, which last longer than one year. If the asset will last less than one year, you simply show the entire purchase price in the expense column for the year you bought the equipment and do not depreciate it. Inventory and consumable supplies are examples of purchases which are expensed immediately because they last less than one year. Equipment and fixtures are examples of items which usually last longer than one year.

Let's say you expect to spend $20,000 for fixed assets to open your business—items like a new toilet, several new walls, a cash register, a small computer, and all your store fixtures. Assuming your accountant agrees that five years is the proper time frame to use for depreciation, you can take $333 as an expense for depreciation each month ($20,000 divided by 60 months). Some items may be depreciated faster and some items slower. Check with your CPA for questions about depreciation and fixed assets. Once you get a realistic figure for depreciation, enter it on Line 12 of your profit and loss forecast.

Lines 13-17 ▪ Other Expenses

Inevitably, you will encounter a number of other expenses, depending on your business. Bad debts, car and truck expenses, commissions, dues and publications, employee benefits programs, freight, laundry and cleaning, legal and professional services, office supplies, postage, repairs and maintenance, taxes, travel and entertainment, utilities, telephone and security systems are common ones. Spend some time thinking about these and any other costs you may incur on Lines 13-16. Naturally, if you expect any of these to be recurring expenses, include a reasonable monthly estimate.

Remember, be prepared to show receipts and justify to the IRS the business nature of all your expenses, particularly travel and entertainment, auto expenses, employee benefits and insurance.

F. Finish and Review Your Profit and Loss Forecast

After all the sales, variable cost of sales, and operating expense numbers are complete, subtract your cost of sales from sales to get your gross profit (Line 3 of your profit and loss forecast). Next, subtract the total of all your expenses (Lines 5-16) from gross profit to get your profit. Do it for each month and for the year. Check your arithmetic by seeing if the monthly profit figures add up to the same figure you get for your yearly total. If they don't add up to the same figure, double check your addition to find the error. If they match, congratulations!

You've now completed your first run through a profit and loss forecast. Date it so you won't get confused if you do another draft. I hope it looks positive. However, if like many people, you find you need to increase profitability to make the business a good economic idea, go

back through all your assumptions. How can you realistically reduce costs or increase volume? Incorporate only those changes you're sure are sound into the forecast. Now look at the profit figures again. Do they show enough profit to make a good living, pay back your money source, and leave some margin for error? If they do, and you're sure the figures are right, you will want to go ahead with your business plans. If the adjusted figures still do not show enough profit, it may be wise to look for another business idea, or change your basic business assumptions. Turn to the following pages to see how the exercise looks for Antoinette.

Notice, for example, that Antoinette's business looks more profitable now than it did in her preliminary analyses in Chapter 2. That's because, while her estimate for cost of sales went up from 50% to 60% (because she realized a lot of her merchandise would be sold at reduced prices), thereby reducing profits, her labor cost estimate dropped more (from $3,300 per month to $1,255 per month). The net effect of these contradictory changes was a slight increase in profit. You can make similar changes in your forecast as long as you're sure you can make them really happen. Additional changes Antoinette might consider, which would reduce her profit somewhat, include the provision for more labor in busy times and showing utilities as a separate line item. In addition, it might also be wise for her to show some freight expense to return defective merchandise and incidental car and truck expense, as well as a provision for a burglar alarm service.

How much profitability is enough to justify going ahead with your business? That's both a good question and a touchy one. Or, put another way, there are almost as many answers as there are business people. My personal response is, I look for a yearly profit (including my wages and return on investment) equal to the amount of capital needed to start the business. If I invest

$40,000 in a business, a conservative profit forecast should show a yearly profit including owner's wage of at least $40,000. Based on this approach, Antoinette should spend $20,000 or less to open the business, since the first year's profits are about $19,000. Of course, it may not be possible to achieve this profit the first year. Nevertheless, if it's going to take much longer than that, you may want to think twice about going into that business.

Another way to approach the issue of profitability is to look at your profit forecast from an investor's viewpoint. A $19,000 profit for the dress shop won't seem like much to them. They will be concerned that the dress shop owner will have a difficult time making it through the inevitable slow times. An investor or lender will probably want her to be able to convincingly demonstrate she has a plan to increase sales enough to raise the profit forecast to a more respectable level—say, the $30,000-$35,000 she shows in the second year.

When Antoinette looks at her Profit and Loss forecast carefully, she may want to change the estimates for telephone expense and think carefuly about whether or not to plan for raises for her employees. But, these are minor points at this stage of the process.

Service Business Note: Many service businesses (e.g., a bookkeeping service or a computer consulting operation) can be started out of one's home on a part-time basis for very little cost. It often takes several years for this sort of business to expand to the point where reasonable levels of profitability are achieved).

G. Your Profit and Loss Forecast and Income Tax Return

Up to now we assumed that your cost of sales is a simple percentage of sales. That's a useful simplification for forecasting purposes, but you'll need to follow more complicated rules when computing actual results for income tax purposes. These tax rules require that you take a physical inventory on a regular basis. This means not only counting all the merchandise in the store, but costing it out as well. You really need to do this anyway to see if anyone's stealing. Since you now know what your cost of sales percentage should be, you will want to know if actual costs are higher. If they are, it may indicate a theft problem, or you may simply be underpricing your merchandise. Here's an example which demonstrates how you do this:

COST OF SALES

Beginning Inventory from physical count	$10,000
Add: Purchases during period	+ 30,000
Subtotal: Goods available for sale	40,000
Less: Ending Inventory from physical count	- 15,000
COST OF GOODS SOLD DURING PERIOD	$25,000

You don't need to get this complicated in your forecast; just remember these other operating rules are there.

In the next chapter, you'll learn to translate these numbers into a forecast of your checkbook cash balance.

ANTOINETTE'S DRESS SHOP PROFIT FORECAST — YEAR 1

	JAN	FEB	MAR	APR	MAY	JUNE	JULY	AUG	SEPT	OCT	NOV	DEC	YEAR 1 #	YEAR 1 %
SALES	12000	13000	17000	15000	20000	17000	15000	15000	18000	18000	20000	24000	195000	100.0
COST/SALES (60%)	7200	7800	7800	9000	12000	7200	9000	9000	10800	10800	12000	14400	117000	60.0
GROSS PROFIT	4800	5200	5200	6000	8000	4800	6000	6000	7200	7200	8000	9600	78000	40.0
OPERATING EXPENSES														
WAGES	1120	1120	1120	1120	1120	1120	1120	1120	1120	1120	1120	1120	13440	6.9
PAYROLL TAXES	135	135	135	135	135	135	135	135	135	135	135	135	1620	0.8
RENT	2000	2000	2000	2000	2000	2000	2000	2000	2000	2000	2000	2000	24000	12.5
ADVERTISING	250	250	250	1250	250	250	250	250	1250	250	1250	250	6000	3.2
INSURANCE	100	100	100	100	100	100	100	100	100	100	100	100	1200	0.7
ACCOUNTING	300	150	150	150	150	150	150	150	150	150	150	150	1800	1.0
INTEREST	200	200	200	200	200	200	200	200	200	200	200	200	2400	1.3
DEPRECIATION	333	333	333	333	333	333	333	333	333	333	333	333	3996	2.2
LEGAL	0	0	0	0	0	0	0	0	0	0	0	0	0	0.0
SUPPLIES	50	50	50	50	50	50	50	50	50	50	50	50	600	0.3
TELEPHONE	30	30	30	30	30	30	30	30	30	30	30	30	360	0.2
OTHER	100	100	100	100	100	100	100	100	100	100	100	100	1200	0.6
TOTAL EXPENSES	4618	4618	4618	4618	4618	4618	4618	4618	4618	4618	4618	4618	58416	30.0
PROFIT	182	582	582	382	3382	182	1382	1382	1582	2582	2382	4982	19584	10.0

ANTOINETTE'S DRESS SHOP PROFIT FORECAST – YEAR II

	JAN	FEB	MAR	APR	MAY	JUNE	JULY	AUG	SEPT	OCT	NOV	DEC	YEAR II #	YEAR II %
1 SALES	14000	15000	15000	18000	23000	15000	18000	19000	22000	22000	24000	28000	233000	100.0
2 COST/SALES (60%)	8400	9000	9000	10800	13800	9000	10800	11400	13200	13200	14400	16800	139800	60.0
3 GROSS PROFIT	5600	6000	6000	7200	9200	6000	7200	7600	8800	8800	9600	11200	93200	40.0
4 OPERATING EXPENSES														
5 WAGES	1120	1120	1120	1120	1120	1120	1120	1120	1120	1120	1120	1120	13440	5.8
6 PAYROLL TAXES	135	135	135	135	135	135	135	135	135	135	135	135	1620	0.7
7 RENT	2200	2200	2200	2200	2200	2200	2200	2200	2200	2200	2200	2200	26400	11.3
8 ADVERTISING	300	300	300	1300	300	300	300	300	1300	300	1300	300	6600	2.8
9 INSURANCE	100	100	100	100	100	100	100	100	100	100	100	100	1200	0.5
10 ACCOUNTING	150	150	150	150	150	150	150	150	150	150	150	150	1800	0.8
11 INTEREST	200	200	200	200	200	200	200	200	200	200	200	200	2400	1.0
12 DEPRECIATION	333	333	333	333	333	333	333	333	333	333	333	333	3996	1.7
13 LEGAL	0	0	0	0	0	0	0	0	0	0	0	0	0	0.0
14 SUPPLIES	50	50	50	50	50	50	50	50	50	50	50	50	600	0.3
15 TELEPHONE	30	30	30	30	30	30	30	30	30	30	30	30	360	0.2
16 OTHER	100	100	100	100	100	100	100	100	100	100	100	100	1200	0.5
17 TOTAL EXPENSES	4718	4718	4718	5718	4718	4718	4718	4718	5718	4718	5718	4718	57616	25.6
18														
19 PROFIT	882	1282	1282	1482	4482	1282	2482	2882	3082	4082	3882	6482	33582	14.4

Chapter 6

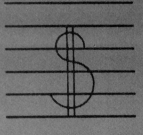

PREPARE YOUR CASH FLOW FORECAST AND CAPITAL SPENDING PLAN

SIX

A. Introduction

In Chapter 5, you drafted your estimated profit and loss forecast. This is like making a moving picture of the financial side of your business with a wide angle lens. While it tells you a lot about the big picture, it leaves you ignorant of many details. One of these simply can't be ignored. If it is, you may go broke, even though your business seems profitable viewed from afar.

The crucial detail has to do with when money will actually come in—or in the lingo of financial planners, "cash flow." In the day-to-day world of starting and operating your business, you will be at least as concerned about short-term cash flow as you will be about long-term profitability. After all, you don't want to go bankrupt ten minutes before you get rich. One new business owner I know even wears a t-shirt which says: "Happiness is positive cash flow."

So, let's put a close-up lens on our camera and focus on cash flow. Here again, it's necessary to get out your pen and play with some numbers.

B. What is a Cash Flow Forecast?

Start by looking at the sample cash flow form in Appendix 4. It's divided into two parts. The top part, entitled "Uses of Cash," deals with things you will spend money on. The bottom section lists the sources of the cash needed to buy all those things.

The "Uses of Cash" section is further divided into those pre-opening expenditures which will occur before you actually begin your business and the monthly expenditures which will occur after you start operations. Things you pay for before you open may include your opening inventory, fixtures and equipment, business licenses, deposits for the building lease and whatever else you need.

The money to pay for your pre-opening expenses is set out in the "Sources of Cash" section of this form. It includes your investment, as well as any loans or investments others make in your business. The total amount of money you have available in this section should comfortably exceed the amount of money you will need to open the business (pre-opening uses of cash), so you have a cushion should you have some slow months and unexpected expenses once you begin.

Commonly, cash flow from monthly sales is not enough to cover monthly expenses for the first few months after a new business opens. If your cash flow forecast shows a negative picture for your business for this period, you need to have extra money set aside. This is called "working capital." Working capital keeps the doors open until cash flow from monthly business becomes positive. If your cash flow forecast shows you'll run a cash deficit for several months, don't be too concerned. Just be sure you have enough working capital to cover it. But, if your cash flow forecast shows a continuing cash deficit, or a deficit which rises over time, your business may have some fatal flaw and you should re-examine the whole idea before making any commitments.

Growth, too, can create problems. Many businesses which grow quickly suffer a severe cash flow shortage because receipts from sales do not come in fast enough to cover needed investment in inventory and accounts receivable. If you find yourself in this situation, you will need to reduce your growth rate or find extra sources of money. See the cash flow discussion below, in Steps 3 and 4 of this chapter for more on this.

Before you start your own cash flow forecast using the blank form in Appendix 4, let's look at the sample we have designed for Antoinette's Dress Shop.

The $30,000 (total sources of cash) Antoinette started with is enough to cover her pre-opening requirements and allow her a surplus of $3,000, which she can use for working capital. To see if this is enough working capital to meet all of her requirements, it will be necessary for Antoinette to complete the monthly operation portion of her cash flow forecast for the first year. See the cash flow forecast that follows. To arrive at her expenses, Antoinette has made certain assumptions about her own need for living expenses on the owner draw line. You will have to do the same. As you can see, Antoinette keeps this amount as low as possible at the beginning.

To complete this part of the cash flow forecast, Antoinette must also make assumptions about how much new inventory she will purchase to replace goods sold, as well as her other monthly expenses. Remember, most of these estimates have already been made as part of her profit and loss forecast in Chapter 5 and can simply be plugged in here. Assuming you have done your profit and loss forecast, you can do the same.

To see if Antoinette has enough working capital to keep her shop going until it develops a positive cash flow, refer to the "Cash Balance" line of her cash flow forecast. This bottom line shows what will happen to her checkbook month by month if all her assumptions turn out to be accurate. Note that Antoinette starts with $3,000 extra cash. Her cash balance then drops to $2,815 at the end of the first month. That's because she had to spend $185 more in the first month than she collected from sales (total spending of $12,518 less total receipts of $12,333). As you can see by examining the cash balance line for subsequent months, Antoinette comes close to zero in the fourth month when her cash balance drops to $660.

Were I Antoinette, this analysis would convince me to try to get another $2,000 in working capital, just in case business was a little slower than I estimated. But, look what happens in the twelfth month. Antoinette's cash balance goes up to $13,380. This occurs because dress shop sales have a seasonal peak around the Christmas season. Should the projection prove out, these strong sales will give Antoinette a comfortable cash cushion to take into the slow months after the Christmas season.

PRE-OPENING CASH REQUIREMENT—ANTOINETTE'S DRESS SHOP

Uses of Cash—Pre-opening

Opening inventory	$16,000
Lease Deposits	2,000
Fixtures, Equipment	4,000
Marketing, Open Promotion, etc.	2,000
Other pre-opening expenses (business licenses, etc., and miscellaneous)	3,000
TOTAL MONEY OUT	$27,000

Source of Funds—Pre-Opening

Bank loan	$15,000
Owner savings	15,000
TOTAL SOURCES OF CASH	$30,000
NET CASH	$3,000

C. Fill Out Your Cash Flow Forecast

Now, let's go through your cash flow forecast line by line. Start by tearing out the blank form provided in Appendix 4. As you fill out your forecast, you may find you need to slightly alter the form we supply. Go ahead. Your form should reflect your business. For an example of a cash flow forecast for a project development, turn to Appendix 3.

Step 1: Pre-Opening Expenditures & Capital Spending Plan

[Lines 1-10 of Your Cash Flow Forecast]

Only you can estimate what you will need to spend in order to open your business. As part of doing this, review your profit and loss forecast in Chapter 5. Also, take a look at Antoinette's cash flow forecast set out above. Just to be on the safe side, however, it is wise to rethink all your pre-opening expenditures one more time. Some of the items you'll buy will be considered capital items which you'll depreciate over their useful lives. It's helpful to think about these in a separate category from operating expenses because of this tax treatment difference, but it isn't really necessary. All the pre-opening expenses represent your investment in the business. Here's a list of most of the items normally considered capital items when acquired before opening your business. If you have doubts, ask your accountant:

CASH FLOW FORECAST FOR ANTOINETTE'S DRESS SHOP — YEAR 1

	PRE-OPENING	JAN	FEB	MAR	APR	MAY	JUNE	JULY	AUG	SEPT	OCT	NOV	DEC	TOTAL YEAR
SOURCES														
LOAN	15000													15000
SAVINGS	5000													15000
COLLECTIONS (SALES)	0	12000	13000	13000	15000	20000	12000	15000	15000	18000	18000	20000	24000	195000
(DEPRECIATION) Non Cash Expense	0	333	333	333	333	333	333	333	333	333	333	333	333	3996
OTHER SOURCES	0													
TOTAL SOURCES	20000	12333	13333	13333	15333	24333	12333	15333	17333	18333	18333	20333	24333	228996
USES OF CASH														
PRE-OPENING														
OPENING INVENTORY	16000													16000
DEPOSITS—LEASE	2000													2000
UTILITIES	0													
LICENSES	0													
OTHER	0													
EQUIPMENT/FIXTURES	4000													4000
LEASEHOLD IMPROV	2000													2000
OPENING PROMOTION	2000													2000
OTHER PRE-OPENING	3000													3000
USES—MONTHLY														
OWNER'S DRAW	0	1000	1000	1000	1000	1000	1000	1000	1000	1000	1000	1000	1000	12000
PURCHASES	0	7000	8000	9000	9000	12000	6000	8000	7000	12000	13000	7000	6000	117000
EXPENSES (fixed+var)	0	4618	4618	4618	4618	4618	4618	4618	4618	4618	4618	4618	4618	58416
PRINCIPAL PAYMENTS (from P+I)	0	100	100	100	100	100	100	100	100	100	100	100	100	1200
ADJUST FOR NON-CASH WITHDRAWAL	0	(200)	(200)	400	(200)	(200)	400	(200)	(200)	400	(200)	(200)	400	0
TOTAL USES	17000	12518	13518	15118	14518	17518	12418	13518	14518	17118	18518	12518	12118	215618
NET CASH	3,000	(185)	(185)	(1,785)	(185)	6,845	(85)	1,815	(185)	(385)	(185)	2,215	12,215	13,385
CUM. NET CASH	3,000	2,815	2,430	845	660	3,475	3,390	5,605	5,325	4,535	4,254	5,915	13,380	

• Equipment, including machinery, larger tools and other large, expensive items;

• Fixtures for retail display areas and office furniture;

• Leasehold improvements or any alterations you make to the building, including walls, bathrooms and carpeting;

• Permanent signs, heaters, air conditioners, cooking and refrigeration equipment;

• Computers, typewriters, adding machines, cash registers, phone systems, etc.; and

• Anything else which has a useful life of more than one year.

Pre-opening costs also include a lot of costs which are considered operating expenses. Here's a list of some common purchases. Naturally, if you know you'll need to purchase something that's not on this list, include it in the cost estimates:

• Opening inventory (sometimes you can get a deferred payment schedule from suppliers, but you will usually have to pay for many, if not most, goods before you sell);

• Lease deposits (landlords normally want some advance rent and security deposits when you sign the lease);

• Tax deposits (some taxing agencies require deposits or bonds before issuing a permit);

• Business licenses and permits (most businesses need a business license from the city or county and perhaps a professional license from the state);

• Opening marketing and promotion (most businesses plan some initial publicity shortly after they open and have worked out the kinks in their system);

• Insurance (if you get a premium financing plan, they'll want about 20% of the first year's premiums in advance);

• Telephone installation (if you lease, start with a basic system, you can always upgrade);

• Utility deposits (sometimes the local utility company requires a cash deposit to establish business service);

• Stationery (you'll need business cards, letterhead and envelopes. Shop around. Some printers will give you a beginning package that includes a free logo); and,

• Reserve (there's always something else, so leave a little extra money).

Assigning specific dollar amounts to this sort of list should give you a good idea of how much cash you need to open your business. Here is an example for Antoinette's Dress Shop.

ANTOINETTE'S DRESS SHOP PRE-OPENING CAPITAL SPENDING PLAN

Item	Amount
FIXED ASSETS (longer than one year)	
10 ea dress racks, Meyer supply, $100 each	$1,000
NCR Cash Register, Model 245 (slightly used)	500
Singer Pro Model sewing machine, new	1,000
5 ea, lite fixtures. Hardware Supply	1,500
Neon Sign, Smith Sign Co. bid	2,000
Leasehold Improvements, Jones Const. bid	3,000
TOTAL FIXED ASSETS	$9,000
EXPENSE ITEMS	
Working capital per cash flow worksheet	$3,000
Misc. Deposits	
	2,500
Opening Inventory	
	16,000
TOTAL CAPITAL REQUIRED TO OPEN	$30,000

Here's an example of a one-man consulting firm's opening cash needs (as you can see, he plans to start with extra cash):

JEFFER'S ASSOCIATES CONSULTING: PRE-OPENING CAPITAL SPENDING PLAN

Item	Amount
FIXED ASSETS (longer than one year)	
Desk, conference tables, chairs	$3,000
Copy machine	2,000
Typewriter	700
Misc. decorative accessories	500
TOTAL FIXED ASSETS	$6,200
EXPENSE ITEMS	
Working capital	5,000
Misc. deposits	2,000
Supplies, stationery	500
TOTAL CAPITAL REQUIRED TO OPEN	$13,700

A pre-opening spending plan should reflect the exact amounts you will spend as accurately as possible. For example, it was okay for Antoinette to use estimates of costs when she thought about her business in general terms, but now she needs to be precise. Why? First, because she should have shopped around for the best deals by now and know them, and second, because if a potential lender asks her why she's spending $100 each for dress racks, she can say, "Because, the used ones from the auctioneer are terminally rusty and the discount ones are shoddy. I want my image to be high quality, and this is the best deal on good racks." In other words, by this time, Antoinette should know the business she is about to open.

Step 2: Pre-Opening Sources of Funds

[Lines 22-27 of Your Cash Flow Forecast]

Here's where you write down how much money you will invest in your business from your savings and how much you will put in from a bank loan or other loan or investment sources. As part of filling out this part of the form, you will arrive at an estimate or SWAG of the amount of working capital you will have in reserve by comparing your projected funds to your projected expenditures. This is the number you will now work with to complete your cash flow forecast.

Example: Millie More thought she needed a large sum to begin a leotard and dance supply shop. After she carefully estimated the costs, however, she found she could open her doors for about $10,000. In addition, it seemed that $2,000 in a working capital reserve was adequate, since she expected a good sales volume from the start. As she had only $5,000 in her savings account, she needed to borrow $7,000 from a relative, bank or some other

funding source. Her local bank wasn't interested, but her ex-father-in-law, Angelo, lived up to his name and became her guardian angel by lending Millie $7,000 at a low rate of interest. As part of making her cash flow forecast, Millie must now see if her $2,000 surplus, after paying her pre-opening expenses, will be enough to carry her through.

Step 3: Monthly Cash Expenditures

[Lines 13-18 of your Cash Flow Forecast entitled "Uses of Cash Monthly"]

The next item to cover as part of making your cash flow forecast is your monthly cash business expenses. First, consider your personal living expenses. This is not the place to reward yourself in a style to which you would dearly love to become accustomed. The idea should be to cover your basic living costs. You can always give yourself a raise later on when profits justify it. So, estimate your bare bones living costs each month and write that amount on the owner's draw line.

The second item to cover is the purchase of goods and supplies to replace what you have sold. If you are in a service business, this will be a minimal cost, unless you plan to sell some product as part of your service. For retailers, an ideal situation is where you are able to sell goods to your customers before you have to pay your supplier. When you order merchandise to replace what you sell, show the amount of your order in the month you actually expect to pay for it. Most suppliers expect you to pay 30 days after receiving the goods; some will wait up to 90 days. Look back at Antoinette's Dress Shop cash flow forecast to see how payment for goods is correlated with high sales months.

Example 1: Bill Gardener plans to open an engine and mower shop in Bangor, Maine in July. Since there is not a huge demand for rototillers and riding mowers in the winter months, the manufacturers agreed to allow Bill to order merchandise to replace his original stock during the following winter but not pay for it until his second July, with no interest costs or other charges. This means Bill would enter the costs to replace his original inventory in the thirteenth month of his cash flow forecast.

Example 2: Gertie's Gift Palace in Pismo Beach, California anticipates two excellent months each year—December and August (i.e., Christmas and clam season). Gertie orders merchandise at the March gift show for her August opening and plans to order again at the July gift show for her busy Christmas time. She receives these shipments in May and October and must pay most of her bills in September and January, except that many suppliers demand a substantial deposit (or full payment) with her first order, as she is a new account. Gertie's pre-opening cash will take care of these initial payments.

The third line under "Monthly Cash Expenditures" (line 15 on your cash flow forecast) can be taken from your profit and loss forecast. Fill in your total monthly expenses just as they appear on the profit and loss forecast.

Withholding Tax Warning: The wage payments shown on the profit and loss forecast in Chapter 5 show the gross amount you will pay the employees. However, the checks you write to the employees will be for less than this total. That's because the IRS requires that you collect money for them on behalf of your employees. It's hard to make exact estimates of how much the average employee will have you withhold for them, but let's assume that you hold back 20% of your employee wages for taxes. If your monthly wage bill is $3,000, that means you'll be holding back $600 every month.

The IRS expects you to pay them quarterly. That means you will have an $1,800 IRS payment every quarter.[1] Many business owners go bankrupt because they forget about these payments. Since you are holding money that belongs to your employees, the IRS has little patience with employers who fail to make these payments.

To make the adjustment for quarterly IRS payments, reduce the wages you pay in each of the first two months of each quarter (for example, January and February) by 20% by reducing the monthly expense amount by that dollar amount (see Antoinette's cash flow forecast earlier in this chapter). In the third month of each quarter, you'll pay the 20%, so you'll show the payment in March for the first quarter. Assuming you guess this amount will be $200 per month, as Antoinette did, this means you will write a $600 check in March. Just the same, you will only show a $400 expense item in your cash flow forecast. Why? Because in the month of March you will have a $200 expense item reduction for money withheld to be paid at the end of the next quarter. This will partially offset the $600 check you send to the IRS, giving a net increase in expenditures of $400 for March. Here's how it goes: January gross wages, $1,120; estimated withholding, $200; net checks in January, $920; February gross wages, $1,120; estimated withholding $200; net checks written, $920; March gross wages, $1,120; estimated withholding for March, $200; net checks written, $920 to employees, $600 to IRS.

Next, write in an estimate of the amount of any monthly principal payments of loans you plan to make. Obtain this number by looking back at your profit and loss forecast and computing your total payment. The key point is to make the interest portion of your monthly

---

[1]Larger businesses must make these payments monthly.

loan payment and the principal portion equal the check you will write. If you have an interest-only loan with scheduled principal re-payment dates, show them here in your expenditure forecast.

Example: Craig and Sue Scott borrowed $50,000 from a bank to help start a bakery-coffee shop. The loan which was designed to allow them to make interest-only payments of $600 per month required that they make principal payments of $10,000 at each annual anniversary of the loan for five years. That big loan payment put a dent in their cash balance in the twelfth month of operation. To get past this deadline, their business plan should show adequate cash coming in to make the payment.

Other cash expenses which would not be included on the profit and loss forecast but which should be included in a cash flow forecast might include the acquisition of additional capital equipment or leasehold improvements. For example, your sales might grow fast enough to justify buying another cash register; that purchase would show on the cash flow forecast, but not the profit and loss forecast. After completing the monthly cash expenditures ("Uses of Cash") section of your cash flow forecast, add all the individual uses and write the total on your "Total Uses" line (line 20).

Inventory Turnover Note—Retailers Only: At this stage, you should be closing in on the amount of cash you need to get started. If you have a service business or restaurant, you should already have a pretty good number for your pre-opening expenditures. However, if you plan a retail business, you have a little more work to do to check your assumptions. This involves estimating your inventory turnover.

The whole subject of inventory management and inventory turnover is what separates the professionals from the amateurs in the retail business, so let's spend a little time on that subject for the readers who are planning to enter the retail business. If you're not planning to enter the retail business or are planning to enter a business where inventory is small or non-existent, skip ahead to the next section.

Inventory is usually the biggest single investment a retailer makes. In other words, that's where most of her cash goes. Commonly, it happens that a retailer shows a high taxable income, but no cash. Why? Because all her cash went into increasing the inventory. You'll see how that can happen as we go through the cash flow worksheets.

The goals of inventory management are:

• To have a wise enough selection of new, fresh merchandise to appeal to customers;

• To quickly reduce or eliminate the items which move slowly from your stock;

• To keep the overall investment in inventory in line with profit expectations.

Good retailers keep current with the merchandise customers want now. They make it a point to always have the popular items in stock. No self-respecting popular music record store would be caught dead without the top ten albums and tapes in stock. Similarly, a record store specializing in classical music or jazz should know what was released last week, as well as last year. A good retailer quickly marks down slow moving items for a quick sale. They then use the cash from selling these dead items to buy new, popular ones and, in the process, improve the look of their store. For example, there is nothing sadder than a small bookstore still trying to sell last year's hard cover best seller when the drug store down the street already has the paperback version. Of course, a good retailer also has a wide enough selection to appeal to most customers. In the bookstore's case, this might mean a strong backlist in several areas of local interest.

Good inventory management also means deciding that some customers just aren't worth catering to. For example, if you wear odd size clothes, you are very aware of this merchandising policy. I wear shirts with 37-inch sleeves because I'm six feet, four inches tall and it has only been in the last five years that I could buy shirts at any place but a tall shop. That's because retailers used to think that 37-inch sleeve shirts never sold. Then the baby boom generation came of age, with many men needing larger sizes, and it became economical to serve these folks.

Good retail managers accomplish all of these ends and also keep the total dollar investment in line with profit goals by carefully managing "inventory turnover." Inventory turnover is how many times per year you completely replace the stock. For example, if your average gross profit is 50% and your sales are $300,000 and your inventory is $40,000, you turn over your inventory 3.75 times per year. Compute it this way. Your cost of sales is $150,000 ($300,000 x .50). Now, divide this cost of sales cost figure by your inventory ($150,000 divided by $40,000) to get 3.75. If your retail business has an inventory turnover of four times per year, you'll be doing pretty well. Many retailers are able to average only one or two turns per year.

Many people who plan new retail businesses expect to start with a fairly small inventory because they don't have much capital to invest. This will very likely cause problems if the sales figures they expect this inventory to produce are too high. For example, if you plan to sell widgets, but can only buy $10,000 worth to start, it would seem unlikely that you could produce sales of $200,000 per year. Even assuming you doubled the price of the widgets, this would mean turning your inventory over ten times in the year. For most businesses, it simply isn't realistic to expect inventory to turn over even seven or eight times a year.

Now, let's return to Antoinette's Dress Shop. Antoinette estimated her first year's sales at $195,000 and her cost of sales at 60%. She also figured her opening inventory at $16,000. Unfortunately, this means she has to turn her inventory 7.3 times per year ($195,000 x .6, or $117,000, divided by $16,000), just to meet her plan. This is not very likely. Antoinette should probably plan for a more realistic inventory turnover of 3.5 times per year. To do this and end up with $195,000, she would need an inventory of $33,000 ($195,000 x .6 = $117,000 divided by 3.5). This would raise her initial cash requirement to $47,000. With that much cash investment needed, her business idea probably is not worth pursuing unless she can generate a good deal more profit than her profit and loss forecast indicates. This would undoubtedly mean raising sales projections, etc.

Many retailers make a similar mistake; some catch the mistake at this stage, some catch the mistake when they have a business consultant review their plan, as discussed in Chapter 8, and some never catch it. They just sink slowly into bankruptcy, wondering why sales never met projections. Slow inventory turnover kills many retailers. What about Antoinette? I shall continue with Antoinette's original assumptions, including those for inventory turnover, for several reasons. First, this book is simply not set up to go back and do all the numbers over. Second, I want Antoinette's problem (the fatal flaw in her plan) to really sink in. I hope Antoinette's predicament will give you a vague feeling of unease as you continue to read her plan. The lesson is this. Just because a business plan appears to be thorough and looks good on paper, that's no guarantee that it will be successful. It pays to be skeptical. If you can't be skeptical about your plan, have a consultant review it. See Chapter 8.

Step 4: Monthly Cash Receipts

[Lines 25-27 of your Cash Flow Forecast]

Some businesses, especially service businesses and wholesale operations, routinely give customers credit. Others, such as restaurants and many retail stores, require cash for all sales. If you're in the retail business, you'll probably want to avoid giving credit to your customers. Most retailers accept cash, credit cards and some personal checks, all of which can be transferred into fairly immediate cash. If your business will sell on cash only, you can write the monthly sales figures on the profit and loss forecast you made out in Chapter 5 on the "Cash Collections" line of the cash flow forecast. Do that now.

If you'll be manufacturing, wholesaling, or in a service business, where cash is collected at a different time than the sale is recorded, you need to make an estimate of when you'll actually get your money. For example, if customers normally pay bills in 60 days in your industry, fill out the cash collection line by writing receipts for sales from your first month of operation (see line 1 on your profit and loss forecast in Chapter 5) in month three of your cash flow forecast.

Example: Mike's Marble Manufacturing company plans to sell to lots of small gift shops. Based on detailed research, Mike estimates that most of his customers will pay in 60 days or less. However, 20%-30% will probably not pay until

90 days, and 3%-5% will either never pay or not pay for an extended period of time. Accordingly, Mike uses this estimate to spread his receipts into the appropriate months.

Credit Note: You should realize that the primary result of selling on credit will be an increase in working capital requirements. If you plan to sell on credit and are not sure when your customers will really pay, be conservative and use 90 days. If you expect payment in 60 days, you'll have at least two months of cash expenses with no cash income. Refer back to Antoinette's cash flow example earlier in this chapter. If she collected for sales three months after the sale, she would need extra working capital equal to the first three month's cash expenses. This would mean extra working capital of $41,154. For a lot of new businesses, this extra working capital requirement may be so large as to make their business plan unworkable. This is the real reason why some businesses hang a sign by the cash register: "In God We Trust, All Others Pay Cash."

Depreciation Note: Remember that you provided for depreciation in the operating expense areas of the profit and loss forecast in Chapter 5. You did that even though depreciation is not a cash expense. That means that you must now adjust the "Uses of Cash" section (Step 3 of your cash flow forecast) to properly reflect depreciation. This is because if you included depreciation as an operating expense (and accordingly wrote down the monthly total of operating expenses in the cash flow section under "Uses of Cash Monthly"), you have overstated the amount of cash you will actually spend.[2] To adjust for that, you now write the amount of depreciation expense under the "Sources of Cash" section of your cash flow forecast. Do it now. This will adjust the "Uses of Cash Monthly" section of your cash flow forecast to reflect the proper disposition of depreciation. On the other hand, if you already eliminated depreciation from the "Uses of Cash section," you will not include any depreciation as a source of cash. In other words, just leave the expenses alone if depreciation has already been removed.

If you expect other sources of cash that do not appear on your profit and loss forecast, include them now. This might include additional loans or investments on your part, or from family or friends. Finally, add up all your sources of cash and write the totals on the line for "Total Uses."

Example: Sharyn Colby plans a landscape gardening consulting business. Her plan shows that her working capital would be pretty much exhausted by her sixth month of operation. Fortunately, she has some real property for sale and expects a sale to close in about four months. This allows her to show an additional cash investment in the fifth month of her cash forecast.

Step 5: Monthly Cash Balance

[Line 31 of Your Cash Flow Forecast]

Here's where we really find out if your business plan makes sense from the point of view of cash flow. The arithmetic is simple. First, subtract your "Total Uses of Cash" from your

───────────────

[2]Remember, depreciation is just a paper expense the government allows you. It is intended to account for the wearing out of fixed assets, but most businesses do not pay out any cash for depreciation since the assets last longer than the government thinks they last.

"Total Sources of Cash" for each monthly period in your forecast. Next, add or subtract the difference to the cash balance you estimated as being available at the beginning of that month. This will show you what will happen to your business checkbook.

Example: The cash flow forecast for Sharyn Colby's landscape consulting business showed that her uses of cash exceeded sources of cash each month for six consecutive months before it began to turn around in the seventh month. The effect of this was that gradually the cash balance she started with dropped until it would have become a negative figure if she hadn't sold her land.

If your cash forecast shows a steady reduction in the cash balance for several months, you may have to increase the working capital needed to start the business. For example, if you show a negative cash balance by the twelfth month of $4,000, but you expect cash receipts to begin exceeding cash expenses about that time, you should allow for at least $5,000 or $6,000 more working capital than you originally planned. There is no magic rule for how much working capital to budget. Use your common sense. To repeat, in planning, the thing to watch is your estimated cash balance. If it gets too close to zero or a negative figure, you'll have to modify your forecast to add more cash, or, as the alternative, reduce expenses or increase sales.

Warning: If you have to make changes to your forecast to produce positive cash numbers, slow down. You need to be sure that any changes you make at this stage are things you can really accomplish. If you make an unrealistic assumption to show a positive cash flow, you may fool the banker or backer, but you'll still have to live with the real results.

Chapter 7

CREATE YOUR BUSINESS PLAN

SEVEN

This is where you create your formal business plan. You have already created many of the components. Now it's time to reduce these to final form and add several important new elements which will help create a coherent document. Prepare everything in draft form first, so that it will be easy to make changes both in the content of your material and the order in which you wish to organize it. Incidentally, don't be afraid of changing your plan. One of the major advantages a small business person has over larger corporations is that the small business owner can take advantage of changed circumstances quickly and easily.

Step 1: Describe Your Proposed Business

Read the description of your business you wrote as part of Chapter 2, Section D. Now modify it to reflect the decisions you made while developing and modifying your financial projections. If you haven't yet written a business description, reread Chapter 2 and prepare one.

To review, your business description should answer the following questions:

• What will you sell, or what service will you provide?

• Who will your customers be?

• What hours of will you be open?

• What kind of atmosphere, service or general approach to business will you emphasize?

• Where will you locate?

Example: Here's how the revised description of Antoinette's Dress Shop might read:

BUSINESS DESCRIPTION
ANTOINETTE'S DRESS SHOP

Antoinette's Dress Shop will be a women's clothing store designed to serve the growing market of women who are out of college but under 40. We will specialize in fashionable but somewhat conservative clothes designed primarily to be worn by the upwardly mobile working woman. This will include business suits, pants suits and dresses for daytime wear, together with normal accessories such as purses and belts. We will not carry shoes, nor will we carry leisure clothing like jeans and jogging suits. We will make minor alterations at no charge and we will do them quickly.

Antoinette's Dress Shop will offer a relaxed atmosphere with personalized attention and unlimited fitting-room time. We will be open six days a week, with evening hours Monday through Friday. The market analysis which follows demonstrates the need for a store which caters to the younger working woman, discusses the target customer in detail, and outlines a plan to inform them of our existence efficiently and inexpensively.

Note: This business description is better written and more thought through than the one set out in Chapter 2. Yours should go through a similar evolution.

ACME PROGRAMMERS
833 Joost St., Vancouver, Wash 98664
(206) 239-0415

Step 2: Write Your Marketing Plan

Here is where you set out all the reasons why your proposed business is sure to be profitable. Some of the specific questions you must answer are:

• What is your competition and how will your proposed business be special or distinctive?

• What do your potential customers need or want that they are not getting from your competition? Or, to phrase the same question in another way, how is the competition failing to exploit the potential market you have identified?

• What is your typical customer's age, income, place of residence, place of employment, family status, taste, etc.?

• How many potential customers are in your geographical area? How many will do business with you and how much of their business can you reasonably hope to get?

• How will you efficiently let your potential customers know about your business?

• Have you talked with potential customers? How many? Have they given you some ideas you hadn't thought of before? If not—were you really listening?

Developing this kind of information requires hard, honest work, but it will pay great dividends in your understanding of your business environment. And, don't underestimate the fact that it will impress the bejeezus out of the bankers and other investors you plan to approach.

In her marketing plan, Antoinette covered several points you should consider in yours. She described a profile of her typical customers and pointed out what those customers look for in a dress shop. She gave some overall statistics for her city and customer profile and talked about future trends. In discussing the competition, she suggested that the needs of her target group were not adequately being met and described several decisions she had made to attract and serve her customers in unique ways—namely adjusting her store hours and location to suit her customers' needs, making prompt free alterations, and adopting several marketing strategies such as fashion shows and clothing tips. In addition, she identified a risk to the business and described how she planned to counter it.

Your marketing plan should address the same issues or similar ones, even though the specifics of your plan will vary greatly depending on your proposed business.

ANTOINETTE'S DRESS SHOP—MARKETING PLAN

Antoinette's Dress Shop will concentrate on developing a clientele consisting primarily of working women in the under-40 market. We are particularly interested in "professional" women who expect to advance in their chosen career. These women require fashionable clothing at reasonable prices. According to the New City Chamber of Commerce, the greater trading areas of this city include some 20,000 women who fit this description.[1] Forecasters expect this market to continue to grow at the same 10% growth rate it has enjoyed for the past five years. We believe the trend towards a higher concentration of professional women in this county may even accelerate because of the increased concentration of professional and management industries locating here.[2]

Personal experience and market research[3] demonstrate that upwardly mobile working women prefer fashionable, but slightly conservative, clothing at moderate prices. In addition, it has been demonstrated that these women prefer to shop where they receive both personal attention (especially prompt, free alterations which, traditionally, have not been provided to women) and frequent sales. Women in this group normally prefer to shop between 5:00 p.m. and 8:00 p.m. or on their lunch hour.

At present, many younger professional women travel 35 miles to South City to shop at Freida's because their needs are simply not being met locally. Currently, our city has only four types of women's clothing stores:

    1. Department stores such as S. Bagnin, Jerry's, and Glendale's.

    2. Teen fashionable stores appealing primarily to the 15 to 25 market, such as Wild Thing, Marian's, and Golden Frog.

    3. Discount and mass-market stores such as J-Mart, I.C. Henney and Stears.

    4. Specialty stores such as those featuring clothes for tall or short people, maternity wear, sports clothing (jogging, tennis, etc.), such as Big Guy, Short Sports, Lady Esquire, the Joggery, and Modern Maternity.

---

[1]Annual survey of business conditions, New City Chamber of Commerce, January 19, 198_.
[2]Bank of New City economic forecast for 198_.
[3]See attached article from the September 27, 198_ issue of "Woman's Monthly."

Some of the consumers we have targeted presently shop at the department stores for the type of business clothes we will sell. However, we believe we can capture a lot of this business for the following reasons:

Generally speaking, the department stores offer a wide mix of merchandise. It isn't easy to find a large selection of appropriate business clothing at reasonable prices in any of them. In addition, Bagnin and Glendale's are only open one evening a week after 6 p.m., the time most people who work 9 to 5 prefer to shop. Further, both department stores offer fairly impersonal services, with a constant turnover of personnel and charge for alterations, which usually take a week or more to complete. Our policy of offering free alterations within 24 hours is sure to appeal to women who put in at least a 40-hour week in addition to maintaining their homes. We should note that the Lady Esquire Shop does offer fairly direct competition. We believe, however, that its pricing policy indicates a decision to cater primarily to women approaching the top of the executive ladder (those who make $40,000 and up). This leaves us plenty of room to compete.

Our location at the Plaza in the center of town puts us within walking distance of major banks, brokerage houses, insurance companies, real estate and law firms. We are only four blocks from the new RST computer center and the related software development businesses that are springing up around it. In addition, we will be next to Jerry's and the Golden Frog. The former is an old-line local department store which carries a lot of clothing and supplies of interest to older women who see themselves as traditional homemakers. We should benefit by comparison. The latter is a popular tops and pants outfit where many of our potential customers already shop for leisure wear.

Antoinette's Dress Shop plans an extensive direct mail campaign to tell our potential customers about our grand opening sale. We will develop our mailing list from the New City Chamber of Commerce membership list, the mailing list of the county business magazine, the membership lists of business women's clubs and the University Woman's Club, and from other appropriate sources. Our direct mail campaign will be supplemented by a modest media campaign targeted to media, such as the New City Monthly, which is popular with our potential clientele. In addition, we plan to have regular fashion shows, and to publish and distribute fact sheets for working women containing tips on such things as choosing clothes appropriate to their job, clothing for business travel, as well as clothes cleaning and maintenance tips. Younger women who read magazines such as "Self," "Savvy" and "Working Woman" are extremely responsive to self-improvement tips.

Step 3: Discuss the Risks Facing Your Business

Every business faces risks. You need to look squarely at yours. In addition, the people whom you will ask for money will want to see that you can not only face reality but can also come up with plans to deal with possible difficulties. Read what follows and add a risk discussion to your plan.

Here are some of the risks you may face:

Competition: Most businesses have competition. How will your business differ in significant and positive ways from your competition? If your competition is strong, don't minimize that fact, but describe ways you will adjust to or use that strength. For example, if you plan to open a restaurant next to an extremely popular one, part of your strategy might be to cater to their overflow. Another might be to open on days or evenings when they are closed.

Pioneering: If you anticipate no direct competition, your business probably involves selling a new product or service, or at least one which is new to your area. This means you'll be a pioneer. How will you avoid going broke trying to develop a market?

Cycles and Trends: Many businesses have cycles of growth and decline often based on outside factors such as those discussed in Chapter 2—taste, trends, etc. What is your forecast of the cycles and trends in your business? For example, if your forecast tells you that your proposed business (e.g., selling a new electronic product) may decline in three years when the market is saturated, can you earn enough money in the meantime to make the venture worthwhile?

Slow Times: Every business experiences ups and downs. Is your business small and simple enough, or capitalized adequately enough, to ride out slow times? Or do you have some other strategy, such as staying open long hours in the busy season and closing during times of the year when business is dead?

Owner's Ability: Nobody knows everything. How do you plan to compensate for the knowledge you're short on? For example, if you've never kept a set of books, you will need to hire a part-time bookkeeper and an accountant to make sure the bookkeeping system is adequate.

Cash Flow: Seeing the money come and go on a daily and weekly basis is very different from looking at a yearly profit and loss forecast (Chapter 5). You also want to be sure that your business can survive long enough so you can enjoy your profits. If you filled out a cash flow forecast such as the one set out in Chapter 6, you should be able to demonstrate that you can survive foreseeable cash flow problems.

Example: Doreen Cook wanted to establish her own restaurant. She had cooked for other restaurant owners for years and knew the practical side of putting good food on the table, inside and out. However, she had little patience with financial matters and was honest enough to admit she didn't want to learn how to keep books. To solve this problem, she invited George, her CPA, to be her junior partner, with full responsibility for financial management. She and George emphasized this connection in her business plan and loan package, which George designed. In addition, George was invaluable in lining up a list of potential lenders.

Write your risk analysis by first thinking of the main dangers your business faces. This shouldn't be hard, as you have probably been concerned about them for some time. Focus on the main ones and don't bog down worrying about all sorts of unlikely disasters. Some of these may be on the list set out above; others will be unique to your business. Once you have identified the principal risks facing your business, write out a plan to counter each.

A Note of Philosophy: This is the stage when remorse or jitters may set in. You may be thinking, "Oh my God! Am I really doing this? Think of all the things that could go wrong. I could lose everything!"

ANTOINETTE'S DRESS SHOP—RISK ANALYSIS

Like every new business, Antoinette's faces several risks. One of these is both immediate and important, the others are less severe.

The primary risk we face is that our concept of an entire store selling business clothing to younger, upwardly mobile, educated women is new to this area. No one else is presently doing exactly what we propose. Although we believe we have identified a market niche which the competition has failed to adequately exploit, our assumption remains to be proven here in New City. On the positive side, the population base of our target customers is more than adequate to support a store of our size and we have based our volume (and profit) projections on low average figures for the industry. In addition, the type of store we propose has been very successful elsewhere. Nevertheless, we must demonstrate that this type store will work here, or, in other words, that it will take sufficient business away from stores with a broader line of merchandise to make a profit.

A secondary risk is that we are thinly capitalized. If our sales volume fails to meet projections in the first year, our small working capital reserve may be inadequate to meet our cash flow needs. On the positive side, however, we believe our sales projections are conservative and that we will have little trouble meeting our sales goals. In addition, by starting with relatively modest capital, we will have no large debt service obligations. Also, we have had several potential investors express an interest in the business. If our working capital reserves are exhausted, but the business demonstrates potential, we should be able to attract investors.[4]

Finally, there is some risk that the population of younger working women in New City will decline. We do not expect this to happen. White collar jobs have doubled here in the last decade and it seems reasonable to expect that the population of working women will continue to grow and that we will profit from that expansion. This projection is based on the fact that many high technology firms have located here and more are expected to do so. Nevertheless, if for any reason this industry declines, or a significant number of computer-related companies fail or move overseas, we could face some problems and might have to change our marketing strategy. This does not seem to be a significant danger, however, as most of the people located here are management staff, not manufacturing personnel.

---

[4]But remember we discovered that, on the basis of the cash flow forecast, Antoinette's has a fatal flaw (Chapter 6, Section C) and her entire plan will need reworking from the beginning.

Your purpose in writing a risk discussion is to force yourself to face your fears and concerns, not to scare yourself out of going into business. If your rational, intellectual analysis tells you that the risk factors are manageable, proceed as hard and fast as you can. You don't have time for useless and unnecessary worry. On the other hand, if you really do get bogged down in worrying about potential disasters, pay attention to your anxieties; they may be telling you that you don't have the personality to handle the risks you'll take in a small business.

The purpose of this book is to help you understand the dimensions of those risks, but you as the potential business owner must put your money and belief on the line. Abe Lincoln said it: "Be sure you're right, then go ahead."

Step 4: Prepare Your Personnel Plan

As part of completing your profit and loss forecast in Chapter 5, you made some assumptions about how many people you will hire and how much you'll pay them. Now it's time to reduce these plans to a narrative. As part of doing this, you will need to answer several questions:

• How many people will you hire?

• What qualifications should each employee have? (e.g., work experience, education, references, etc.)

• How many hours will each work?

• What will you pay them?

• What will each employee do?

• How do you know you can hire the kind of people you need for the money you plan to pay?

• If you're hiring several people, will one supervise the others?

ANTOINETTE'S DRESS SHOP PERSONNEL PLAN

Antoinette's Dress Shop will employ the following: One assistant manager and one part-time sales clerk. The assistant manager will be Sally Walters. Her resume is attached. I have known Sally Walters for several years and believe we will work well together. Until recently, she was the assistant manager of the dress department of a large department store, where she helped modernize the merchandise line. Her department increased sales by 25% in two years. She will be paid $5.75 an hour to start. I have promised her more money and a profit-sharing plan as soon as the business is profitable. My goal is to fully involve Sally[5] in the business so that I will feel comfortable leaving her in charge when I take time off, etc.

Sally Walters' work responsibilities will be as follows. She will work a 40-hour week primarily assisting customers. She will also assist in ordering decisions. Sally will sometimes open and close the shop and make bank deposits, although she will not have to do so regularly. She will work from 12:00 p.m. until 8:00 p.m. Wednesday and Thursday, and all day Friday and Saturday.

The part-time sales clerk will be paid slightly above prevailing wage. She must be personable, presentable and have some prior retail sales experience. This clerk will work two evening hours Thursday through Saturday. She will be available to help Sally and myself during peak selling times. They will also assist in keeping the store attractive by stocking, cleaning and developing window displays. Sally and I know several acceptable candidates and

---

[5]Some people may prefer to be more formal and always refer to people as Mr., Mrs., or Ms. in their personnel profile. I find that, for most small businesses, this is artificial. I prefer to use people's given names after first identifying them by their full name.

the local unemployment office indicates that many more are available.

I will work six days at the start, but will consider closing the store on Mondays if that proves to be a slow day. I will act as seamstress until business expands significantly. If business expands more rapidly than forecast, additional part-time clerks and a part-time seamstress will be hired as appropriate.

Antoinette's will not offer health insurance or other employee benefits until the profit picture warrants those considerations.

Example: A Small Manufacturer's Personnel Plan

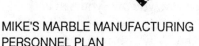

MIKE'S MARBLE MANUFACTURING
PERSONNEL PLAN

Based on expected sales volume (as confirmed by initial orders), MMM will begin operations with the following employees:

Secretary/order and billing clerk;
Three hourly production workers;
Shipping clerk-packer.

The owner will take responsibility for sales ordering and production scheduling. He will be in the office at least half of each day to supervise general operations.

The secretary/clerk will be responsible for billing customers, taking telephone orders and handling routine correspondence. She will report directly to the owner.

The production workers will report to one of their number who shall be designated "lead man." They will be hired jointly by the owner and the lead man and

trained by the lead man. They are responsible for meeting the production schedule established by the owner and assuring quality control is maintained to the satisfaction of the shipping clerk, as a preliminary screen, and the owner, as the final quality control check.

The shipping clerk will ship all orders after inspecting them for quality control. He will consult with the lead production worker about production schedules and any problems with quality. He will deliver order documentation to the secretary for billing purposes.

The secretary/clerk shall be paid $1,150 per month and will work from 8:00 a.m. to 4:30 p.m., Monday through Friday. The shipping clerk will be paid $6.00 per hour. Every effort will be made to assure him of 40 hours per week, but his hours will be reduced if orders are slow. The production lead man shall be paid $8.00 per hour and guaranteed a 40-hour week. In slow times, he will do routine maintenance on the equipment. Production workers will be paid $5.00 per hour, when work is available. Hourly workers will be eligible for overtime and time-and-a-half for the first twenty hours of overtime and triple time over 60 hours per week. However, it is expected that there will not be large amounts of overtime, as additional production workers will be hired if the business warrants it.

MMM will offer employees the opportunity to join a group medical insurance plan paid for by MMM. In addition, a bonus plan will be established whereby employees with a year or more of employment will be eligible to divide up to 25% of the company's profits over the profit target for the year. The profit target will be announced in the first month of each year. Employees are eligible for one week's paid vacation after one full year of steady work. Should they work for MMM longer than one year, they will be eligible for two weeks of paid vacation after the second year of work.

An outside bookkeeping service will prepare statements and tax returns from data provided by the secretary/clerk.

Example: A Small Service Business
Personnel Plan

ACME PROGRAMMERS: PERSONNEL PLAN

Acme Programmers will employ one full-time person,
Steve Sharpnik, whose job will be to locate computer
programming jobs and arrange work schedules with
Acme's programmer consultants. Steve will also
interview, screen and test Acme's computer
programmers, all of whom will be paid by the hour on
a work-for-hire basis, based on their experience and
the nature of the programming work undertaken. The
general range will be $20 to $35 per hour. It is
expected that the programmer consultants will be
available 10 to 30 hours per week and that their work
with Acme will constitute a second job. In the event
that any programmer works more than an average of
25 hours per week on a regular basis, they will be
treated as employees and paid a regular salary,
which will be negotiated.

Step 5: Outline Your Personal Goals

This is a tricky part of your plan. Your
lenders and backers want you to be happy in
your new venture. If you are not, you are
unlikely to make it a success. However, people
who back you will also want to be sure that
you're truly committed to the financial success of
your project. They don't want to back a bee
keeper who loves bees so much she can't stand
to disturb them by removing the honey from the
hive.

Ideally, your personal goals and
commitments will tie into the business goals

exactly. In reality, you probably have at least
some personal goals that don't have much to do
with business profitability.

Reread the personal goal worksheet you
prepared as part of Chapter 1, Section B. If for
some reason you haven't accomplished this, do it
now. Examine your personal goals with a critical
eye to see if any of them interfere with achieving
the financial goals you have established. It's
often helpful to have an objective outside
observer read your personal goal statement as
well. They may help you recognize your blind
spots. For example, if you plan to sell low- to
moderately-priced food but are personally
committed to using both premium ingredients
and a time-consuming and labor-intensive
preparation and cooking process, you may have
a problem.

If your personal goals seriously conflict with
your proposed business, and they are really
priority items for you, you owe yourself and
your potential backers the favor of modifying
your business plan. Why? Because, if the things
that make you happy really conflict with what it
takes to make your particular business work,
you probably shouldn't be in the business.
Experience shows that small businesses need the
personal dedication of the owner to succeed. By
the time you write your statement of personal
and business goals, you should have resolved all
serious conflicts that will interfere with your
business success. Here's an example of a
personal goal statement which includes a
frivolous (but honest) goal which may well
interfere with the business.

Example 1: "My reasons for starting this
business are to make a good living, prove I can
be successful, enjoy the freedom of
independence, and have lots of free time to work
on my car collection. In addition, I would like to
create a business which I can bequeath to my
children."

The problem, of course, is that most people starting small businesses are tied to them full time (if not more) and it's probably unrealistic to think that there will be a lot of time left to tinker with a car collection. Assuming our budding entrepreneur is willing to postpone most of his tinkering until his business is established, here's how this statement could be re-written to sound a little better to a potential backer.

Example 2: "My personal and business goals coincide to a great degree. Successful implementation of this business plan will enable me to meet the following personal goals: provide a good living for my family; work in a field I know and like; achieve the personal satisfaction of seeing my plan come true; enjoy the prestige and independence accruing to a successful business owner; provide a legacy for my children; and provide the means to a richer and more fulfilling life for both myself and my family."

Notice that in Example 2, "time to work on cars" was translated to "provide the means to a richer life." Perhaps your statement will neither be this lyrical nor obfuscatory, but hopefully you get the picture. Now let's look at Antoinette's statement.

ANTOINETTE GORZAK
—PERSONAL GOAL STATEMENT

 I want to start Antoinette's Dress Shop for the following reasons:

I want to prove that I can create a successful business by drawing on my educational background and work experience;

I want to do something I regard as worthwhile and feel that choosing and selling good clothes at a fair price will be an honest service to my customers and the community generally;

I want the chance to make a better living than I can make by working for others;

I want the responsibility and freedom to be my own boss; and

I want to spend my time working with customers and people in the clothing business who share my values and life style.

Step 6: Your Business Plan Introduction and Request for Funds

Finally, it's time to write the introduction to your business plan loan package proposal. You may wonder why we have waited until last to do this. It's simple. Your introduction is a kind of summary of your entire package, emphasizing the high points. I have found it's easier to do this after you have created all the parts of your package.

Pay Attention! There is one thing we want you to understand before we go further. Many people will never read your entire package. They will make their preliminary decision as to whether to lend you money or invest in your project on the basis of the introduction. Others will decide to read the rest of your materials only if your introduction engages their interest. So be sure to put all your strong points in the first few paragraphs, saving the details for later. In addition to creating an introduction which outlines the high spots of your business plan and loan proposal and emphasizes the positive, you should absolutely follow two additional rules:

- Keep it short
- Be specific

In an age of media over-kill, few people read more than one page with attention. Your job is to tell your reader who you are, what you want to do, and how much money you need, all on one page.

Prepare to write your introduction by rereading all the data you have already prepared. Now, organize the high points into a coherent pattern that will tell the story of your proposed business. Some people find it helpful to photocopy all materials and then cut out key information and reorder it with tape or staples. Or, you can do the same job by making an outline. Either way, after you put your points in order, have a friend look them over and make suggestions for change. Once you are satisfied with your outline of key points, make a note of the most positive feature of each. This is the material that will go into your introduction. Remember, you've got one page to sell your idea.

Here is Antoinette's preliminary outline of the high points of her business plan. Remember, at this stage she is only doing this exercise for herself, so she has no need to be fancy:

INTRODUCTION TO BUSINESS PLAN—OUTLINE

Dress shop catering to working women under 40;

20,000 potential customers in the city;

Growing market;

No competitor exploits market systematically;

Risks such as newness of my concept to our community appear moderate and I have a plan to overcome all identified risks;

I have a good friend with solid qualifications to be assistant manager;

My background includes responsibility and knowledge in all critical areas;

My personal goals coincide with the financial success of the business;

Detailed financial projections show that I can start the business and reach my goals with a loan of $15,000, which I can secure with home equity;

Creative marketing ideas include free alterations, clothing tips for working women, occasional fashion shows, etc.

Next, Antoinette rearranges these highlights in logical order. Here is how her second version looks:

INTRODUCTION TO BUSINESS PLAN—OUTLINE #2

1. Open a dress shop catering to young professional working women/ need $15,000 to do it;

2. My market analysis demonstrates the concept is sound and that I have more than enough potential customers (20,000) to make it work;

3. I have several unique marketing ideas which should attract customers;

4. No competitor exploits market systematically;

5. Personal qualifications prove that I can do it; both my qualifications and Sally's;

6. Financial projections show the loan can be paid back with ease;

7. The money will be well-used for opening inventory, equipment, working capital and the other things necessary for starting the business;

8. Conclusion: statement of desire.

Here then is Antoinette's introduction:

INTRODUCTION

Here is my plan to open a dress shop catering to younger working and professional women and my application for a personal loan of $15,000.

Changes in the work force in New City have resulted in a large growth in the number of younger working women who identify themselves as "professionals." There is currently no store in New City which adequately caters to the needs of this group for moderately priced, stylish clothing to be worn at work. I propose to open Antoinette's Dress Shop to fill this need. My goal is simple: to sell good quality, moderately-priced clothing to the upwardly mobile younger woman, to provide free alterations to that clothing, and to provide several services that will help my customers dress well for a reasonable cost.

My qualifications include three years experience as a clothing buyer and assistant merchandise manager for the Rack-a-Frax Department store here in New City. During my tenure, the Designer Dress Department, which was my principal area of responsibility, showed a 35% sales increase. I will be assisted by Sally Walters, who has five years experience in the field, the last three being in the dress department at Glendale's.

My loan request is based on a detailed financial projection which demonstrates that by combining $15,000 of my savings with $15,000 of borrowed money, I can begin business at a favorable location on the west side of the town mall with a solid inventory. I will consider securing the loan with a second trust deed (mortgage) on my home, which has an equity of $45,000. My detailed financial projections show the loan being repaid in 36 equal monthly payments at competitive interest rates at the same time that there will be sufficient profit to meet my twin goals of providing myself with both an adequate living and return on my investment.

The funds I wish to borrow will be allocated to procure my initial inventory as well as equipment, fixtures, leasehold improvements, advertising and working capital as indicated in this proposal. I hope to open my new store by Labor Day of 19__. I am committed both to serving the younger professional women of New City and meeting my personal financial goals.

Dated:

_____

Antoinette Gorzak

Investor's (Venture Capitalist's) Note: In our sample introduction for Antoinette's Dress Shop, we propose a loan payback formula since Antoinette plans to borrow the money she needs from a bank. However, if you plan to solicit equity investors instead of applying for a loan, you'll need a different statement delineating what they will receive for their money. As a small business, you will almost certainly not propose selling stock to the public at large. Therefore, you will need to propose that investors will receive a significant share of ownership of the business and perhaps some monthly or annual cash payment as well.

Example: An investment of $20,000 in John's Roof Repair business will result in the investor receiving a 33% interest in the business. Present plans are to distribute one-half of the annual profit of the company to the owners each year. Based on projections contained in this proposal, this means a person who invests $20,000 will receive $5,000 the first year, $17,500 the second year, and $25,000 each year thereafter. In addition, investors will be entitled to have any necessary roof repairs done to their homes or business buildings and those of immediate family members at 50% off the regular rate.

Note on Raising Equity Finance: In Chapter 3, I presented an overview of what's involved in raising equity capital through the use of small, closely-held corporations and partnerships. The actual setting up of these organizations is beyond the scope of this book.

Step 7: Gather Your Supporting Evidence

If you have any documentation which supports claims you make in your business plan, include it in an appendix or "exhibits" section to your business plan. For example, in Step 2 of this chapter, Antoinette referred to a magazine

article supporting her marketing strategy, as well as a New City business survey and economic forecast. A copy of these materials should be included in the appendix.

In deciding what to include in your appendix, and how to prepare it properly, follow these common sense rules:

• Include documentation of points that a potential lender or investor would be likely to question (e.g., horse shoeing is a growth industry);

• Do not include support for obvious statements (e.g., people like ice cream);

• Present your material in a well-organized way. Don't be afraid to edit by cutting and pasting, as long as you don't unfairly change the meaning;

• Organize your material in logical order and include a title page. This should read as follows:

APPENDIX 1: DOCUMENTATION IN SUPPORT OF THE BUSINESS PLAN OF

_____.

Then list the materials you include.

Here are several things that you should commonly include in your appendix:

1. Copies of proposed lease agreements;

2. Copies of bids for any needed construction work;

3. Plans for construction work;

4. Drawings of business signs or logos;

5. A list of what will be purchased for your opening inventory;

6. Copies of any newspaper stories or other publicity you have received which relates to your business. This is particularly important for people who are entering service businesses, where they are their own main product.

ANTOINETTE'S APPENDIX

TABLE OF CONTENTS

1 Annual Survey of Business Conditions, New City Chamber of Commerce, January 19, 198_.

2. Bank of New City Economic Forecast for 198_.

3. Article from September 27, 198_ issue of "Woman's Monthly" concern ing the need for specialized clothes for the working woman.

4. Newspaper articles and picture of Antoinette when she put on large and successful fashion show for working women at the Rack-a-Frax Department Store.

5. Copy of proposed store lease (critical pages only, others available on request).

6. Planned fixture layout for Antoinette's Dress Shop.

7. Antoinette's Dress Shop sign drawing and bid, Smith Sign Co.

8. Leasehold improvements bid for shop, Jones Const. Co.

9. Quote from Meyer Supply on dress racks and cash register.

Now that you have a first draft of all the parts of your business plan, the next step is to assemble them into a logical and presentable order. We will assist you to do this in the next chapter.

Chapter 8

REFINING YOUR BUSINESS PLAN
AND LOAN PROPOSAL

EIGHT

Personal experience indicates that most people only pay attention to funding proposals that are well-presented. Think of it this way. When you go to the bank to present your proposal, chances are you will comb your hair and dress in appropriate attire. Give your business plan the same courtesy.

Step 1: Organize Your Business Plan and Loan Proposal

Now you're ready to assemble your materials. After you do this, you will be ready for your final edit.

Start by reading through everything you've written to spot any inconsistencies or obvious goofs. Make necessary corrections. By now, your material should be typed, doubled-spaced, in semi-final form. Your tables and charts can either be prepared with a typewriter or word processor, or printed neatly by hand. If you are using a word processor, and plan to use it for your final draft, make sure it has a letter-quality printer. Most low cost dot matrix printers do not produce acceptable results. Each semi-final copy of your proposal should be placed in a three-hole binder or folio. Duo Tang makes a good one.

Arrange the components of your plan in the following order:

Example 1:

BUSINESS PLAN AND LOAN REQUEST FOR

ByteRight: The Computer Consultants

December 15, 198_

Submitted by:

A. 'John' Smith
1234 Avenue Street
Milpitas, CA 95555

Example 2:

BUSINESS PLAN AND LOAN REQUEST

Antoinette's Dress Shop

Submitted by:

Antoinette Gorzak
555 Marden Road
New City, OREGON 98765

1. **Title Page:** This should be a separate page with the title of your business plan and loan request, the date, and your name.

2. **Introduction Page:** I recommend putting your one-page introduction here. You prepared this in Chapter 7, Step 6. However, as an alternative, you may want to put your introduction after the Table of Contents.

3. **Table of Contents Page:** For now, just list the headings for the major sections of your plan. Later, when you assemble your plan and number the pages, come back and put the appropriate page number next to each heading. If your report is thick, use divider pages with colored tabs to mark each section, so readers can find what they want quickly.

4. **Business Description:** Next comes the business description you wrote in Chapter 7, Step 1.

5. **Marketing Plan:** The marketing plan you wrote in Chapter 7, Step 2 comes next.

6. **Business Risk Analysis:** Put this section after your marketing plan. If your analysis is detailed, make it a separate section. If not, include it as part of your marketing discussion.

7. **Personnel Plan:** Next comes the personnel plan you wrote in Chapter 7, Step 4.

8. **Business Owner's Resume and Financial Statement:** Now insert your own resume and personal financial statement which you designed in Chapter 4.

9. **Key Employee Resumes:** After your resume, include those of your key employees. Again, you did this in Chapter 4.

10. **Capital Spending Plan:** Here you include the capital spending plan which you designed in Chapter 6, Section C, Step 1. Remember, this should set out the details of what you will buy, including prices, model numbers of equipment and suppliers.

11. **Profit and Loss Projections:** Next, include the profit and loss forecasts you made in Chapter 5. You need to explain all the major assumptions you used in making these projections, as discussed.

12. **Cash flow Forecast:** Here is the place for the cash flow forecast you made in Chapter 6, Section C. This should include an introduction explaining your assumptions.

13. **Appendix:** Now include any information which supports your concept--fashion trends, newspaper articles about competition in the area, demographics, personal materials about your business successes, and anything else you want potential backers to see. I discussed this in Chapter 7, Step 7.

Now that your plan is arranged in order, make at least one photo copy of the entire document. You will use this as your working copy, or perhaps we should say, your "re-working" copy.

Step 2: Complete Your Final Edit

Put your completed and organized business plan aside for a day or two. You want to come back to it as fresh as possible. When you do, here are some things to look for:

Check for consistency one more time. Your plan should say the same things in the financial section that it says in the business description, and so on. For example, Antoinette, who says she will do free alterations as part of her business plan, should be sure she has budgeted enough time for sewing, as well as carrying out all her management and sales tasks.

Assess the overall business message of your proposal. Does it make sense? Would you lend money on the strength of it? Can you make it more convincing by strengthening some of its sections? If so, do it.

Can you document all the claims you make? If someone asks you to back-up a point or elaborate on it, are you ready with facts and figures?

Finally, does your package look and sound good? It may seem obvious, but good writing, good organization, and good spelling can make all the difference. If you have any doubts about this, have it reviewed and perhaps rewritten by a professional writer. This needn't be expensive. If you don't know an experienced technical writer, ask at the local newspaper or an ad agency, or the English department at the local high school or college. For a modest fee, you may well be able to improve your work substantially. You needn't go overboard, however. Your principal concern should be if your prose is clear and to the point.

Step 3: Review Your Plan With a Business Consultant

It is often wise to have your plan reviewed by an experienced business consultant after you think it is in good shape. For a modest fee, a good small business consultant, or C.P.A. who specializes in the area, may either be able to save you from a costly mistake or point out additional profit opportunities. At the very least, they should be able to make suggestions as to how to improve the way your information is presented. I suggest that you wait until this stage for a review, so the consultant will be able to see your entire concept quickly. If minor suggestions of form or presentation are offered, you can incorporate them easily. If the suggestions are more major, give them some thought before making changes. Remember, this is your

business and your proposal, and it's up to you to make the final decisions.

Here are some things to look for in a business consultant:

• Several years experience owning a business or counseling with businesses of similar size and type to yours. A consultant familiar with General Motors isn't likely to be much help in opening a one-person employment agency.

• A good reputation in the community for professionalism and longevity. You can establish this by checking references.

• Personal compatibility with you. This usually translates as having a sincere interest in helping you establish your business. If you don't like a person, don't work with him, no matter how well-recommended. In addition, beware of the consultant who adopts a "me expert, you peasant" attitude. This is your business plan and loan package. For lots of reasons, from getting experience in practical problem-solving to saving money, you probably want to do the lion's share of the work yourself.

You can find a business consultant specializing in small businesses by talking to people with businesses you respect in your area.[1] Banks that specialize in loans to small businesses should also be able to make helpful suggestions. Speak to the business loan

---

[1]Several small business consultants who I know and trust helped me with this book. They are available to review business plans for reasonable fees. Peg Moran (see Chapter 11 on resources for reviews of Peg's books) specializes in helping women who are starting their first business. She can be reached in Rohnert Park, CA at (707) 795-5642. Roger Pritchard teaches group workshops and advises individual small businesses in Berkeley, California. His business is called Financial Alternatives, and he can be reached at (415) 527-5604. Finally, I, too, advise many small business clients using many of the tools presented in this book. My office is in Santa Rosa, California and I can be reached at (707) 576-1181.)

manager, not just a neighborhood branch manager. An alternative is to contact your local Chamber of Commerce. Another source of potential help is the Service Corps of Retired Executives (SCORE). SCORE is a Small Business Administration-sponsored group of retired business people who help small business owners at little or no cost. Occasionally, some of the retired executives are so used to doing things their own way that they are unable to see the advantages and risks inherent in a new approach. Others, however, are extremely helpful. To contact SCORE, write or phone your local Chamber of Commerce or the nearest Small Business Administration office.

Step 4: Last Steps

Make your final changes and take yourself out for a terrific dinner with someone whose company you enjoy. You deserve it.

ANTOINETTE'S DISCOURAGING MOMENT

Antoinette was pleased with her plan after putting it together, reviewing and polishing it. She was convinced she had a winner. Almost as an afterthought, she decided to have a business consultant review her business plan before taking it to the bank. She was glad she did. In brief, here is what the consultant told her:

"Antoinette, you have written a fine business plan and have a good idea for a business, but your financial projections contain one serious error. I believe that you have underestimated the amount of inventory you will have to carry by $15,000 to $20,000. Unfortunately, changing this number will influence all your other financial projections and will mean you have to rethink your entire plan."

The consultant then discussed the same inventory turnover problem we discovered in Chapter 6, Section C, Step 3. Reread this discussion if you have forgotten it. The consultant then suggested that Antoinette take a few days to decide if she wished to try and raise more money and rework her entire plan or drop the idea. Antoinette was stunned. She was expecting to discover some minor flaws, not a possibly fatal one. Nevertheless, after much soul-searching, she was relieved to have discovered the problem before, not after, she began her business. She decided that raising the extra money for inventory wasn't an insurmountable problem. The question was could she reasonably increase her sales projections enough to justify the increased inventory. To make this decision, she decided to again talk to a number of women in the target audience to get a better idea of how often they might patronize her store. I shall leave the decision to you as to whether Antoinette decides to proceed with her plans or decides to go back to work for a salary. After all, it's much the same sort of difficult choice you are likely to have to make about your own business.

Chapter 9

SELING YOUR BUSINESS PLAN

NINE

A. How to Ask for the Money You Need

Now that your business plan has been polished to perfection, you're ready to use it as part of your campaign to get financing. Your first task is to decide where you'd ideally like to get the money you need, and whether you prefer to get it from a lender or an investor. We discuss this in detail in Chapter 3. Chances are you have long since decided whom to approach first. If you haven't, decide on your list of priorities now. For example, you might decide to first approach your father, then the Bank of Newcastle, then the Small Business Administration, etc.

Before you actually begin to call people and make appointments, give some thought to a few preliminaries. The most important is that, like it or not, you're now a salesperson. Your task is to sell your plan. Don't let this discourage you, even if your experience with selling has been negative. There are all sorts of good ways to sell things, most of which depend on a good product and an honest, straightforward presentation. We can't tell you exactly how to approach selling yourself and your plan, but we can give you one bit of essential advice. You must ask for the sale. Don't make the common mistake of discussing your plan in generalities and then saying "thank you" and walking out the door, or hanging up the phone.

As part of every presentation, you must ask the potential source of funds if he will invest in your venture or lend you the money. Repeat this phrase:

"Thank you for listening to my business plan. Will you invest/lend me the money I need to get started?"

If you are turned down, don't hang your tail between your legs and slink away in a puddle of embarrassed perspiration. Ask why. Sometimes the reasons why a person won't help finance your business will be more valuable to you than the money—especially if the person who turns you down misunderstood your concept.

Here's another important hint to help you sell your plan. Be sure you explain exactly what your backer will get in return for her investments. Or, to put it another way, sell the benefits of the investment. For example, bankers want to hear that their loan will be soundly secured and paid back with no problem. Your relatives, on the other hand, may be as interested in family solidarity or the prestige of a family-owned business, as in receiving tangible monetary benefits. A small business investor who sees himself as a budding venture capitalist may well want to be part of an exciting project that promises high returns for a small investment.

In Chapter 3, we discussed some general ideas about how to convince different types of funding sources to support you. In addition to being a convincing salesperson, this usually boils down to offering investors/lenders a fair return, as much security as possible, and a little romance. By romance, I mean to emphasize the fact that investing and lending money are very personal activities. Your backer wants to feel good about you and your project and to help you meet your goals. Your backer also wants to share in your excitement. So, in addition to presenting a potential lender or investor with a sound financial plan, make sure he knows what makes the project exciting for you.

Now, let's look at some of the ways you might approach specific types of backers.

1. Friends and Relatives

Reread Chapter 3, Section E(2) on raising money from relatives. Remember, the first rule of borrowing money from people close to you is that you want to be very sure they can afford to lend it to you and that you will be able to pay it back. Everyone who works with small business financing can tell horror stories about situations in which business owners had to deal with both the failure of their enterprise and a bunch of angry relatives. Put simply, it's no fun.

But assuming you do want to ask a relative or friend for a loan, how should you go about it? Obviously, much of this depends on the people involved and your relationship to them. We can't tell you much about either of these areas. Here are some general suggestions, however:

• Approach your loan request in a business-like way. Don't just spring it on the person in a social context;

• Give your friends or relatives an idea of what you want to talk about well in advance and make an appointment to talk business. It's sometimes a good idea to give them a copy of your loan package and business plan in advance so they can review it independently;

• Remember, the person you are talking to knows you well. So, while you should obviously be well-organized, business-like, and enthusiastic, you can save the hyperbole for someone else. You may also want to modify your business plan package slightly to make it a little less formal. For example, your brother may know what's in your resume as well as you do, so you can safely skip that;

• Above all, give the person you're talking to a graceful way not to lend or invest. Remember, this is a business proposition, not proof as to whether someone cares for you. Once everyone is assured an easy exit if for any reason they aren't excited about your project or just don't have the money to invest, or for any other reason, you may find they will be relaxed enough to give you a fair hearing.

2. Supporters

As you will remember from Chapter 3, these are people who care—often deeply—about the subject area of your business. Your best approach is to try to enlist this enthusiasm and to honestly involve these people in your dream. If you do, it won't be hard to get financial help. Often it's best to involve supporters at an early stage so that you really get the full benefit of their good ideas.

If you have a business—anything from a music store, to opening a dentist's office in a rural area where there is no dentist now—where you think potential supporters exist, but you don't know them, check it out. Figure out ways to get the word out in the correct circles about your plan. If people care, they will respond, and if your business plan is otherwise sensible they may well extend financial help.

Mike's
Marble
Manufacturing

1707 Pebble Way, Boulder, Colo. 80302 (303) 478-2109

3.   Banks

Again, reread Chapter 3. The main point to remember about banks is that they lend money, they don't invest it. Banks simply don't make enough on the money they lend to take substantial risks. A banker will want to know all about you and your business, but when it comes to saying "yes" or "no," the security of the loan will be paramount on their minds.

In approaching a bank for the first time, it is important to understand that within all banks, responsibility for different tasks is divided. You want to talk to the loan officer in charge of small business loans, not the trust officer or the person in charge of getting the automatic teller machine to work right. The ideal way to meet a bank lending officer is to know a bank vice-president socially and have her refer you to the loan officer. Bankers, like almost everyone else, prefer dealing with people they know. However, if you are like most other mere mortals and don't have any old school ties or country club connections to trade on, you will have to be creative. Think about whom you know with friendly contacts at a local bank. Almost anyone who owns a successful small business will qualify, as will accountants, business consultants, etc. See if you can arrange an introduction, or at least get permission to use your contact's name. If all else fails, call the bank and ask the receptionist the appropriate person with whom you should talk.

Once you have a name, follow these introductory steps. Telephone for an appointment and briefly describe the subject matter you'll want to discuss. Show up on time with your loan package and business plan. Open the discussion by talking about your personal business and/or employment history. Highlight your community involvement while trying to discover common interests and acquaintances. Maybe you both have children in Little League, maybe you both belong to the Rotary Club or the Symphony Association or the Volunteer Fire Department. Who you are in the community and what you have accomplished in other jobs or businesses is an important part of the loan application process. While it's important to be business-like, it's also important to take your time. Again, refer to the discussion on bank loans in Chapter 3, Section E(6) for an idea of what the banker is likely to say. Obviously, he is not going to approve your plan immediately. Expect lots of checking and probably a series of meetings. But never forget rule number one. To get a loan, you have to ask for it. As part of each meeting with the bank, ask politely but specifically about the status of your loan.

Here are a few things to emphasize when talking to bankers:

• **Your other bank business:** If you don't already patronize the bank in question, make sure the lending officer knows you plan to do so if you get the loan.

• **Security:** Again, remember, the banker wants to lend money, not invest it. Save your fantasies about the big returns you expect to get in exchange for your risk for the venture capitalists. Tell the banker how sure he is to get his money back with interest. If you can offer security for the loan, emphasize it.

• **Be persistent:** There are lots of banks. For all sorts of reasons, some may be more willing to make small business loans one year and others the next. So, if you are turned down by one bank, keep trying. Make sure you understand why you were rejected, however, and, if possible, change the items in your proposal that caused this rejection. Pay extra attention to aspects of your plan which continue to receive negative comments. People who work with small businesses in your area can probably save you time by suggesting the banks which specialize in lending to businesses like the one you plan to start.

Note: Be realistic! Your banker wants to be assured about your knowledge and enthusiasm about your business. But she also needs to know that you have your feet on the ground—bankers are like that. So don't exaggerate your expectations. If you puff too hard, the banker is almost sure to be turned off.

4. Equity Investors (Venture Capitalists)

Start by rereading Chapter 3, Section C(2). Remember, we use the term "venture capitalist" a bit loosely to include people who invest relatively small amounts of equity financing. These may be relatives, acquaintances, or anyone else with money to invest in what looks to be a profitable business. We are not talking about the venture capital firms organized to lend huge sums. If you are talking to these folks, you need more help than we can give you in this book.

As you should know from reading the discussion in Chapter 3, the primary distinction between a venture capitalist and a lender involves risk, security and amount of return. The venture capitalist is traditionally willing to take more risk. In exchange for doing that, she will want a chance to make a large profit. In short, to catch the interest of potential investors, you need to emphasize the possibility of a healthy return if your project is successful. Ask yourself whom you know that would be more attracted to the

notion of making a substantial profit than lending you money at a normal interest rate.

Here are some suggestions:

• **Prepare a summary of what you are offering:** In addition to the business plan you have already designed, you need to tell the equity investor both what you are offering (partnership, limited partnership, shares in a corporation, etc.) and what the projected return is;

• **Ask for names of others who might invest:** If you are turned down for any reason, ask if the person you are talking to knows someone who might be interested in investing. Don't be shocked if someone suggests that he can put a deal together for you for a fee. This is common practice. If you're interested in this possibility, check references carefully to be sure you are dealing with a reputable person. A fee of 5% to 10% of the money raised is normal. Avoid people who ask for fees before you receive the loan. Often the reason this sort of request is made is that the money finder fears he can't perform. Be careful;

• **Do not promise a certain return:** If your potential investor is unsophisticated, emphasize in writing that there is always some risk associated with a high potential return. Make certain the investor knows your projections are just that—projections. In short, never guarantee what you may not be able to deliver. The person putting up the money should even understand there is a possibility she may lose the entire investment if things go very badly.

5. Government Agencies

The hardest thing about getting money from the government is finding out which program can help you. The second hardest thing is finding out who in that agency can make a decision for or against your proposal. Compared to these two, filling out the forms is easy.

Start by asking your local bankers who work with the agencies. Most will have some experience with at least one of the agencies, such as the Small Business Administration, and can steer you in the right direction. If you run into a wall, try your local elected representatives. They have aides whose business it is to help people like you. If you do find a program that looks good, be sure your elected representative knows about your application.

B.   What to Do When Someone Says "Yes"

Your first job when someone indicates his interest in loaning you money or investing in your plan is simple—don't faint. It's fine to prepare for a negative result so you are not too disappointed if you are rejected, but remember to be prepared for a positive reception, too. If your proposal is good, it will be funded sooner or later

One good approach is to have a number of answers ready, depending on what the lender or investor offers. It's a little like being a major league baseball outfielder in a close game, with several men on base. Depending on where the ball is hit, you need several alternative plans as to how to respond. You can see some pretty funny plays when a fielder fails to think ahead and throws to the wrong base.

If you're asking for a loan or a set amount of money at a certain interest rate, and the lender says "yes," presumably you will too. But, what should you do if the lender offers you less than you want, or asks for higher payments than you expect, or proposes a different financial formula entirely?

First, make sure you understand exactly what the proposal is. Second, don't answer on the spot. Take the proposal home and see if you can live with it. If you can't, meet with the person again and explain exactly what you can't accept and why. Then propose changes. If this doesn't result in agreement, start looking for other funding sources. It's far better to say "no" than to accept a disadvantageous deal. Anyone who has been in business for a while will tell you the times he turned down poor business proposals were at least as important to his ultimate success as the ones to which he said "yes."

Example: Charlie wanted a loan of $20,000 to start a limousine service. The bank offered him $20,000, but wanted equal monthly payments of $1,018 over two years. Charlie had expected to make payments of $530 per month over five years. After he ran the different loan payments through his cash flow schedule, he discovered that he couldn't pay his own rent and grocery bill if he had to pay $1,018 per month on the loan in the first two years. After he explained his problem to the loan officer, the bank offered Charlie interest-only payments for the first two years. That was a much better deal and Charlie took it.

C.   Plan In Advance For Legal Details

Whatever loan or equity investment you arrange will have to be reduced to writing. If you deal with a bank or other institutional lender, they will have the necessary forms. However, if your arrangement is with a friend, family member, or private investor, these details will probably be up to you.

Writing up a simple loan agreement isn't difficult. You may already know how. If not, consult an attorney or someone else familiar with the law and forms required. While a course in contract law is beyond the scope of this book, here are several sample notes which may help you focus on this task.

If your note is simple (so much money, at so much interest, to be paid at regular intervals), you can safely design it yourself. However, if it's complicated and involves default provisions, security, balloon payments, etc., you and the person you are dealing with would be wise to have it checked by an attorney. If you have done most of the work, this shouldn't be too expensive. Negotiate the fee in advance.

If you plan to arrange for an equity investment, you have considerable work to do beyond the scope of this book. In short, you need to have a detailed plan for the legal form of organization you prefer. We talk about partnerships, limited partnerships and small corporations in Chapter 3. All require that you do considerable work on your own, or hire a lawyer. Either way, the preliminary work should be done prior to arranging your financing so the deal can close promptly. See Chapter 11 for references to several helpful resources.

Example 1

PROMISSORY NOTE

Robert Lee of 1411 South St., Homer, Alaska and Gertrude Fox of 123 Main St., Fairfax, Alaska, agree that Gertrude Fox hereby loans Robert Lee the sum of Fifty-Six Thousand ($56,000) Dollars to be repaid on the following terms:

1. Principal and interest of 10% per year will be paid in ___ equal monthly installments on the first day of each month beginning the first day of September 198_ and continuing through the first day of August, 198_;

2. On September 1, 198_, the entire unpaid balance of principal and interest shall be due and payable in full;

3. Should Robert Lee tail to pay an installment on the date due, as set out in Paragraph 1 of this agreement, the whole sum of the principal and interest then outstanding shall, at the option of Gertrude Fox or any subsequent holder of this note, immediately become due and payable;

4. Should Robert Lee fail to meet any condition of this agreement, and should Gertrude Fox or any subsequent holder of this note take legal action to collect it, Robert Lee shall be responsible for all attorney's fees.

Date: _____   _____
                               Robert Lee

Date: _____   _____
                               Gertrude Fox

Example 2

$8,639.00   July 30, 198_

PROMISSORY NOTE

For value received, the undersigned promises to repay to Sebastian Grazowtski, of New City, Oregon, the sum of EIGHT-THOUSAND SIX-HUNDRED AND THIRTY-NINE DOLLARS ($8,639.00) including interest at 12% per year. This money is to be paid in __ equal monthly payments of $315.00 (principal only) commencing on September 1, 198_ and continuing until November 1, 198_, at which time the monthly payments will increase to $440.61 per month until the entire balance of principal and interest is paid.

Should default be made in the payment of any installment when due, then, at the option of the holder of the note, the entire amount of the principal and interest shall become immediately due and payable. In the event of any default on this note, the holder shall be entitled to recover all costs of collection of same, including reasonable attorneys fees and costs.

Date: _____

                                          _____
                                          Sebastian Grazowtski

Date: _____   _____

                                          Virginia Woo

Example: Wilhelmina Whalen needed $35,000 to start a coffee shop. She decided to form a small corporation and sell an investor 25% of the company for that amount. If the coffee shop succeeded, as she expected, the 25% investment would be worth $100,000 in three years. Harrison Flyright liked Wilhelmina and her business idea. He offered $25,000 but wanted 50% of the company. Wilhelmina thought that was too high a price and said "no." Sometime later, Harrison increased the amount to $32,000, and Wilhelmina agreed to give him 50% of the stock. As a California resident, Wilhelmina incorporated her business using *How to Form Your Own California Corporation,* by Anthony Mancuso (Nolo Press). She issued half the stock

to Harrison in exchange for his cash and was off and running.

Congratulations! Now you have a complete business plan and are ready, willing and able to achieve your goals. May the force be with you! In the next chapter, I offer some thoughts about what may happen once you open your business. This material isn't related to designing your loan package and business plan, but nevertheless, I hope you will take the time to read it.

Chapter 10

AFTER YOU OPEN—
SOME THINGS TO CONSIDER

TEN

Here I am concerned with some of the things that can happen after you open your business. My message takes the form of several short stories. Each is roughly based on a real situation. This material is not meant to take the place of the excellent books on small business management described in the next chapter. It is meant to remind you that getting your business started should be seen as the beginning of your long march towards realizing your dream. Or, in other words, even though you have come a long way, you still have miles to travel.

Many small business start-up books take fairly extreme approaches. Two common ones can be summarized as follows:

1. Here comes another lamb to the slaughter; hopefully this book can frighten him out of his dumb idea; or,

2. Anybody can find fame and fortune in a small business; just read this book and get a big strongbox in which to store your surplus gold.

I hope to steer a middle course by offering you both encouragement and caution. In my view, small business is one of the last great frontiers of both individualism and opportunity, but like the prairies of yesteryear, there are more than a few rattlesnakes among the poppies.

Let's look at some of the ways to avoid the rattlers.

A. Running Your Business After It Opens

To illustrate the importance of planning for the operation of your business after it opens, I'd like to share the experiences of Molly, a friend and former student, who wanted to open a bath supply shop. Molly encountered a long series of depressing obstacles on the way to getting the money to open her business. But since she was both stubborn and a fighter, each made her even more determined. In truth, before long, getting the necessary money had become an obsession. Finally Molly succeeded. Unfortunately, at this point she became strangely lethargic. While her new business wasn't terrible, it clearly needed both energy and an ability to innovate to really succeed. Molly simply had little energy left for the demanding job of competing in a changing marketplace. Her business closed in twelve months, which was just about how long it took to start it. She lost a lot of money and a lot of pride.

Moral: This book focuses on the steps needed to open a business, but running a small business profitably requires much more than this. You need a coherent plan of action of what to do after opening. As part of designing your business plan in Chapter 7, you began this task. Don't stop once the doors open. You will need a continuing operating plan which you should be ready to modify on the basis of experience. It's particularly important to be ready to change your business plan if business isn't good. Many people kid themselves into thinking that business is sure to improve soon. In my experience, it usually doesn't, unless you make it happen.

B.   Set Goals and Respect Them

Success in a small business involves meeting your objectives, especially the one that says you have a positive cash flow by a specific date. How long should it take to know whether your business will meet your objectives? The answer is, normally, not very long. Again, many people make the mistake of waiting a year or two to see whether the business will succeed. I think that's a mistake. Figure out how long it should take for your potential customers to hear about your opening and then add a month or two. That's usually no more than three to six months in a retail business, depending on the type of business and how good a promoter you are. Put another way, your sales will probably level out in three or four months after opening. People in service, wholesale, and small manufacturing businesses may expect a longer start-up cycle. For example, a real estate agency normally takes six to twelve months for money to begin coming in. That's how long it takes to find clients, negotiate deals, and generally get known in the community.

Moral: The point here is to establish in advance a time when you will review your business performance to see if you are meeting your goals. Put this date on your calendar before you open your doors. This forces you to compare your results to your plan and not fool yourself into postponing what may turn out to be an unpleasant job. If you face up to the fact that your business is not doing as well as it

should be early, you still have a chance to make changes before your money and energy run out.

C.   Have a Plan For When Your Business Meets or Exceeds Objectives

Now let's assume your business succeeds. Why shouldn't it? After all, you've planned carefully and worked hard. When it happens, be sure you relax and enjoy your success for a while before you think about expanding. Everyone needs to know how to take a vacation, especially small business owners. Should you ultimately decide to expand, consider this. Some of the wisest people I know would rather make a decent profit with a small business than make a much bigger business with many more headaches and, perhaps, only a little more profit.

Let me illustrate this point with the story of two men I know well. Fred and Fritz opened a breakfast restaurant several years ago. After they learned the ropes, they made a good profit. Best of all, they went home everyday at 3:00 p.m. Then they opened a second breakfast restaurant and things were twice as good. Next, they made plans to open two more, on the theory that if two are good, four will be better. This meant they had to run the two existing restaurants while building the new ones. Inevitably, hired help ended up managing the existing restaurants. About then, interest rates went up and there was a recession. Finally, they got all four restaurants open. The only problem was that without their personal attention, business had dropped 40% at the original locations and was less than half of what was expected at the two new ones. Within two years, they both lost their homes as well as their businesses and were back to working for someone else. Not surprisingly, their new boss thought it unreasonable for his employees to go home at 3:00 p.m.

Moral: Bigger is not necessarily better. It all depends on your personal objectives, of course. If your objectives are to make your business bigger, however, you need to plan as carefully as you did when you began. Resist the urge to over-expand. Just because you have done well so far, does not mean you are a budding business genius. You will very likely continue to do well if you expand slowly and sensibly.

6444 alexis way
ann arbor, mi 48103
(313) 654-8471

D.   If Your Business Doesn't Meet Your Objectives

Sadly, the best laid plans of mice and men rather regularly go astray. What do you do when your sales are less than half you expected after you have been operating four months? Do you triple the advertising budget and hope that sales will pick up? I hope not. A more sensible approach is to make another business plan adjusted to the sales you are actually getting. This is psychologically difficult for many people to do. It's all too easy to get hung up on proving that your original plans were right, rather than accepting what the numbers tell you.

To illustrate, let me introduce Pierre, who has a degree in hotel management and is an accomplished chef. Pierre, who never ran a restaurant, or any other business for that matter, bought a failed cafe. He projected $30,000 a

month in sales, and budgeted accordingly. Actual, sales in that first three months were $12,000, $18,000 and $16,000. Then sales leveled off at the $14,000 per month level for the next several months. Pierre lost $60,000 in the first quarter. Then he cut back to where he was only losing $2,000 or $3,000 per month for the next three months, but stuck to the idea that he could generate sales of $30,000 per month. In the meantime, he sold his house and his wife's jewelry to keep up with the bills. Many people suggested that he make further economies so that he could make a profit on $14,000 per month or, as an alternative, sell the restaurant. So far, he has refused. Perhaps eventually he'll take in a $30,000 month. If he doesn't, he'll go broke. Pierre's approach is not one I would recommend.

Moral: Here is how I would approach this sort of problem. I would take the first four month's total sales and divide by four to get a monthly average. Then I would design a profit-and-loss forecast such as the one you did in Chapter 5 to make a profit at that level of sales. To do this, I would have to cut back. I would also pay a lot of attention both to the quality of my food and techniques to get the word out in the community. If Monday and Tuesday evenings were slow for example I might close the restaurant and start a cooking class those nights. If my efforts to generate more business failed, I would think about closing. It's far better to close with a small loss than to hang on and end up in bankruptcy.

E.   A Plan to Get Out of Business

What should you do if you have already scaled down your expenses, tried a number of innovative marketing techniques, and made sure your product or service is truly a quality one, but you still lose money? Again, the answer is to either fundamentally change your business, or get out of it. You'll be well-advised to make these tough decisions promptly if circumstances indicate.

If you decide to close your business, you have four basic options:

1. You can lock the doors and disappear. But unless you plan never to come back, that will create more problems than it solves, not to mention the human problems you will cause your landlord, your lender, your other creditors, and your friends. Disappearing is almost always a bad idea.

2. If your business makes a small profit (or sometimes, even if it doesn't), you may be able to sell it to someone who will be satisfied with less than you are, or has visions as to how to make it profitable. In order to see whether selling is a viable alternative, make a balance sheet for your business similar to the personal financial statement you made in Chapter 4. A simplified version might look like this, though, of course, you will want to do it in more detail.

In this example, if Sally can sell her business for at least $16,000 cash, she can pay her creditors and come out clean. Remember, when you sell a business, your creditors will all line up to be paid. If you can't raise enough cash to pay your creditors and they aren't willing to take less than the face amount of what you owe them, you may have to declare bankruptcy just to get rid of the business.

3. You can declare bankruptcy. If you're in a position where payments from current bills can be easily met from current cash flow, but you have a stack of bills from past slow times that are bogging you down, you may find the Federal bankruptcy laws will help you. Here is a brief overview of how to think about this.

SALLY'S BOOK SHOP: BALANCE SHEET

Assets

Cash	$ 200
Inventory at cost	32,000
Fixtures and equipment at estimated sales price	5,000
TOTAL ASSETS	$37,000

Liabilities

Accounts payable	$15,000
Income taxes and withholding payable	1,000
TOTAL LIABILITIES	$16,000

Chapter 11 of the Federal Bankruptcy Act provides you with court protection from your creditors while you continue to operate the business and work on a plan to pay the past due bills. This is a formal process and probably requires that you work with an attorney to file the necessary forms and appear with you in court. It also requires that you provide the court with frequent financial statements on how your business is doing and obtain court approval of any changes. If you can operate the business on a current basis and develop a plan to settle your past due bills that the court and your creditors will accept, Chapter 11 is a way for you to keep the business.

Another option is to offer creditors a fractional payment for their bills in exchange for them releasing you from any further liability. Most creditors know they'll be lucky to get 10 cents on the dollar at liquidation, so if you can offer substantially more, you may have a lot of flexibility in negotiating a deal.

Finally, there is Chapter 7 of the bankruptcy law, otherwise known as straight bankruptcy. Here, you simply close down and the court sells whatever property you have left to the highest bidder. The proceeds are then parceled out to your creditors and your debts are discharged. *Bankruptcy: Do It Yourself*, by Janice Kosel, is a good source of information about this option.

4. One other option for a retail business is to have a going out of business sale. This usually involves selling all your merchandise at or below cost. There are firms who make a business of liquidating businesses, or you can do it yourself. For certain types of retailers, a liquidation sale can sometimes be a better idea than selling a business. Take Sally's book shop, for example. If she could sell her assets at cost, she could pay all her creditors and end up with $21,000 in cash. Even if she only got 60 cents on the dollar, she would come out clean. Auctioneers and liquidators have lots of tricks to get the best prices for everything. It's worth investigating if you're thinking about a sale, especially if you have a lot of inventory.

Chapter 11

GOOD BOOKS FOR
SMALL BUSINESSES

ELEVEN

Here we refer you to a few books and pamphlets relevant to starting a small business which I think are particularly helpful. There are several others that are also good. This is my list, not a comprehensive study of the subject. Oh, and one more thing. Several of the books I list are also published by Nolo Press. That's because Nolo Press concentrates on how-to-do-it books and avoids the double talk that makes many business books virtually unreadable. I recommend their approach highly, especially if you don't have a graduate degree in business administration; after all, a wise man once said that if you can't explain something to a twelve-year-old child, you probably don't know your subject thoroughly.

A. About Small Business Generally

There are two books everyone thinking about starting a small business should own. The first is *Honest Business* by Michael Phillips and Salli Rasberry, Random House, 201 E. 50th St., N.Y.C. 10021. This book might as well be entitled, *Zen and the Art of Small Business Success*. It is a remarkable book focusing on the personal and psychological qualities it takes to succeed in a small business. Much of Phillips' and Rasberry's advice stands conventional small business wisdom on its head. A must-read.

Small Time Operator by Bernard Kamoroff, Bell Springs Publishing (P.O. Box 640, Laytonville, CA) is currently in its fully updated 19th printing with excellent reason. It gives you the basics of keeping books, paying taxes, renting a building, becoming an employer, etc., even down to the type of calculator to buy, more thoroughly and better than anyone else. If you never buy another business book, buy this one.

Other material which I have found very helpful includes:

The Small Business Handbook: A Comprehensive Guide to Starting and Running Your Own Business, Irving Burstiner, Prentice-Hall, Inc. This book is just what the title says. I used it as a textbook in a small business management class with good results. Good practical advice. Its only fault is that it tries to cover all aspects of running a business, which sometimes results in hitting the high spots, rather than the in-depth coverage many of these areas deserve. But each chapter has an extensive bibliography of more detailed sources which readers will find valuable.

Successful Small Business Management by David Seigel and Harold Goldman, Fairchild Publications (7 East 12th Street, New York, NY 10003). It is a fact that certain personality types are more likely to succeed in a business than others. This excellent 340-page book identifies and discusses these human traits in a logical and well-organized manner. It covers pre-start up, getting started, different types of businesses, pricing, selling, advertising, and even accounting, from the personal perspective of the business owner. The authors emphasize that you need to understand the common-sense basics of operating a business (which they explain well), but you also need to offer a quality product or service, and you need to treat your customers honestly and with respect.

Home-Based Business by Beverly Neuer Feldman, Till Press (P.O. Box 27816, Los Angeles, CA 90027). A good general introduction to running a business out of your home. Another good book in this field is *Mail Order Moonlighting* by Cecil C. Hogue, Ten Speed Press (Box 7123, Berkeley, CA 94707).

Straight Talk About Small Business by Kenneth Albert and *Setting Up Shop* by Randy Smith, both published by McGraw Hill (1221 Avenue of the Americas, New York City 10020), are both excellent books for budding business people. Read both before you start.

Small Business Administration Pamphlets: The SBA publishes a good many useful books and pamphlets covering everything from finance to insurance to exporting and franchising. One of the best is "Starting and Managing a Small Business of Your Own." Most pamphlets are available in the reference section of your library. Or, you can get a list from Superintendent of Documents, U.S. Government Printing Office, Washington D.C. 20402. Ask for order form 115B (for Sale Management Assistance Publication).

Bank of America Pamphlets: The Bank of America offers an unusually well-written series of pamphlets on a number of small business topics, such as "How to Buy or Sell a Business," "Financing Small Businesses," "Understanding Financial Statements," "Steps to Starting a Business," and many more. Single copies are free at Bank of America branches in California. If you are out of state, write Small Business Reporter, Bank of America, Dept. 3401, Box 3700, S.F., CA 94137 and ask for order information.

Expenses in Retail Business: This is a sales tool put out by the NCR corporation to help sales people sell cash registers. Nevertheless, it has some very good information on typical ratios of expenses to sales in various businesses. Use it to see if your projected expenses are in line with industry averages. Available from your nearest NCR Corporation office.

B.   Women in Business

Invest In Yourself: A Woman's Guide to Starting Her Own Business (Doubleday, 1984), by Peg Moran, is an attractive workbook which helps you take stock of your interests, talents and resources. It then gives you practical information about starting a business, with dozens of exercises to help you plan the entire scope of the project. I recommend it highly.

Surviving the First Two Years: A Woman's Guide to Running Her Business Successfully, by Peg Moran, is the sequel to *Invest In Yourself*, and is due to be published by Doubleday in February, 1985. Peg continues her workbook style to re-evaluate your original business plan based on what you have learned in the first year or two. This is a good book.

C.   Small Business and the Law

As I discussed in Chapter 3, you may want to organize your business as a partnership, limited partnership or closely held corporation. The following materials will prove helpful.

The SBA publishes a free leaflet, "Incorporating a Small Business." You can get one from Box 15434, Fort Worth, Texas.

Unfortunately, the best self-incorporation books are only available in three states. *How to Form Your Own California [Texas, Florida or New York] Corporation* by Anthony Mancuso includes full instructions on how to incorporate a new or already existing business. The book comes complete with all tear-out forms necessary, including articles, bylaws and stock certificates. Nolo also publishes a similar book for professional corporations and a third for non-profit corporations. These latter two books are only available in California editions (order and price information for all Nolo books is at the back of this book). Nolo Press and Legisoft, Inc. also publish *California Incorporator*, a software package that lets you do the incorporation paperwork with minimum effort. You answer questions on the screen and *California Incorporator* prints out the 35-40 pages of documents you need to make your California corporation legal.

Nolo Press also publishes a comprehensive book specifically about legal aspects of partnerships, called, appropriately, *The Partnership Book: How to Write Your Own Small Business Partnership Agreement*, by Denis Clifford and Ralph Warner. The book includes just about everything a small business person needs to know to establish his or her own partnership. The book also discusses limited partnerships, but in less detail. (See back of this book for order information.)

People planning partnerships will also want to read:

• "Tax Information on Partnerships," IRS publication 541.

• *Partners in Business: How to Choose and Build the Relationship Most Vital to Your Success*, by Melvin Wallace, Enterprise Publishing (725 Market St., Wilmington, Del 19801). This book focuses on the interpersonal side of partnerships. It is really a psychology book, but a good one.

• *Small Business Legal Problem Solver*, by Arnold Goldstein, Inc., CBI (286 Congress St., Boston, MA 02210). This book answers a number of questions about business law, from bank accounts to bankruptcy. The information about contracts, sales agreements, etc. is excellent. A good general reference.

• A good book on doing your own legal research (something that small business people should really know how to do) is *Legal Research: How to Find and Understand the Law*, by Stephen Elias, Nolo Press (order information at the back of this book).

• Should you ever find yourself holding a handful of bad checks, you will want to grab a copy of *Everybody's Guide to Small Claims Court*, by Ralph Warner (Nolo Press). It is the best guide on how to properly prepare a small claims court case—which is far more than half the battle. It also contains good advice on who, where, and how to sue.

D. Magazines—Continuing Small Business Help

Most big business publications, such as *The Wall Street Journal, Business Week,* and *Forbes,* are not directly helpful to the little guy. Several publications I find of more value to start-ups are:

• *Inc.* (38 Commercial Wharf, Boston, MA 02110). This is primarily oriented towards big small businesses (or small big ones), but nevertheless is well put together and helpful.

• *In Business* (Box 323, Emmons, PA 18049). A bi-monthly magazine devoted entirely to small business. It has lots of articles on tax, financial and legal matters. Probably the best of the bunch for start-ups.

• *Entrepreneur Magazine.* This magazine is normally available from your local newsstand. It covers a great many business opportunities in depth and purports to give all the secrets needed to be successful in the hottest new fields. Also,

each issue has an order form to order past business studies. They can be very useful, although they tend to gloss over the difficult parts. If you are planning to enter a business they have already studied, it's a must-read, but check out all their assumptions and statements before spending any money. If you can't find it on the newsstand, write: *Entrepreneur Magazine* 2311 Pontius Avenue, Los Angeles, CA 90064.

• *Mother Earth News* (Box 70, Hendersonville, N.C. 28739): The other end of the spectrum from *Entrepreneur,* this bi-monthly magazine features "cottage industry" home business ideas and does so very sensibly.

E. Computers

Don't get involved with one until you read the *Whole Earth Software Review* (Box 428, Sausalito, CA 94966). Most computer publications have an axe to grind. One way or another they have a financial interest in pushing one software or hardware product or another. This one doesn't. Read it.

Appendix 1

A Business Plan and Loan Package for a Small Service Business

Here is a business plan for a small personnel agency located in a city of about 70,000, which plans to specialize in placing people in secretarial, clerical and word processing positions. Basically, all you need to get started in this business is a state license (in many states), a desk and telephone. However, as in most other businesses, to do well you also need to know the business intimately, be able to manage your time effectively, have good sales ability and be convinced that you will succeed.

This plan is designed to do two things:

• Show you how to write a plan for business where personal service is the only product; and,

• How to write a plan for a business to be started with a small investment.

Note: This plan is based on the business concept of an acquaintance of mine. It is more informal than Antoinette Gorzak's plan for at least three reasons:

1. Antoinette's plan is designed for presentation to bank loan committees and is necessarily more complete;

2. I have used Antoinette's Dress Shop plan to illustrate each of the elements of a thorough business plan, where as the employment agency plan that follows is designed for presentation to relatives and personal friends and can be a little less complete; and,

3. The dress shop is a more risky venture, since it is a brand new business, whereas Eleanor has already proven her profit-making potential—now she is just changing location.

BUSINESS PLAN

CENTRAL PERSONNEL AGENCY

By: Eleanor Buss

March 3,198_

TABLE OF CONTENTS

[NOTE: We omit page numbers here, but be sure to include
them in your own Table of Contents.]

A. Introduction and Request for Funds

This is a request for a loan of $6,000 to establish the Central Personnel Agency as my sole proprietorship. Central Personnel will specialize in providing South City employers with secretarial, clerical and computer (word processing) skilled personnel. I am presently a junior partner in Mid-Mountain Personnel Services, a similar type of personnel agency with headquarters in North City. I manage the branch office in South City. Mid-Mountain provides me with an office in a good, downtown location and a moderate salary. I like what I do and feel that helping people find work is a creative and satisfying activity.

The $6,000 loan, which I am hereby requesting, will enable me to open my own employment agency, make my own business decisions, and substantially increase my income. To do this, I will be competing with my former employer, Ms. Jackie McCabe (dba Mid-Mountain Personnel Agency), to some extent, even though her headquarters is, and will remain, in North City. To minimize any hostility that could hurt business, I have kept Ms. McCabe informed of my plans. She supports them, has agreed to allow me to take over the lease on the South City Office, and is enthusiastic about working out a referral plan under which we will work cooperatively when we are dealing with employers located in each other's prime geographical area.

My best estimate of sales revenue and cash flow (both of which are spelled out in detail in this plan) shows that even using conservative estimates, I will earn a significant profit once my new business has been underway six months. My background experience in the personnel agency field, and past record of success, support my view that I will succeed. I am eager to begin.

B. My Experience and Background

As my resume sets out in detail, since 198_ I have worked for three different employment agencies in this area, successfully finding jobs for many people. This has given me the opportunity to learn the personnel agency business thoroughly, including how to find employers needing workers, and how to locate and screen desirable employees.

During the years I was acquiring this valuable experience, I always planned to open my own business. Last year, in the hope of achieving this goal, I formed a partnership with Ms. Jackie McCabe, who has operated Mid-Mountain Personnel Service in North City for several years. As a junior partner, my responsibility was to open a South City branch office, which I did. My goal was to increase my income, and, to have more control over business decisions than I had as an employee. While the personal relationship between Ms. McCabe and myself is cordial, the partnership has not worked to our mutual satisfaction. This has been largely because Jackie's main office in North City has grown so fast it has consumed all of her energy. This has left me operating the South City branch largely by myself, at the same time that a substantial portion of the profits I have generated go to Jackie under the terms of our partnership agreement.

As part of terminating our partnership agreement, Jackie and I have agreed that I will retain the lease on the present Mid-Mountain office in South City. In addition, we have signed a written agreement (available upon request) which provides that we will share all fees and commissions when one of us places an employee with an employer in the other's primary market area. Having made this agreement, I need accomplish only two more tasks before I can open my business. The first is to take and pass the state personnel agency license examination. I expect to do this in February with little difficulty, as I have received top grades in the preparatory course given by North State Community College. My other task involves the purpose of this proposal. I need to borrow enough money to begin business.

C. Resume: Eleanor 'Ellie' Buss

RESUME OF ELEANOR 'ELLIE' BUSS

Address: 564 Sampson Avenue, South City, ORE 96785; Telephone 567-8976

Business Address: c/o Mid Mountain Personnel Services, 453 Second Street, Suite 300, South City, ORE; Telephone 765-8970

Marital Status: Single

PROFESSIONAL EXPERIENCE

May 1983 to Date: Junior Partner; Mid Mountain Personnel Services. As account executive, I locate employers needing assistance, meet with employers to ascertain their personnel requirements, screen, counsel and evaluate applicants and refer qualified applicants to employer. Also, I assist applicants in preparing resumes and in preparing for interviews. I average ten placements per month, of which one-half are positions where the applicant pays the fees; my gross average billings are $3,500 per month.

1982 to 1983: Account Executive; Woodshaft Personnel Agency. Responsible for all the same functions as listed above. Average gross billing was $3,500 per month, which represented an average of ten placements per month.

1982: Trainee Account Executive; Yolo Personnel Agency. Screened and evaluated applicants; solicited job openings with appropriate clients; completed placements; average billings $2,500 per month.

1981: Purchasing agent; Parsifone Electric. Ordered material and inventory to coincide with contract process, estimated commercial and residential jobs; negotiated all materials purchased to assure cost control and maintain profit margin on bids.

1980 to 1981: Scheduler; Graphicscan. Production scheduling for printing and graphic studio; estimated jobs for clients.

1975 to 1980 Production Schedule; Acme Pre-Built Components Co. Scheduler/coordinator for large manufacturer of structural components; coordinated finish room schedule with customer priority and transportation availability; interface with other departments and sales staff to ensure customer satisfaction.

D. Business Description of The Central Personnel Agency

Central Personnel will specialize in secretarial, clerical, word processing, and computer operator jobs, a field in which there is constant turnover. I will also provide services for technical and mid-management jobs, but expect it to take several years before these latter areas provide a substantial portion of my income.

My particular specialty will be women re-entering the work force after completing family-raising responsibilities. In this connection, I have developed a successful liaison with the South City Women's Resource Center. This group, which is partially funded by grants from local businesses, provides training, seminars and counseling for re-entry women and will provide me with a source of many highly-motivated potential employees.

Because of my two-year history in the personnel business in South City, I have placed many employees and expect that the already developing trend toward much of my business coming from repeats and referrals will continue. Also, in cooperation with the Women's Resource Center, I shall continue to provide detailed counseling to applicants (especially those who have been out of the labor market for several years or more) on how to compose resumes and take interviews, as well as on which jobs to seek. In addition, I plan to work closely with employers to assist them in determining what type of employee they need, how much they should pay, etc. I want employers to feel that my pre-screening is honest and thorough and that by dealing with me they can save time by not having to interview clearly unsuitable candidates.

E. Central Personnel Agency Marketing Plan

1. How I Will Find Qualified Employees

The secret to success in the personnel business in South City is finding high quality employee applicants. Because of the relatively rapid turnover among clerical employees, and because the South City economy is expanding, it is relatively easy to place suitably highly-motivated employees with good skills once they have been identified. Because of my prior two years in this business and this area, many of my initial candidates will come from repeats and referrals from people I have placed. Others will be referred as part of my work with the Women's Resource Center

In my experience, there are several other effective marketing techniques to develop a wider community base. Classified advertising of job openings develops many prospective employees. Also, maintaining an active presence in the Chamber of Commerce and other traditional business and civic organizations enables prospective employers to recognize me as a person of integrity and stability. In addition, as discussed above, I shall continue to expand by association with the South City Women's Resource Center, a group that counsels women re-entering the labor force. I also intend to provide free seminars of my own on "How to Find a Satisfying Job." Finally, I will regularly mail a brief newsletter to all major area employers listing all the job areas for which I have qualified applicants.

2. Competition

South City has three active personnel agencies in addition to the branch of Mid-Mountain, which I now run and which will close as part of the opening of my new business

a. Bill's Personnel Services: This is the oldest and largest in the city. Recently, Bill's has suffered from their own high employee turnover, largely because it is run by an absentee owner. Bill's traditionally advertises heavily and depends on aggressive pricing policies to compete. They provide little employee counseling and, in my opinion, do not screen potential employees with sufficient thoroughness. At Mid-Mountain, I have already demonstrated that my personal approach to the needs of both employers and employees as opposed to Bill's high volume approach is welcomed by the South City market place.

b. Strictly Business: This firm was recently acquired by an experienced professional counselor who heads a staff of three good counselors. Its primary emphasis is on technical management people and it handles clerical and computer operator jobs only as a sideline. Eventually, Strictly Business will be a competitor as I develop more mid-level management clients, but initially, they will not be a problem as our markets are so different.

c. <u>The Woodshaft Organization</u>: This agency has a staff of three and is directly competitive. Woodshaft spends about $1,000 per month on advertising, but does little work with community organizations such as the South City Women's Resource Center. The owner's husband died recently and as an understandable result, the business seems to lack energy. I believe that the Woodshaft Organization will offer the most competition over the next several years. However, because of the expanded South City job market, my own proven track record at Mid-Mountain, and my commitment to hard, creative work, I feel there is plenty of room for my new enterprise to prosper.

3. Market Growth

South City has a large number of the type of jobs I specialize in, with plenty of growth potential. Most of the other agencies are more interested in technical job categories. South Cities' growth as a regional financial and market center will insure commensurate growth in job openings and should encourage the trend for women to re-enter the job market. My approach to counseling both employers and employees is unique locally and I expect a continuing growth from my commitment to individual service; because this approach saves everyone time and expense in the long run.

My new downtown location (the office I will take over from Mid-Mountain) is already established, convenient, and close to the Women's Resource Center, with whom I work closely.

[**Note**: If you plan a large service business and need to borrow more money, it would be wise to back up this section with growth projection statistics. These are probably available from local banks, the Chamber of Commerce, etc.]

F. Financial Projection

1. Introduction

The key to the prosperity of Central Personnel Agency lies in quickly getting the business into the black and then building on that initial success.

The profit and loss and cash flow forecasts in Section F of this proposal show a significant profit and positive cash flow from the beginning of operations. These results depend on my ability to generate revenue at the rate of $4,000 per month for the first two months and $5,000 for each month thereafter. I have no doubt about my ability to do this based on the job orders already on the books. This is because I have most of the employee applications necessary to fill these jobs on file and know how to locate the rest. And even if my revenue forecasts for the first two months are off by as much as $1,500 per month (37.5%), I will still be able to pay business expenses, service the loan, and cover my basic living expenses.

2. Loan Security

My personal financial statement is included on the page immediately following the profit and loss forecasts. I believe my personal signature is more than enough security for a loan of $6,000, since I have substantial assets. Nevertheless, I will consider the possibility of pledging some assets as additional security if appropriate. Incidentally, my past personal credit reports will show that several years ago I got behind on my payments on several accounts (I have never defaulted or declared bankruptcy). During the period in question, I was helping several family members who were experiencing emergencies (e.g., illness, sudden loss of work, etc.). These necessitated the diversion of the maximum amount of my financial resources to members of my family who were in greater need. All these problems have since been resolved, the money repaid me, and I am happy to say that all my accounts are current.

3. Central Personnel Agency Profit and Loss Forecast, Year 1

CENTRAL PERSONNEL AGENCY: PROFIT & LOSS FORECAST — YEAR I

	MAR	APR	MAY	JUNE	JULY	AUG	SEPT	OCT	NOV	DEC	JAN	FEB	YEAR I
	1984										1985		
PLACEMENT REVENUE	4000	4000	5000	5000	5000	5000	5000	5000	5000	5000	5000	5000	58000
OPERATING EXPENSES													
RENT	515	515	515	515	515	515	515	515	515	515	515	515	6180
ADVERTISING	300	300	300	300	300	300	300	300	300	300	300	300	3600
TELEPHONE	30	30	30	30	30	30	30	30	30	30	30	30	360
SUPPLIES/POSTAGE	10	10	10	10	10	10	10	10	10	10	10	10	120
INTEREST	150	150	150	150	150	150	150	150	150	150	150	150	1800
TRAVEL/ENTERTAIN.	50	50	50	50	50	50	50	50	50	50	50	50	600
TOTAL EXPENSES	1055	1055	1055	1055	1055	1055	1055	1055	1055	1055	1055	1055	12660
PROFIT BEFORE TAXES	2945	2945	3945	3945	3945	3945	3945	3945	3945	3945	3945	3945	45340

CENTRAL PERSONNEL AGENCY: CASH FLOW FORECAST — YEAR I

	PREOPENING	MAR	APR	MAY	JUNE	JULY	AUG	SEPT	OCT	NOV	DEC	JAN	FEB	YEAR I
USES OF MONEY														
LICENSES/DEPOSITS	1100													1100
WORKING CAPITAL	2000													2000
PRINTING/ADVERTISING	1500	1055	1055	1055	1055	1055	1055	1055	1055	1055	1055	1055	1055	14160
PRINCIPAL REPAYMT.	0-	50	50	50	50	50	50	50	50	50	50	50	50	600
FURNITURE/TELEPHONE	700													700
OWNER'S DRAW	700	1200	1200	1200	1200	1200	1200	1200	1200	1200	1200	1200	1200	15100
TOTAL USES	6000	2305	2305	2305	2305	2305	2305	2305	2305	2305	2305	2305	2305	33660
SOURCES OF MONEY														
LOAN	6000													
REVENUE		4000	4000	5000	5000	5000	5000	5000	5000	5000	5000	5000	5000	58000
TOTAL SOURCES	6000	4000	4000	5000	5000	5000	5000	5000	5000	5000	5000	5000	5000	64000
NET CASH	0-	1695	1695	2695	2695	2695	2695	2695	2695	2695	2695	2695	2695	30340

G. Personal Financial Statement: Eleanor 'Ellie' Buss

PERSONAL FINANCIAL STATEMENT: ELEANOR 'ELLIE' BUSS

ASSETS: at market value:	
Cash in banks	$ 400
Stocks	
United Inc.	450
Universal Corp.	300
Household furnishings	6,000
China collection	2,000
2 Horses	4,000
Horse trailer	1,500
Surrey and buggy	3,000
Tack	1,000
Car, Mazda RX	7,000
Residence	95,000
Total Assets	$ 120,650

LIABILITIES:	
First on property, $771 per month	$ 76,000
Auto loan, $250 per month	6,000
Credit Cards: Visa $80 per month	1,500
Macy's $40 per month	700
Business Loan, $50 per month	3,000
Total Liabilities	87,200

NET WORTH	33,450

ANNUAL INCOME:	
Professional fees	28,000
Dividends	600
Total Income	28,600

ANNUAL EXPENSES:	
Loan Payments: 1st	9,252
Car	2,000
Visa	960
Macy's	500
House Related Expenses (food, rental, etc.)	4,000
Property taxes	950
Insurance	300
Living expenses	10,000
TOTAL EXPENSES	27,962

H. Business Risk Analysis

Every business faces risks. Central Personnel Agency is not an exception. However, I believe that the risks facing my business are manageable. I see nothing that will seriously threaten the business.

Here are the major risks I anticipate and how I plan to deal with them:

1. **Partner Problems**: When faced with the prospect of my leaving and taking an income source away from her, my current partner, Jackie McCabe, the owner of Mid-Mountain Personnel Services, was initially somewhat angry. However, when we discussed the fact that she had more work on her hands in North City than she could cope with and that we could cooperate on future job placements, she became supportive of my starting my own business. Nevertheless, Jackie could still open a competitive agency at any time—which might threaten my new accounts. Therefore, I am volunteering to pay her a one-third share of all future job orders developed from connections I made while the partnership was active. My budget will support this concept as long as my payments to Jackie do not exceed one-third of revenues. I do not expect this to happen, but should it, Jackie had indicated she will accept a deferred payment plan. Within six months to a year, I expect the great majority of my businesses will stem from new contacts and I will no longer need to pay Jackie.

2. **Competition**: There are several competing employment agencies in South City, as discussed in Section E, above. As I am aiming for a slightly different market than the other agencies and have a track record of success in my target area, I do not feel that the competition will hurt me. Even if the other agencies expanded their clerical placements, I think my personal rapport with my clients and the Women's Resource Center should prevent me from suffering any real problem.

3. **Slow Times**: People are hiring now and times are good. When the economy slows down, as it inevitably will, so too will new hires, although because of the high turnover, there is always some demand for clerical help. However, I plan to put aside money when times are good to cushion against future bad times. Also, I plan to reduce the effect of slow times by keeping my overhead low.

4. **Owner's Ability**: I have never operated an independent business before. However, I have been paid on a straight commission basis for some time and am used to the need to perform in order to be paid. I can see no insurmountable problems resulting from being on my own and have already determined the licenses, tax permits, etc. I will need to begin. I plan to use the same bookkeeper and accountant who do the books for Mid-

Mountain Personnel to help with paperwork. In addition, I have a friend who is a small business consultant and I can rely on her advice should I need it.

In short, I believe that I have addressed the major risks facing my business and have demonstrated that those risks are manageable.

I. Capital Spending Plan

Most items of equipment will be leased or rented, so there will be little need for capital beyond working capital and some fees and printing costs:

Printing/stationery	$ 500
Initial advertising	1,000
License application fee	250
Employment agency license fees	250
Business license	50
Insurance deposit	50
First & last month's rent & deposit	1,030
Phone installation	200
New furniture	500
Working capital	2,000
TOTAL CAPITAL	$5,830

Other capital items and most of the furniture have already been paid for. The office building provides a receptionist and copy service as part of the rent.

J. Personal Goals

After trying various careers, I discovered a career I am very good at and which provides me great personal satisfaction. I feel a deep sense of personal accomplishment when a client pays a fee for completing a job hire. That validates my ability. My goal in opening the Central Personnel Agency is to make some money while doing work I basically love.

Appendix 2

Business Plan for a Manufacturing Business

The business plan for DAY INTERNATIONAL, INC. that follows is roughly based on a real plan, although I have changed many details, including the financial projections. And because of space limitations, I have omitted a number of charts and exhibits contained in the appendix to the original plan.

Here, the founders of the company are asking for $75,000 to complete the task of bringing their product to market. They expect sales of nearly a million dollars by the end of the second year of operations. While these numbers may be somewhat larger than those you expect, this plan should serve as a good guide if you plan to operate a manufacturing business. If you use it as a general guide, you should be well-served.

When reading what follows, note the effort that has been put into developing a rational basis for estimating sales volume. The reason for this concentration on sales is the simple fact that the large majority of new products introduced into the marketplace do not sell well enough to produce a profit. Investors and lenders know this, of course, and therefore will want to see solid data to support your claim that your product will be different. Therefore, any plan for a manufacturing business, no matter how small, should answer the question, "Will people buy my product?"

You will see that this business plan calls for the manufacture of two different products using the same technology. The first is aimed at the commercial market and is reasonably costly; the second targets the consumer market and carries a somewhat lower price.

The founders of DAY INTERNATIONAL believe that a successful business needs more than one product to survive.

While there are some exceptions to that rule, diversification can achieve powerful benefits if one product meets resistance in the marketplace.

You may also note that this plan does not discuss marketing or advertising in detail. This is because DAY INTERNATIONAL, INC. plans to have their distributors and sales representatives handle a great deal of these activities. Were this my business, I would pay a little more attention to marketing. I've learned that a new small business which leaves marketing to someone else often courts disaster. The reason for this is simple. When a product is new, no sales representatives, wholesale or retail outlets have much of a stake in its success. Until they do, they are unlikely to do much to push it.

Finally, you will note that this plan varies somewhat in structure from the ones discussed in the text. This reflects two factors:

• This plan is for a very different type of business (manufacturing rather than retail); and

• The personalities of the founders are different.

Antoinette Gorzak's method of promoting her business idea was to sell herself first and then her business. Frederick Jones and Phillip Court, the principals in DAY INTERNATIONAL, INC. take an approach more compatible with their scientific backgrounds—they concentrate on selling their new technology and the manufacturing specifics that will bring it to market, and keep themselves in the background. Either approach can be effective, although in the case of DAY INTERNATIONAL, INC., I wouldn't mind knowing a little bit more about why the founders think they will be good business people. The important thing these varied approaches illustrate, however, is that there is no one right way to prepare a business plan and loan package. Just as it's important to follow the general rules set out in this book, it is also important to be yourself.

DAY INTERNATIONAL, INC.

AN INVESTMENT OPPORTUNITY

APRIL __ , 198_

DAY INTERNATIONAL, INC.
123 Smith Place
San Jose, CA
Telephone (408) 777-1212

TABLE OF CONTENTS

[**Note:** We have omitted page numbers here, but be sure you include

the appropriate page numbers in your own Table of Contents.]

A. Introduction

After several years of development work, DAY INTERNATIONAL, INC. is ready to market two unique electronic devices, both of which use the same patented new technology. This technology utilizes computerized optic displays to create a programmable message. In commercial application, this is valuable in creating commercial signs and displays which use a scrolling technique to attract and inform customers. As a recreational product, computerized optical displays using this technology can be made to respond directly to music and voice patterns. In other words, full color visual displays result from sound. This product application is particularly attractive to young people.

Extensive market research suggests a large market for both the commercial (Kinet-O-Scroll) and the recreational (Kinet-O-Scope) applications of this product. The commercial programmable sign market already exceeds one million dollars in the United States and is sure to grow quickly. Many units are purchased by retailers for what amounts to instant in-store advertising. In this application, the retailer can program a sign with information on that day's specials, and presto, he has created his own attractive electronic display. The product, which is described more fully in the accompanying Product Description (Section E, below), has several features not now commercially available, including a wide choice of type styles. It will also have a substantial price advantage over other products now on the market. The consumer recreational market for this product is not fully tested, but there are a number of exciting potential uses (see Section E, Product Description).

DAY INTERNATIONAL, INC. is incorporated under the laws of the state of California and is ready to begin operations. The founders have spent several years of hard work preparing for this time and have made substantial personal investments. They are eager to proceed. However, because their personal financial resources are not adequate to manufacture and distribute sufficient units, they are prepared to offer a one-third share of the corporation for an equity investment of $75,000. The enclosed financial projections demonstrate that if projections are met, there will be a very profitable return for the investor.

B. Company Description

DAY INTERNATIONAL, INC. was incorporated in California on June 1, 198_ as an outgrowth of Day Kinetics, a partnership formed in November of 198_. The corporation was organized to manufacture and sell several electronic display items for commercial and recreational purposes. The technology on which these products is based is covered by U.S. Patent (Smith #5676890123), for which an exclusive license has been obtained by the corporation. DAY INTERNATIONAL's offices are at 123 Smith Place, San Jose, CA, and the telephone number is (408) 777-1212. All stock is held by Frederick R. Jones and Phillip Court who, along with several family members, occupy seats on the Board of Directors.

Two seats on the Board of Directors are still to be filled. A minority shareholder, or shareholders who invest $75,000, will be permitted to seat two directors by majority vote. The majority shareholders are willing to prepare a formal shareholder's agreement, with the idea of protecting the interests of the minority shareholders.

C. Patent Status

Phillip Court, one of the directors and officers of DAY INTERNATIONAL, INC., obtained an exclusive license to the U.S. Patent on which the Kinet-O-Scroll and Kinet-O-Scope are based (Smith #5676890123) in 198_. This license was granted by the original inventor of the process, Elmo Smith, for 2% of any eventual sales of either product during the term of the patent, until Smith receives $200,000, 1.5% until Smith receives a total of $400,000, and 1% thereafter. This license is cancelable if Smith does not receive $20,000 per year with the first payment, due November 198_. The license excludes certain applications of the Smith patent which are not related to the corporation's products.

In 198_, Phillip Court assigned an exclusive sub-license for the remaining term of the patent (10 years) to DAY INTERNATIONAL, INC. The payment to Court for this sub-license is 2% of the sales, expiring when sales of $100 million have been attained. In addition, the corporation has assumed the obligation for the royalty payment to Smith. All patent documentation, license agreements and contracts are available to the potential investor or his agent upon request.

D. Corporation Management

The founders of DAY INTERNATIONAL, INC. are: Phillip V. Court and Frederick R. Jones, Jr.

The directors, officers and key employees of this corporation are as follows:

1. Frederick R. Jones, Jr., President, Treasurer and Director;

2. Phillip V. Court, Vice-President, Secretary, and Director;

3. Edmund R. Jones, Project Manager, Accounts Payable Manager.

Frederick R. Jones, Jr., age 52, has over 25 years of experience as an engineer, project engineer, program manager, proposal manager, marketing specialist, department head, program director, marketing manager, etc. His specialty has been in automatic control systems and advanced display systems for manned aerospace vehicles. Mr. Jones' prior associations have been with Butterworth Aircraft (1954-1969), Vokar Electronics (1969-1979), and National Computer (1979 to date).

Phillip V. Court, age 46, has over 19 years of experience as an analog design engineer and manager. He is presently Engineering Manager of Data Conservation Products at a major corporation headquartered in Santa Clara, California. Prior to this, he was the first vice-president of engineering of Ultradesign, a $200M sales semi-custom integrated circuit house. Mr. Court has authored numerous applications, brochures, several articles for a national electronics publication, and holds three U.S. patents.

Edmund R. Jones, age 23, holds a Bachelor of Science degree in marketing from the University of California, Irvine. He has gained valuable work and customer interface experience at such companies as Reliable Insurance, VSV Associates and West Coast Semiconductor. In addition to his varied work experience, he has demonstrated community service and leadership capabilities, most significant of which are his leadership of a troop of explorer scouts and his membership in several regional opera societies. Edmund R. Jones is the son of Frederick R. Jones, Jr.

E. Product Description

The corporation plans to manufacture two products, both based on the Smith Patent. One of these is the Kinet-O-Scroll, which is designed for commercial applications. The other is the Kinet-O-Scope, which is designed for home recreational use. They are more fully described as follows:

The Kinet-O-Scroll: This consists of a scrolling "Times Square" type message sign. Using its patented technology, DAY INTERNATIONAL can produce a moving sign that is more versatile, attractive and economical than existing units. Basically, the Kinet-O-Scroll displays alphanumeric, graphic and animated characters in full color. While the sign can be manufactured in numerous sizes, we plan to start with a unit with a screen measuring three feet vertically and four feet horizontally. All sorts of businesses, including restaurants, bars, banks, stores, real estate offices, airline terminals, bus stations, etc., can use the Kinet-O-Scroll sign to inform customers of special events or offers at a comparatively low cost. The cost of the unit may further be reduced by users who make arrangements (tie-ins) for reimbursement by advertisers. This could be the case where companies that manufacture products or services that a retailer sells (e.g., clothing, insurance, soft drinks) pay for advertising or provide their product at a better discount in exchange for advertising. There are hundreds of thousands of potential locations for such a low-cost merchandising tool.

The Kinet-O-Scroll is completely developed, and tested. The first 100 production units have been completed and a production capacity of over 200 units per month is established. It is projected that the sales rate will rapidly build to a minimum of 100 units per month. This sales estimate, as well as long-term sales projections for the Kinet-O-Scroll, are based on extensive research into the need for this type of product, as well as into the sales history of existing (but inferior) products. This research has also involved consumer studies in which potential customers were asked to rate a variety of existing products with our new product.

In outline form, here is what we believe to be an objective summary of the "strip sign" market and the sales potential of the Kinet-O-Scroll:

• The Kinet-O-Scroll is unique in its mode of operation and its technical capacities. For example, it provides at least twice the visual resolution of other scrolling signs.

• There are at least a dozen manufacturers of programmable strip signs that can perform a somewhat similar but less efficient function. The total annual sales of these products has been estimated (*Advertising Graphics Magazine,* Fall 198_) to be $10,000,000. This represents a 27% increase from last year.[1] The existent products are all very similar. No one manufacturer commands a dominant share of the market.

• The published prices of the strip signs that come the closest to having features similar to the Kinet-O-Scroll are in the $1,500 to $2,000 range. As a result of efficiencies of design inherent in the patented technique used in the Kinet-O-Scroll, DAY's published list price is under $1,000.

• DAY's service contract (available on request) is above average for the industry.

• DAY's warranty policy (available on request) is above average for the industry.

The accompanying chart shows the sales volume of programmable signs in the United States in millions of dollars. In

----

[1]Many small manufacturing operations will have a local marketing strategy at least to start. Don't let the sort of marketing survey presented here intimidate you. The same sort of approach can be used for any manufacturing business. For example, if you plan to make a better raisin-chocolate chip cookie, or a crisper lemon tortilla chip for local distribution, think about ways you can convincingly tell a potential lender or investor that it will sell.

198_, the total market for programmable signs is estimated to be $12,000,000. The corporation forecasts sales of 1,200 Kinet-O-Scroll units by the second year of production at a wholesale price of $550. These sales forecasts are considered conservative in that they are based on a market penetration of only five percent.

The Kinet-O-Scope: The Kinet-O-Scope features a small-sized screen which produces optic displays in response to both the human voice, music and other sounds. The display is in full color and the patterns created in response to sound are stunning. It is particularly attractive to young children experimenting with the sound of their own voice, although this is by no means the only market. People who love music, for example, are commonly fascinated by the Kinet-O-Scope. To accurately estimate the sales potential of the Kinet-O-Scope in the consumer market is difficult, as no directly comparable products exist.

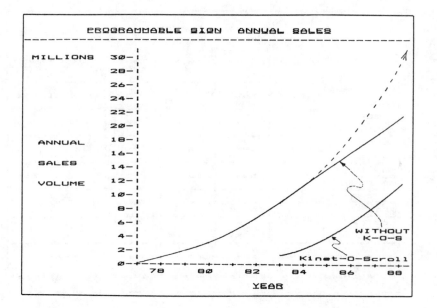

In an effort to arrive at as accurate an estimate as possible, extensive consumer interviews were conducted. The Kinet-O-Scope Market Research Chart which follows summarizes the results of these interviews. When compared directly with the most similar products available (these are not nearly as good, but there is nothing else), 56% of the people asked preferred the Kinet-O-Scope. Even more persuasive, 49% of those tested would buy it for themselves, while 62% of those tested would buy it for a gift.

While there are no specific competitive products to the Kinet-O-Scope, it is clear that there is a distinct market for products of this type. This conclusion is arrived at by looking at good sales figures for Light Organs, Infinity Lights, Wave

Devices, Volcano Lights, Rain Lamps, and other products which use
light in innovative and creative ways.

Perhaps the best example of the size of the market is the
Lava Light, a less technically advanced, but lower cost product.
According to its manufacturer, Volcano Simplex International, over
6,000,000 units have been sold in four years, with 3,000,000 sold
last year. If we consider a wholesale average selling price of
$90, this represents over $270,000,000.

DAY INTERNATIONAL, INC. conservatively estimates that it
will sell about 2,800 units of the Kinet-O-Scope in the second
year of operations, for a wholesale dollar sales volume of $420,000
($150 per unit). Further sales growth is expected in later years.
Note that this unit volume is a tiny fraction of the Volcano
Lights' sales volume for last year.

```
+-----------------------------------------------------------------+
|                      MARKET - RESEARCH                          |
|    -------------------------------------------------------------|
|             | WAVE | KINET | RAIN  | LIGHT | LAVA  | INFNY       |
|             |      |  -O-  | LAMP  | ORGAN | LIGHT | LIGHT       |
|             |      | SCOPE |       |       |       |             |
| ------------|------|-------|-------|-------|-------|-------       |
| PREFFWRED   |      |       |       |       |       |             |
| THIS        |  9%  |  56%  |  9%   |  1%   |  10%  |  13%        |
| PRODUCT     |      |       |       |       |       |             |
| ------------|------|-------|-------|-------|-------|-------       |
| CHECK       |      |       |       |       |       |             |
| IF YOU      |  2%  |  0%   |  2%   |  3%   |  4%   |  0%         |
| OWN IT      |      |       |       |       |       |             |
| ------------|------|-------|-------|-------|-------|-------       |
| WOULD       |      |       |       |       |       |             |
| BUY IT      | 32%  |  49%  |  18%  |  9%   |  16%  |  24%        |
| FOR SELF    |      |       |       |       |       |             |
| ------------|------|-------|-------|-------|-------|-------       |
| WOULD       |      |       |       |       |       |             |
| BUY IT      | 43%  |  52%  |  18%  |  11%  |  5%   |  31%        |
| AS GIFT     |      |       |       |       |       |             |
| ------------|------|-------|-------|-------|-------|-------       |
| ESTIMATED   |      |       |       |       |       |             |
| RETAIL      |  *   |104.52 |  *    |  *    |  *    |  *          |
| PRICE       |      |105.54 |       |       |       |             |
| ------------|------|-------|-------|-------|-------|-------       |
| NOTICE      |      |       |       |       |       |             |
| OF          |      | 12%   |       |       |       |             |
| AVAIL       |      | 5.3x  |       |       |       |             |
| ------------|------|-------|-------|-------|-------|-------       |
| AGE: UNDER 16=3%   16-20=10%   21-34=41%   35+=45%              |
|                                                                 |
| *  AVERAGE TOTAL ESTIMATE= $168.69 ACTUAL= $160.00             |
+-----------------------------------------------------------------+
```

F. Marketing Plan

The channels of distribution for the Kinet-O-Scroll and
Kinet-O-Scope will include direct sales by corporate personnel to
selected major accounts, and the use of manufacturer's
representatives (sales reps), distributor's dealers (wholesalers)
and international trading companies to reach the rest of the
market. We do not anticipate establishing our own factory sales
force. With regard to international sales, except for "opportunity
sales," we will not launch our formal effort until we have
adequately penetrated the domestic market. However, we will
explore licensing our technology abroad.

In the beginning, DAY will team with a limited number of sales reps and wholesalers who have proven abilities in successfully introducing new electronic products. At first, the emphasis will be on developing market penetration in a few carefully chosen regions near our manufacturing facility. The reason for this approach is to properly identify effective pricing techniques and marketing strategies. Information gathered will be used to fine tune stocking requirements, manufacturing rate requirements, etc. for general North American distribution. In short, we want to be sure we are walking with a firm and steady tread before we begin to run.

It is particularly important that we work with good sales reps. To this end, we have contacted a number of people knowledgeable in the field (retailers, several small manufacturers of retail products, and two major wholesalers) for recommendations. We have received a number and plan to hold interviews soon. We also plan an aggressive campaign of marketing and consumer electronics and related trade shows. To this end, we have designed and built an attractive display booth that will effectively demonstrate both products in operation. We plan to attend up to ten trade shows in the next six months and will use them as a showcase around which to meet potential sales reps, wholesalers, and customers. In addition, this will be our opportunity to introduce our products to the consumer electronics industry press. To this end we have hired an experienced media consultant to work with us in developing a press package. She has already arranged for several articles about the Kinet-O-Scroll to appear in several popular electronics magazines.

DAY INTERNATIONAL, INC. anticipates expanding the principal sales areas toward the end of the first year of operation. As part of doing this, we hope our higher manufacturing volume will allow us to lower prices as well as to improve our products based on feedback from buyers. In subsequent years, DAY will continue to use sales reps and wholesalers as our main sales force, since they provide many advantages over employee salespeople. The principal one, of course, is that these people are paid a commission (sales reps) or fixed percentage (wholesalers) of each sale, but receive no salary.

Wholesalers have been included in the overall merchandising effort because they offer an established way to get our product onto the retailer's shelves. Many have been in business for years and offer retailers local delivery, computerized ordering and other valuable services. They are expected to play a supportive role to our sales reps, who will have the primary responsibility to call on retailers, write orders, etc. Many of these orders will be forwarded to the wholesaler to be filled (depending on the territory and our contractual relationship with the wholesaler), while others will be processed directly by DAY. It is important that the sales reps and the distributors work as a team. The representatives will be brought on early enough to have a strong voice in distributor selection.

G. Company Facilities

DAY INTERNATIONAL, INC. presently occupies a leased facility of slightly over 1,800 square feet at a very reasonable rental. We use this for both manufacturing and offices. We rent an additional 150 square feet of storage space nearby. There is no concern for the continuation of the lease on our principal location, as it contains three yearly options to renew at the same rate, plus a percentage increase equal to the yearly increase in the consumer price index. The existing space is adequate to support production of at least 400 Kinet-O-Scrolls per month. Nearby space is available for expansion at reasonable rates when we need it. An adequate work force of assembly workers and shipping room personnel is available. We expect to pay between $4.50 and $8.00 per hour to hourly employees, depending on their duties.

Several additions to the corporation's existing manufacturing equipment are required. Assuming, however, that the Kinet-O-Scroll production rate does not exceed 400 units per month, these expenditures will not exceed $30,000. When production increases above 400 units per month, we expect to show enough profit that a bank loan to finance more equipment will be easy to obtain. We can supply a potential investor with more details about these estimates upon request.

H. Product Development Status

Phillip Court began development work based on the Smith Patent in 198_. The idea was to develop operational prototypes of both the Kinet-O-Scroll and Kinet-O-Scope to prove manufacturing feasibility. After design and operation of several early prototypes of each product, a full set of engineering drawing and parts specifications was prepared for each in 198_. Parts were procured from suppliers and a number of units assembled. Next, units manufactured and assembled were subjected to life testing. With some minor modifications, an operational life of up to 4488 hours without failure was achieved for the Kinet-O-Scope. This compares to an expected typical homeowner's usage of 1,000- to 2,000 hours. We are confident from these results that with some minor material changes, which are now in the works, and the introduction of improved mechanical alignment techniques, which we plan to do soon, a 10,000-hour design goal is achievable. This is our goal.

The Kinet-O-Scroll must, of course, be designed to meet far more stringent requirements. We aim to market a product that will last at least four years, even if used 24 hours a day. Tests based on time simulations indicate that we have achieved this goal.[2]

The Kinet-O-Scroll is already in production (units are available for testing), as described in Section I of this proposal, just below. The Kinet-O-Scope can be in production within 120 days after additional financing is obtained.

I. Production Status

The Kinet-O-Scroll is the first and only DAY product currently in production. Here is a summary of both how things are going on the shop floor and how our marketing efforts are developing, as of June 1, 198_.

Material: There is no difficulty obtaining parts for the Kinet-O-Scroll. The two parts with the longest order lead time are the motor and keyboard, which at present take about eight weeks to get. There has been some recent indication of possible stretch-outs on certain semiconductor products we have been getting on a next-day basis, but this is not expected to be a significant problem. Just in case, however, we have identified several alternative suppliers.

Inventories: The first one-hundred Kinet-O-Scroll units have been committed to production. At the time of this writing, 35 are complete and the remainder are 90% finished, requiring only cabinets and final assembly. All materials, with the exception of the cabinets, which should arrive in ten days, are in stock to complete these units, as well as an additional 100 units. The first 100 units are primarily for demonstration purposes. We will use several at trade shows, give others to the electronics press for evaluation, and use still others as samples for our sales reps and wholesalers.

Credit Terms: Although DAY has established 30 day terms with over half of its suppliers, we are presently on cash terms with the rest, due to our low-cash position and because we are a new corporation with no proven credit history. We expect to arrange 30-60 day terms with all our suppliers within six months. New financing will help us accomplish this.

J. Financial Statement and Projections

As DAY INTERNATIONAL, INC. is still in the start-up phase, we have yet to develop positive cash flow.[3] As the attached profit

---

[2] Test results are based on the brush/slip ring life—methods at three times normal speed which has been independently monitored and are available upon request.

[3] Since DAY is already in operation, it would be normal practice to include a balance sheet of operations to date. I do not do this here both because of space limitations and because we have not

and loss projection and cash flow forecast indicate, however, we expect the corporation to begin to generate a positive cash flow and profit before the end of the first year of operations. To accomplish this, however, the corporation needs a total infusion of $150,000 equity capital. The founders have contributed half of that amount and are seeking additional investors for the balance. In exchange for a seventy-five thousand dollar investment, the investor would receive a one-third interest in the company. This would take the form of one-third of the stock in DAY INTERNATIONAL, INC. and one-third representation on the Board of Directors. As noted in Section B above, the existing shareholders are willing to design a shareholders' agreement to protect the interests and representation of the minority shareholders.

Profit projections show that if all goes according to plan, the investor can expect no return of his investment in the first year of operation and substantial profit in the second. (The accompanying profit and loss forecast shows a $338,225 profit for DAY INTERNATIONAL, INC. by the second year.) While the dividend policy of the corporation will be to pay modest dividends to investors in order to generate capital for growth, it can be expected that some of the available profits will be distributed to the shareholders. In addition, the investor can expect significant capital gains should the corporation make a public stock offering. The founders plan to do this after several years of profitable operations.

Warning! Heretofore you have read an optimistic review of DAY INTERNATIONAL, INC. and its chances for future success. However, you should realize that the electronics business is a risky one. Many new products fail, while others succeed for a brief time, only to be supplanted by new technology, changing public taste, or foreign competition. While we believe we have planned carefully and well for each of these eventualities, we want to emphasize one thing loud and clear. Anyone who invests in DAY INTERNATIONAL, INC. is taking a substantial risk. While we believe chances of success are excellent, this is by no means guaranteed. In short, please do not invest money that you can't afford to lose.

K. Product Selling Prices and Costs

The projections included in this business plan are based on several assumptions about product selling prices and costs.

---

discussed balance sheet in the text. If your business is in operation, ask your bookkeeper or accountant to help you prepare a balance sheet and include it.

WHOLESALE SELLING PRICE

Kinet-O-Scroll	(Commercial Unit)	$550.00
Kinet-O-Scope	(Recreational Unit)	150.00

DIRECT (VARIABLE) COST OF EACH UNIT

	Packaging	Direct Labor	Direct Material	Total Cost
Kinet-O-Scroll	$11.00	$24.00	$100.00	$135.00
Kinet-O-Scope	2.00	12.00	30.00	44.00

These figures do not allow for any corporation overhead, such as rent, management costs, etc. They are based solely on the cost of producing each unit. All costs and selling prices have been developed through extensive market research and profitability analysis. They reflect the realities of the market place, as well as the price objectives of management.

DAY INTERNATIONAL PROFIT & LOSS FORECAST — YEAR 1

YEAR I	JAN	FEB	MAR	APR	MAY	JUNE	JULY	AUG	SEPT	OCT	NOV	DEC	YEAR TOTAL
SALES - UNITS KISS	10	20	30	40	50	60	70	80	90	100	100	100	750
KISP	1	1	1	1	1	1	1	1	1	1	1	1	
KIOL	1	1	1	1	1	1	1	1	1	1	1	1	
SALES $	5500	11000	16500	22000	27500	33000	38500	44000	49500	55000	55000	55000	412500
COST OF SALES	1340	2680	4020	5360	6700	8040	9380	10720	12060	13400	13400	13400	100500
GROSS PROFIT	4160	8320	12480	16640	20800	24960	29120	33280	37440	41600	41600	41600	312000
OPERATING EXPENSES													
ADMIN. EXP. INCL. RENT	15000	15000	15000	15000	15000	15000	15000	15000	15000	15000	15000	15000	180000
PROMOTIONAL EXPENSE	3500	3500	3500	3500	3500	3500	3500	3500	3500	3500	3500	3500	40000
SALES COMMISSIONS	0	0	550	1100	1650	2200	2750	3300	5500	5500	5500	5500	33550
ROYALTY	0	0	450	880	1320	1760	2200	2640	4400	4400	4400	4400	26840
TOTAL EXPENSES	18500	18500	19490	20480	21470	22460	23450	24440	28410	28410	28410	28410	282390
PROFIT	(14340)	(10180)	(7010)	(3840)	(670)	2500	5670	8840	9040	13200	13200	13200	29610

YEAR II	JAN	FEB	MAR	APR	MAY	JUNE	JULY	AUG	SEPT	OCT	NOV	DEC	TOTAL YEAR
SALES-UNITS KISS	100	100	100	100	100	100	100	100	100	100	100	100	1200
KISP	50	75	100	125	150	200	250	300	350	400	400	400	
KIOL	—	—	—	—	—	—	—	—	—	—	100	200	300
SALES $	62500	66250	70000	73750	77500	85000	92500	100000	107500	115000	117500	120000	1,087,500
COST OF SALES	15650	16775	17900	19025	20150	22400	24650	26900	29150	31400	32700	34000	290700
GROSS PROFIT	46850	49475	52100	54725	57350	62600	67850	73100	78350	83600	84800	86000	796800
OPERATING EXPENSES													
ADMIN. EXP incl. RENT	20000	20000	20000	20000	20000	20000	20000	20000	20000	20000	20000	20000	240000
PROMOTIONAL EXPENSE	8250	8250	8250	8250	8250	8250	8250	8250	8250	8250	8250	8250	99000
SALES COMMISSIONS	3750	3975	4200	4425	4650	5100	5500	6000	6450	6900	7020	7200	65170
ROYALTIES	3125	3312	3500	3688	3875	4250	4625	5000	5375	5750	5875	6000	54375
TOTAL EXPENSES	35125	35537	35950	36363	36775	37600	38375	39250	40075	40900	41145	41450	458545
PROFIT	11725	13938	16150	18362	20575	25000	29475	33850	38275	42700	43655	44550	338255

Business Plan For a Project Development

The business plan that follows is based on numerous project development plans I have analyzed, with the scale reduced somewhat to fit the small entrepreneur (in this case, John Reynolds) who plans to fix up one house. To make it interesting, I have burdened my house example with inadequate plumbing and the need for electrical work. In addition, because the house has been unoccupied for several years, most of the windows are broken and the flowers are in sad shape.

To sum up briefly, John hopes to purchase and fix up an old house. His plan is to invest $5,000, pay himself a salary of $1,500 per month for the three months the house is being refurbished, and then sell it for an immediate cash profit of $12,445 plus a note from the buyer for an additional $12,000.

The documentation presented here is fairly extensive because the entrepreneur in question will need to borrow money from a bank to complete the work. Occasionally, if a person has private financing, it's possible to complete a development project with less data. While this presentation is for a real estate development project, specifically fixing up and reselling a single family residence, all of the same processes are used for other development projects. Regardless of the project specifics, the developer must establish his ownership of the property or concept, back up his assumption about its projected selling price and the terms of sale, and verify his estimates of the costs necessary to complete the project. Copies of many of the documents referred to in this example have not been included because they are all imaginary. Of course, for a real project, all relevant documents should be included. In this instance, John Reynolds would surely include copies of the preliminary title report, showing him as property owner, copies of a title insurance policy, showing that the title is good, a copy of the note in favor of the Jones, showing that the balance due them is really $55,000, and copies of all bids from the subcontractors who will do the work. In addition, the bank will surely require that a written appraisal of the property be included. If the bank has experience with John Reynolds on other house rebuilding projects in the particular area, they may accept his judgment as to the amount of work needed to put the house in a condition to justify the projected selling price. If not, he may have to provide a written report from the city inspector's office, stating what work must be done to get an occupancy permit.

Loan Request for Single Family

Residential Reconstruction

November __ , 19__

Jonathan Reynolds

847 Market Street

Chicago, Illinois

Telephone (312) 555-7896

Introduction

This is a request for a loan of $30,000 for the purpose of improving a single family residence at 2246 1/2 Hamilton Street, Chicago, Illinois. This house has been condemned by the City because of faulty plumbing and wiring, and because it has been unoccupied for about three years. As a result, there is substantial work to be completed before the house can be legally and profitably sold. According to City inspectors and a private structural engineer, the house is basically sound, except for the items referred to. Specifically, the City has stated they will issue an occupancy certificate once the tagged items are completed to their satisfaction.

Upon completion, the house will have a market value of $120,000 based on comparable sales in the area. Since I have acquired the house for $60,000, the proceeds from the sale of the house will be more than enough to pay the existing note on the house and to pay back the new loan.

Market Value of the House on Completion

Although I have not yet acquired a formal appraisal of the value of the house, a study of recent sales of comparable property in the area supports the value of $120,000. This area of Chicago is undergoing the "Gentrification" process whereby younger, upwardly mobile families are buying older houses and fixing them up to live in or resell. People in the market appear to be willing to pay a premium for a rebuilt house, both in terms of selling price overall and on a square foot basis. And appraisal can be obtained from any number of qualified appraisers at the lender's request.

Comparable Values

Address	Sold For	Sq. Ft.	Features	Age	$/Sq. Ft.
2357 7th St.	$119,000	1,3385	3 br, 1 ba	50+	85.92
406 Bean Ave.	125,000	1,500	3 br, 2 ba	45	83.33
2765 9th St. (This house was condemned also)	75,000	1,200	2 br, 1 ba	50+	62.50
567 Bacon Ave. (This house was condemned; the developer thinks he will sell it for $130,000 upon completion of work)	50,000	1,400	3 br, 2 ba	60+	35.71
1988 7th St. (This house just sold after being fixed up)	135,000	1,450	3 br, 2 ba	40+	93.10

Terms of the Expected Sale

Lenders in this neighborhood have be lending 80% of the appraised value of a first mortgage. Buyers normally expect to make a down payment of 10% to 15% of the selling price. Many sellers are willing to carry a second mortgage on the houses for up to 10% of the selling price. This loan request is based on that set of assumptions about the terms of the resale.

Title to the Property

As evidenced by the preliminary title reports and policy of title insurance issued to me by Chicago Title Insurance, I presently own the property. The escrow closed on October __, 19__ at the Third National Bank. A copy of the escrow documents and title policy are available upon request. I bought the property for a total price of $60,000, by making a down payment of $5,000 in cash with the seller, Mr. and Mrs. Jones of 2336 South Whale Drive in Joliet, agreeing to carry back a $55,000 mortgage on the property The mortgage calls for monthly payments of $800 until October __, 19__, one year from the close of escrow, when the entire remaining amount of $52,500 becomes due and payable.

Costs to Remodel the Property

    As previously discussed, the house needs new plumbing and
wiring, a new roof and other repairs, including replacing most of
the windows, refinishing the floors, and making improvements to
the kitchen to make it marketable for the $120,000 value. I plan
to have the electrical and plumbing, floor, roof and kitchen work
done by licensed subcontractors and to do most of the additional
cosmetic work myself.

    Here is a summary of the low bids I have received so far to
the portion of the work to be completed by outside contractors.
Copies of the bids are available on request.

   Plumbing: Install new water and gas pipe, install new
        water heater, use existing sinks and tub, but install new
        faucets and toilet

        Low bid from Smith Brothers,
        114 Prince William St., Gary, Indiana $ 2,998.00

   Electrical: Pull new wiring throughout, install good quality
        fixtures and outlets, using existing boxes and wall holes
        wherever possible, all to code.

        Frank Rochioloi, Chicago, Illinois $ 5,006.00

   Roof: Install four ply roof over entire house
        with 20 yr. guarantee, to code.

        Johnson Roofing, Chicago, Illinois $ 800.00

   Flooring and Carpeting: Repair flooring and install
        new wall-to-wall carpeting and/or linoleum throughout.

        Acme Floors, Chicago, Illinois $ 4,958.00

   Kitchen Cabinets: Build and install new cabinets in kitchen.

        Urizola Cabinets, Chicago, Illinois $ 1,995.00

   Range and Refrigerator:

        Gordon's Appliances, Chicago, Illinois $ 1,398.00

        Total Bid Items $17,155.00

    I plan to do some of the cosmetic work myself during the
three months construction time. That work will include painting
inside and out, replacing window glass and other miscellaneous
items as the need arises. Cost of materials for those items will
be about $500. Building permits and fees for the electrical,

plumbing and roof work will add another $500. This will put the
total costs, excluding finance costs, at $18,155. As seen on the
project profit and loss projection on the next page, I have
estimated financing and other costs to total an additional
$10,200.

In making my financial projections, I make the following
assumptions:

• That the house will be sold within six months of the start
of construction and that the Jones's note will then be paid off.
(The interest portion of this $800 note is $550.)

• Costs of the new loan of $30,000 secured by a second
mortgage are assumed to be two points, which amounts to a $600
loan origination fee.

• Interest is assumed to be at a 12% annual rate for a six-
month total interest cost of $1,800 for that loan.

• Finally, I assume that I shall pay myself a salary of
$1,500 per month during the time I actually work on the house.

Profit and Loss Forecast for the Remodeling and Resale of

Single Family Residential House at 2246 1/2 Hamilton St., Chicago

Item	$
Sales Price	120,000.00
Less 6% Commission	7,200.00
Net Proceeds	112,800.00
Less	
Cost to Acquire House	60,000.00
Plumbing	12,998.00
Electrical	5,006.00
Roof	800.00
Flooring and Carpeting	4,958.00
Kitchen Cabinets	1,995.00
Range and Refrigerator	1,398.00
Miscellaneous Supplies	500.00
Building Permit, City Fees	500.00
Subtotal Costs	78,155.00
Carrying Costs 6 months Interest on mortgage	3,300.00
Interest and loan fees on new loan, 6 months	2,400.00
Developer Overhead (3 months living expense at $1,500)	4,500.00
Total Project cost	88,355.00
Project Profit	$24,445.00

Sales Price

The sales price of the 2246 1/2 Hamilton St. house, after remodeling, is forecast to be $120,000, with a 6% real estate commission paid in cash from the proceeds of the sale. We expect to carry back a new second mortgage in favor of the buyer of approximately $12,000, which means the seller will pay a cash down payment of $12,000 and obtain a new first mortgage of $96,000 from a bank or savings and loan. The new first mortgage will pay off the existing first and second loans on the property. Thus, at the conclusion of the transaction, I expect to receive the cash difference between the total of all outstanding loan balances,

sales commissions and other cash expenses. In addition, I shall
have a second mortgage on the property in the amount of $12,000.

Cash Flow

As seen on the attached cash flow for this project, there
are only three infusions of cash into the project. The first one
is the money from my savings account with which I made the down
payment on the property and with which I obtained the engineering
studies which convinced me that the project will make money. The
second infusion will be the proceeds from the loan being applied
for here. The third and final infusion will be from the sale of
the property, and that will be sufficient to pay off the other
loans on the project and leave a cash profit of $12,445. The
difference between the cash profit and the book profit shown
earlier is accounted for by the $12,000 second mortgage I'll carry
in favor of the buyer.

Based on demand for housing in the subject area, I believe
that the house will probably sell far more quickly than I have
forecast; in fact, I have already had two inquiries about selling
it. Based on my experience with remodeling houses of this age and
location, I am sure that the $30,000 requested will be adequate to
complete the repairs necessary to increase the value of the house.

PROJECT DEVELOPMENT CASH FLOW — REMODEL HOUSE AT 2246½ HAMILTON

	PRE-CONSTR.	MONTH 1	MONTH 2	MONTH 3	MONTH 4	MONTH 5	MONTH 6	TOTAL COST	TOTAL HOUSE SALE
SOURCES OF CASH									
SAVINGS	5300								
NEW SECOND		30000							
SALE - DOWN PAYMENT - NEW									120000
- FIRST									96000
TOTAL SOURCES	5300	30000							168000
USES OF CASH									
PRE-CONSTRUCTION									
DOWN PAYMENT TO BUY HOUSE	5000								
CITY INSPECTION FEE	100								
ENGINEER CONSULT.	200								
TOTAL PRE-CONST.	5300								
CONSTRUCTION									
CONTRACTORS		5718	5718	5718				17155	
SUPPLIES		167	167	166				500	
PERMITS, FEES		250	-	250				500	
INTEREST ON OLD FIRST MORTGAGE		550	550	550	550	550	550	3300	
PRINCIPAL IN OLD FIRST MORTGAGE		250	250	250	250	250	250	1500	
LOAN FEES ON NEW 2ND		600						600	
INTEREST IN NEW 2ND		300	300	300	300	300	300	1800	
DEVELOPER O HEAD		1500	1500	1500				4500	
TOTAL CONSTRUCTION		9335	8485	8735	1100	1100	1100	29855	
SALE - PAYOFF									
SAVINGS OF JR.									5000
PAYOFF OLD FIRST									52500
PAYOFF NEW 2ND									30000
SALES COMMISSION									7200
TOTAL SALE									95700
NET CASH	-0-	20665	<8485>	<8735>	<1100>	<1100>	<1100>	<29855>	123000
CUMULATIVE NET CASH	-0-	20665	12180	3445	2345	1245	145	145	12445

Appendix 4

Blank Forms

Appendix 4 contains the blank forms you will need to fill out for your business plan and loan package. We have provided only one copy of each form, so you may want to xerox the forms and use the xeroxes as you worksheets.

You can use the Profit and Loss Forecasts and Cash Flow Forecasts we have provided as worksheets also. We recommend that you use the standard-size forms available at any office supply or stationery store for your final copies; they'll be easier to work with.

PERSONAL FINANCIAL STATEMENT—ASSETS

CASH

Cash on Hand   Amount

Cash in Banks—Savings

Bank Name	Account #	Date	Balance
1.			
2.			

TOTAL SAVINGS

Cash in Banks—Checking

1.

2.

3.

Money Market Accounts

1.

2.

Miscellaneous Cash
  (Drawers, Safety Deposit Box)

TOTAL CASH AT

STOCKS AND BONDS

STOCKS (Including Mutual Funds)

Name of Stock	No. of Shares	Exchange	Market Price	Date	Market Value
1.					
2.					
3.					
4.					

TOTAL MARKET VALUE OF STOCKS AT

BONDS

Name of Bond	No. of Bonds	Market Price	Date	Market Value
1.				
2.				

TOTAL MARKET VALUE OF BONDS AT

REAL ESTATE PROPERTY

Description	Date	Market Value
1.		
2.		
3.		

TOTAL MARKET VALUE OF REAL PROPERTY AT

TRUST DEEDS AND MORTGAGES

Note Description	Monthly Payments	Current Balance
1.		
2.		

TOTAL CURRENT BALANCES ON TRUST DEEDS AND MORTGAGES

CASH VALUE OF YOUR LIFE INSURANCE

Policy Description	Cash Surrender Value
1.	
2.	

TOTAL CASH VALUE

ACCOUNTS AND NOTES RECEIVABLE

Note/Account Description	Monthly Payments	Currently Owed
1.		
2.		
3.		

TOTAL NOTES/ACCOUNTS RECEIVABLE

OTHER PERSONAL PROPERTY

Description	Date	Value
1.		
2.		
3.		
4.		
5.		

TOTAL PERSONAL PROPERTY

TOTAL ASSETS

TOTAL ASSETS $ _____

PERSONAL FINANCIAL STATEMENT—LIABILITIES AND NET WORTH

PERSONAL NOTES PAYABLE TO BANKS

Bank	Terms	Payment	Monthly Amount Owed
1.			
2.			

TOTAL NOTES TO BANKS

REAL ESTATE LOANS

Bank (or other lender)	Terms	Payment	Owed
1			
2.			

TOTAL REAL ESTATE LOANS

PERSONAL PROPERTY LOANS

Description	Terms	Payment	Owed
1.			
2.			

TOTAL OTHER ASSETS

LOANS AGAINST LIFE INSURANCE POLICIES

Insurance Co.	Terms	Monthly Payment	Amount Owed
1.			

TOTAL INSURANCE POLICY LOANS

CREDIT CARD AND REVOLVING ACCOUNT BALANCES

Name of Creditor	Average Monthly Payment	Amount Owed
1.		
2.		
3.		

TOTAL CREDIT CARD & REVOLVING CREDIT

ANY OTHER LIABILITIES

Name of Creditor	Terms	Monthly Payment	Amount Owed
1.			
2.			

TOTAL OTHER LIABILITIES

TOTAL LIABILITIES

TOTAL LIABILITIES $ _____

TOTAL LIABILITIES $_____

NET WORTH $_____

TOTAL ASSETS AND LIABILITIES $_____

PERSONAL FINANCIAL STATEMENT
ANNUAL FAMILY INCOME AND EXPENSES

My Annual Income
SALARY AND WAGES

Source	Annual Amount
1.	
2.	
3.	
4.	
TOTAL SALARY AND WAGES	

PEOPLE WHO OWE ME MONEY

Person Owing	Terms	Amount Owed	Annual Payment
1.			
2.			
3.			
TOTAL ANNUAL PAYMENT			$_____

INCOME FROM RENTAL PROPERTY

Source	Annual Amount
1.	
2.	
TOTAL ANNUAL INCOME FROM RENTAL PROPERTY	

DIVIDENDS AND INTEREST

Source	Annual Amount
1.	
2.	
TOTAL DIVIDENDS AND INTEREST	

INCOME FROM BUSINESS OR PROFESSION

Description   **Amount**

1.

2.

TOTAL INCOME FROM BUSINESS OR PROFESSION $_____

OTHER INCOME

Description   **Amount**

[If there are payments or other problems here, attach an explanation.]

TOTAL OTHER INCOME

TOTAL ANNUAL INCOME

TOTAL ANNUAL INCOME $ _____

Annual Living Expenses

REAL ESTATE LOAN PAYMENTS

Creditor	Monthly Payment	Annual Amount
1.		
2.		
3.		

TOTAL REAL ESTATE LOAN PAYMENTS OR RENT

PROPERTY TAXES AND ASSESSMENTS

Property Taxes	Annual Amount
1.	
2.	
3.	

TOTAL PROPERTY TAXES

FEDERAL AND STATE INCOME TAXES

Description	Amount
1.	
2.	

TOTAL TAX PAYMENTS

OTHER LOAN PAYMENTS (Amount Paid in 198_)

Creditor	Monthly Payment	Annual Amount
1.		
2.		
3.		

TOTAL OTHER LOAN PAYMENTS

INSURANCE PREMIUMS

Insurance Companies	Type Policy	Annual Payment
1.		
2.		
3.		

TOTAL INSURANCE PREMIUMS

LIVING EXPENSES

Description	Annual Total

TOTAL LIVING EXPENSES

OTHER EXPENSES

Description	Annual Expenses
1.	
2.	
3.	

TOTAL OTHER EXPENSES

TOTAL ANNUAL EXPENSES

TOTAL ANNUAL EXPENSES $ _____

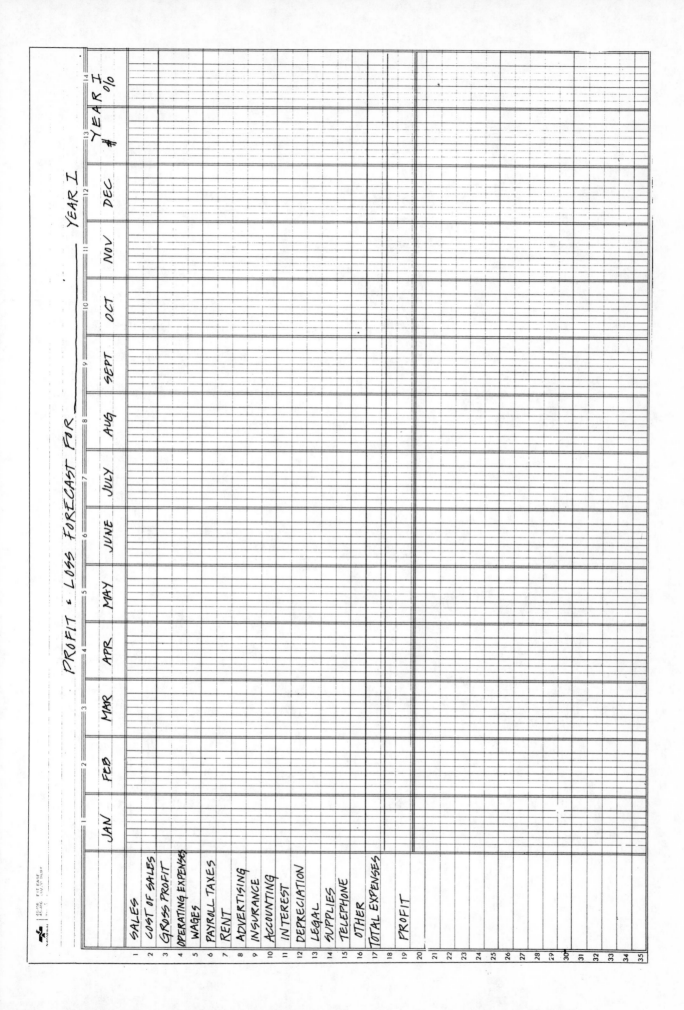

PROFIT & LOSS FORECAST FOR _____ YEAR I _____

	JAN	FEB	MAR	APR	MAY	JUNE	JULY	AUG	SEPT	OCT	NOV	DEC	YEAR I #	YEAR I %
1 SALES														
2 COST OF SALES														
3 GROSS PROFIT														
4 OPERATING EXPENSES														
5 WAGES														
6 PAYROLL TAXES														
7 RENT														
8 ADVERTISING														
9 INSURANCE														
10 ACCOUNTING														
11 INTEREST														
12 DEPRECIATION														
13 LEGAL														
14 SUPPLIES														
15 TELEPHONE														
16 OTHER														
17 TOTAL EXPENSES														
18														
19 PROFIT														

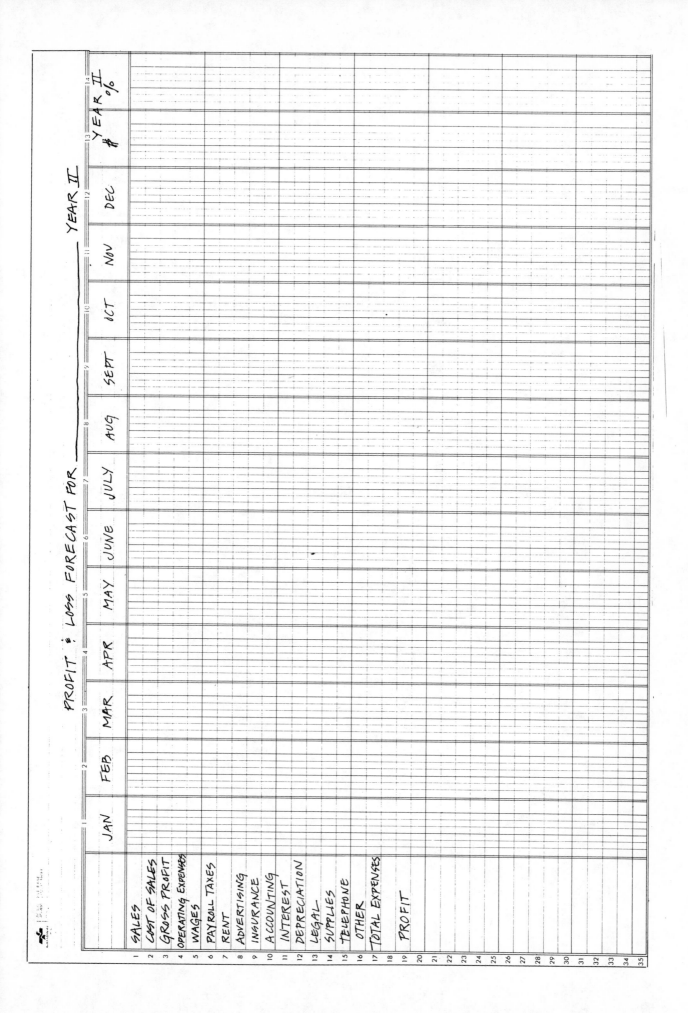

PROFIT & LOSS FORECAST FOR _____ YEAR II

	JAN	FEB	MAR	APR	MAY	JUNE	JULY	AUG	SEPT	OCT	NOV	DEC	YEAR II #	YEAR II %
1 SALES														
2 COST OF SALES														
3 GROSS PROFIT														
4 OPERATING EXPENSES														
5 WAGES														
6 PAYROLL TAXES														
7 RENT														
8 ADVERTISING														
9 INSURANCE														
10 ACCOUNTING														
11 INTEREST														
12 DEPRECIATION														
13 LEGAL														
14 SUPPLIES														
15 TELEPHONE														
16 OTHER														
17 TOTAL EXPENSES														
18														
19 PROFIT														

CASH FLOW FORECAST FOR   YEAR I

	PRE-OPENING	JAN	FEB	MAR	APR	MAY	JUNE	JULY	AUG	SEPT	OCT.	NOV	DEC.	TOTAL YEAR
1	USES OF CASH – PRE-OPENING													
2	OPENING INVENTORY													
3	DEPOSITS – LEASE													
4	UTILITIES													
5	LICENSES													
6	OTHER													
7	EQUIPMENT/FIXTURES													
8	LEASEHOLD IMPROVE													
9	OPENING PROMOTION													
10	OTHER PRE-OPENING													
11														
12														
13	USES – MONTHLY													
14	OWNER'S DRAW													
15	PURCHASES													
16	EXPENSES (from P&L)													
17	PRINCIPAL PAYMENTS													
18	ADJUST P&L FROM QUARTERLY WITHHOLDING													
19	OTHER													
20	TOTAL USES													
21														
22														
23	SOURCES													
24	LOAN													
25	SAVINGS													
26	COLLECTIONS (SALES)													
27	NON-CASH EXPENSE (DEPRECIATION)													
28	OTHER SOURCES													
29	TOTAL SOURCES													
30														
31	CASH BALANCE													
32														
33														
34														
35														

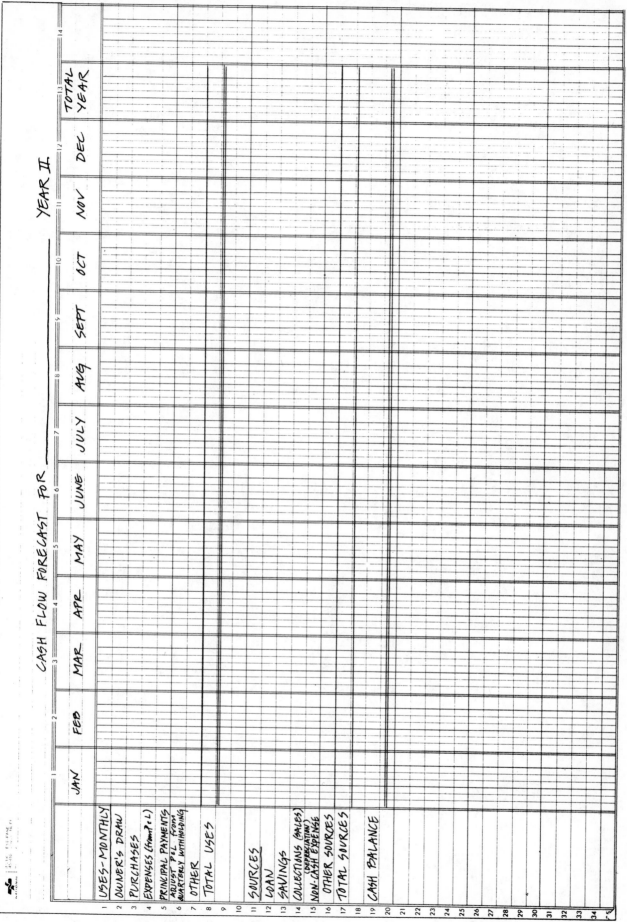

CASH FLOW FORECAST FOR _____ YEAR II.

SOFTWARE

willmaker

Nolo Press/Legisoft

Recent statistics say chances are better than 2 to 1 that you haven't written a will, even though you know you should. WillMaker makes the job easy, leading you step by step in a fill-in-the-blank format. Once you've gone through the program, you print out the will and sign it in front of witnesses. Because writing a will is only one step in the estate planning process, WillMaker comes with a 200-page manual providing an overview of probate avoidance and tax planning techniques. National 3rd Ed.

Apple, IBM, Macintosh	$59.95
Commodore	$39.95

california incorporator

Attorney Mancuso and Legisoft, Inc.

About half of the small California corporations formed today are done without the services of a lawyer. This easy-to-use software program lets you do the paperwork with minimum effort. Just answer the questions on the screen, and California Incorporator will print out the 35-40 pages of documents you need to make your California corporation legal.

California Edition (IBM)	$129.00

the california nonprofit corporation handbook— computer edition with disk

Attorney Anthony Mancuso

This is the standard work on how to form a nonprofit corporation in California. Included on the disk are the forms for the Articles, Bylaws and Minutes you will need, as well as regular and special director and member minute forms. Also included are line-by-line instructions explaining how to apply for and obtain federal tax exempt status—this critical step applies to incorporating in all 50 states. California 1st Ed.

IBM PC 5 1/4 & 3 1/2	$69.00
Macintosh	$69.00

how to form your own texas corporation— computer edition with disk

AttorneyAnthony Mancuso

how to form your own new york corporation— computer edition with disk

AttorneyAnthony Mancuso

More and more business people are incorporating to qualify for tax benefits, limited liability status, the benefit of employee status and financial flexibility. These software packages contain all the instructions, tax information and forms you need to incorporate a small business. All organizational forms are on disk. 1st Ed.

IBM PC 5 1/4 & 3 1/2	$69.00
Macintosh	$69.00

for the record

By attorney Warner & Pladsen. A book/software package that helps to keep track of personal and financial records; create documents to give to family members in case of emergency; leave an accurate record for heirs, and allows easy access to all important records with the ability to print out any section National Edition

Macintosh	$49.95
IBM	$49.95

ESTATE PLANNING & PROBATE

nolo's simple will book & nolo's simple willbook with tape

Attorney Denis Clifford

We feel it's important to remind people that if they don't make arrangements before they die, the state will give their property to certain close family members. If you want a particular person to receive a particular object, you need a will.It's easy to write a legally valid will using this book.

National 1st Ed.	$14.95
wi/30-min audio cassette	$19.95

plan your estate: wills, probate avoidance, trusts & taxes

Attorney Denis Clifford

A will is only one part of an estate plan. The first concern is avoiding probate so that your heirs won't receive a greatly diminished inheritance years later. This book shows you how to create a "living trust" and gives you the information you need to make sure whatever you have saved goes to your heirs, not to lawyers and the government.

National 1st Ed.	$17.95

the power of attorney book

Attorney Denis Clifford

The Power of Attorney Book concerns something you've heard about but probably would rather ignore: Who will take care of your affairs, make your financial and medical decisions, if you can't? With this book you can appoint someone you trust to carry out your wishes.

National 2nd Ed.	$17.95

how to probate an estate

Julia Nissley

When a close relative dies, amidst the grieving there are financial and legal details to be dealt with. The natural response is to rely on an attorney, but that response can be costly. With How to Probate an Estate, you can have the satisfaction of doing the work yourself and saving those fees.

California 3rd Ed.	$24.95

the california nonprofit corporation handbook

Attorney Anthony Mancuso

Used by arts groups, educators, social service agencies, medical programs, environmentalists and many others, this book explains all the legal formalities involved in forming and operating a nonprofit corporation. Included are all the forms for the Articles, Bylaws and Minutes you will need. Also included are complete instructions for obtaining federal 501(c)(3) exemptions and benefits. The tax information in this section applies wherever your corporation is formed.

California 5th Ed. $29.95

how to form your own corporation

Attorney Anthony Mancuso

More and more business people are incorporating to qualify for tax benefits, limited liability status, the benefit of employee status and the financial flexibility. These books contain the forms, instructions and tax information you need to incorporate a small business.

California 7th Ed. $29.95
Texas 4th Ed. $24.95
New York 2nd. Ed. $24.95
Florida 1st Ed. $19.95

1988 calcorp update package

Attorney Anthony Mancuso

This update package contains all the forms and instructions you need to modify your corporation's Articles of Incorporation so you can take advantage of new California laws. $25.00

california professional corporation handbook

Attorney Anthony Mancuso

Health care professionals, marriage, family and child counsellors, lawyers, accountants and members of certain other professions must fulfill special requirements when forming a corporation in California. This edition contains up-to-date tax information plus all the forms and instructions necessary to form a California professional corporation. An appendix explains the special rules that apply to each profession.

California 3rd Ed. $29.95

marketing without advertising

Michael Phillips & Salli Rasberry

Every small business person knows that the best marketing plan encourages customer loyalty and personal recommendation. Phillips and Rasberry outline practical steps for building and expanding a small business without spending a lot of money.

National 1st Ed. $14.00

the partnership book

Attorneys Clifford & Warner

Lots of people dream of going into business with a friend. The best way to keep that dream from turning into a nightmare is to have a solid partnership agreement. This book shows how to write an agreement that covers evaluation of partner assets, disputes, buy-outs and the death of a partner.

National 3rd Ed. $18.95

nolo's small business start-up

Mike McKeever

Should you start a business? Should you raise money to expand your already running business? If the answers are yes, this book will show you how to write an effective business plan and loan package.

National 3rd Ed. $17.95

the independent paralegal's handbook: how to provide legal services without going to jail

Attorney Ralph Warner

A large percentage of routine legal work in this country is performed by typists, secretaries, researchers and various other law office helpers generally labeled paralegals. For those who would like to take these services out of the law office and offer them at a reasonable fee in an independent business, attorney Ralph Warner provides both legal and business guidelines.

National 1st Ed. $12.95

getting started as an independent paralegal (two audio tapes)

Attorney Ralph Warner

This set of tapes is a carefully edited version of Nolo Press founder Ralph Warner's Saturday Morning Law School class. It is designed for people who wish to go into business helping consumers prepare their own paperwork in uncontested actions such as bankruptcy, divorce, small business incorporations, landlord-tenant actions, probate, etc. Also covered are how to set up, run, and market your business, as well as a detailed discussion of Unauthorized Practice of Law.

National 1st Ed. $24.95

29 reasons not to go to law school

Ralph Warner & Toni Ihara

Lawyers, law students, their spouses and consorts will love this little book with its zingy comments and Thurberesque cartoons, humorously zapping the life of the law.—Peninsula Times Tribune Filled with humor and piercing observations, this book can save you three years, $70,000 and your sanity.

3rd Ed. $9.95

murder on the air

Ralph Warner & Toni Ihara

Here is a sure winner for any friend who's spent more than a week in the city of Berkeley…a catchy little mystery situated in the environs and the cultural mores of the People's Republic.—The Bay Guardian

Flat out fun…—San Francisco Chronicle $5.95

poetic justice

Ed. by Jonathan & Andrew Roth

A unique compilation of humorous quotes about lawyers and the legal system, from Socrates to Woody Allen. $8.95

collect your court judgment

Scott, Elias & Goldoftas

After you win a judgment in small claims, municipal or superior court, you still have to collect your money. Here are step-by-step instructions on hwo to collect your judgment from the debtor's bank accounts, wages, business receipts, real estate or other assets.
California 1st Ed. $24.95

chapter 13: the federal plan to repay your debts

Attorney Janice Kosel

For those who want to repay their debts and think they can, but are hounded by creditors, Chapter 13 may be the answer. Under the protection of the court you may work out a personal budget and take up to three years to repay a percentage of your debt and have the rest wiped clean.
National 3rd Ed. $17.95

make your own contract

Attorney Stephen Elias

Here are clearly written legal form contracts to: buy and sell property, borrow and lend money, store and lend personal property, make deposits on goods for later purchase, release others from personal liability, or pay a contractor to do home repairs.
National 1st Ed. $12.95

social security, medicare & pensions: a sourcebook for older americans

Attorney Joseph L. Matthews & Dorothy Matthews Berman

Social security, medicare and medicaid programs follow a host of complicated rules. Those over 55, or those caring for someone over 55, will find this comprehensive guidebook invaluable for understanding and utilizing their rightful benefits. A special chapter deals with age discrimination in employment and what to do about it.
National 4th Ed. $15.95

everybody's guide to small claims court

Attorney Ralph Warner

So, the dry cleaner ruined your good flannel suit. Your roof leaks every time it rains, and the contractor who supposedly fixed it won't call you back. The bicycle shop hasn't paid for the tire pumps you sold it six months ago. This book will help you decide if you have a case, show you how to file and serve papers, tell you what to bring to court, and how to collect a judgment.
California 7th Ed. $14.95
National 3rd Ed. $14.95

billpayers' rights

Attorneys Warner & Elias

Lots of people find themselves overwhelmed by debt. The law, however, offers a number of legal protections for consumers and Billpayers' Rights shows people how to use them.
Areas covered include: how to handle bill collectors, deal with student loans, check your credit rating and decide if you should file for bankruptcy.
California 8th Ed. $14.95

for sale by owner

George Devine

In 1986 about 600,000 homes were sold in California at a median price of $130,000. Most sellers worked with a broker and paid the 6% commission. For the median home that meant $7,800. Obviously, that's money that could be saved if you sell your own house. This book provides the background information and legal technicalities you will need to do the job yourself and with confidence.
California 1st Ed. $24.95

homestead your house

Attorneys Warner, Sherman & Ihara

Under California homestead laws, up to $60,000 of the equity in your home may be safe from creditors. But to get the maximum legal protection you should file a Declaration of Homestead before a judgment lien is recorded against you. This book includes complete instructions and tear-out forms.
California 6th Ed. $8.95

the landlord's law book: vol. 1, rights & responsibilities

Attorneys Brown & Warner

Every landlord should know the basics of landlord-tenant law. In short, the era when a landlord could substitute common sense for a detailed knowledge of the law is gone forever. This volume covers: deposits, leases and rental agreements, inspections (tenants' privacy rights), habitability (rent withholding), ending a tenancy, liability, and rent control.
California 2nd Ed. $24.95

the landlord's law book: vol. 2, evictions

Attorney David Brown

Even the most scrupulous landlord may sometimes need to evict a tenant. In the past it has been necessary to hire a lawyer and pay a high fee. Using this book you can handle most evictions yourself safely and economically.
California 1st Ed. $24.95

tenants' rights

Attorneys Moskowitz & Warner

Your "security building" doesn't have a working lock on the front door. Is your landlord liable? How can you get him to fix it? Under what circumstances can you withhold rent? When is an apartment not "habitable?" This book explains the best way to handle your relationship with your landlord and your legal rights when you find yourself in disagreement.
California 10th Ed. $15.95

the deeds book: how to transfer title to california real estate

Attorney Mary Randolph

If you own real estate, you'll almost surely need to sign a new deed at one time or another. The Deeds Book shows you how to choose the right kind of deed, how to complete the tear-out forms, and how to record them in the county recorder's public records.
California 1st Ed. $15.95

dog law

Attorney Mary Randolph

There are 50 million dogs in the United States—and, it seems, at least that many rules and regulations for their owners to abide by. *Dog Law* covers topics that everyone who owns a dog, or lives near one, needs to know about dispute about a dog injury or nuisance.

National 1st Ed. $12.95

the criminal records book

Attorney Warren Siegel

We've all done something illegal. If you were one of those who got caught, your juvenile or criminal court record can complicate your life years later. The good news is that in many cases your record can either be completely expunged or lessened in severity.

The Criminal Records Book takes you step by step through the procedures to: seal criminal records, dismiss convictions, destroy marijuana records, reduce felony convictions.

California 2nd Ed. $14.95

draft, registration and the law

Attorney R. Charles Johnson

This clearly written guidebook explains the present draft law and how registration (required of all male citizens within thirty days of their eighteenth birthday) works. Every available option is presented along with a description of how a draft would work if there were a call tomorrow.

National 2nd Ed. $9.95

fight your ticket

Attorney David Brown

At a trade show in San Francisco recently, a traffic court judge (who must remain nameless) told our associate publisher that he keeps this book by his bench for easy reference.

If you think that ticket was unfair, here's the book showing you what to do to fight it.

California 3rd Ed. $16.95

how to become a united states citizen

Sally Abel Schreuder

This bilingual (English/Spanish) book presents the forms, applications and instructions for naturalization. This step-by-step guide will provide information and answers for legally admitted aliens who wish to become citizens.

National 3rd Ed. $12.95

how to change your name

Attorneys Loeb & Brown

Wish that you had gone back to your maiden name after the divorce? Tired of spelling over the phone V-e-n-k-a-t-a-r-a-m-a-n S-u-b-r-a-m-a-n-i-a-m?

This book explains how to change your name legally and provides all the necessary court forms with detailed instructions on how to fill them out.

California 4th Ed. $14.95

legal research: how to find and understand the law

Attorney Stephen Elias

Legal Research could also be called Volume-Two-for-all-Nolo-Press-Self-Help-Law-Books. A valuable tool for paralegals, law students and legal secretaries, this book provides access to legal information—he legal self-helper can find and research a case, read statutes, and make Freedom of Information Act requests.

National 2nd Ed. $14.95

family law dictionary

Attorneys Leonard and Elias

Written in plain English (as opposed to legalese), the Family Law Dictionary has been compiled to help the lay person doing research in the area of family law (i.e., marriage, divorce, adoption, etc.). Using cross referencs and examples as well as definitions, this book is unique as a reference tool.

National 1st Edition $13.95

intellectual property law dictionary

Attorney Stephen Elias

This book uses simple language free of legal jargon to define and explain the intricacies of items associated with trade secrets, copyrights, trademarks and unfair competition, patents and patent procedures, and contracts and warranties.—IEEE Spectrum

If you're dealing with any multi-media product, a new business product or trade secret, you need this book.

National 1st Ed. $17.95

the people's law review: an access catalog to law without lawyers

Edited by Attorney Ralph Warner

Articles, interviews and a resource list introduce the entire range of do-it-yourself law from estate planning to tenants' rights. The People's Law Review also provides a wealth of background information on the history of law, some considerations on its future, and alternative ways of solving legal problems.

National 1st Ed. $8.95

the living together kit
Attorneys Ihara & Warner
Few unmarried couples understand the laws that may affect them. Here are useful tips on living together agreements, paternity agreements, estate planning, and buying real estate.
National 5th Ed. $17.95

how to do your own divorce
Attorney Charles E. Sherman
This is the book that launched Nolo Press and advanced the self-help law movement. During the past 17 years, over 400,000 copies have been sold, saving consumers at least $50 million in legal fees (assuming 100,000 have each saved $500—certainly a conservative estimate).
California 14th Ed. $14.95
Texas 2nd Ed. (Sherman & Simons) $12.95

california marriage & divorce law
Attorneys Warner, Ihara & Elias
For a generation, this practical handbook has been the best resource for the Californian who wants to understand marriage and divorce laws. Even if you hire a lawyer to help you with a divorce, it's essential that you learn your basic legal rights and responsibilities.
California 9th Ed. $15.95

practical divorce solutions
Attorney Charles Ed Sherman
Written by the author of *How to Do Your Own Divorce* (with over 500,000 copies in print), this book provides a valuable guide both to the emotional process involved in divorce as well as the legal and financial decisions that have to be made.
California 1st Ed. $12.95

how to modify and collect child support in california
Attorneys Matthews, Siegel & Willis
California has established landmark new standards in setting and collecting child support. Payments must now be based on both objective need standards and the parents' combined income. Using this book, custodial parents can determine if they are entitled to higher child support payments and can implement the procedures to obtain that support.
California 2nd Ed. $17.95

your family records
Carol Pladsen & Attorney Denis Clifford
Most American families keep terrible records. Typically, the checkbook is on a shelf in the kitchen, insurance policies are nowhere to be found, and jewelry and cash are hidden in a coffee can in the garage. Your Family Records is a sensible, straightforward guide that will help you organize your records before you face a crisis.
National 2nd Ed. $14.95

a legal guide for lesbian and gay couples
Attorneys Curry & Clifford
A Legal Guide contains crucial information on the special problems facing lesbians and gay men with children, civil rights legislation, and medical/legal issues.
National 4th Ed. $17.95

how to adopt your stepchild in california
Frank Zagone & Mary Randolph
For many families that include stepchildren, adoption is a satisfying way to guarantee the family a solid legal footing. This book provides sample forms and complete step-by-step instructions for completing a simple uncontested adoption by a stepparent.
California 3rd Ed. $19.95

how to copyright software
Attorney M.J. Salone
Copyrighting is the best protection for any software. This book explains how to get a copyright and what a copyright can protect.
National 2nd Ed. $24.95

the inventor's notebook
Fred Grissom & Attorney David Pressman
The best protection for your patent is adequate records. The Inventor's Notebook provides forms, instructions, references to relevant areas of patent law, a bibliography of legal and non-legal aids, and more. It helps you document the activities that are normally part of successful independent inventing.
National 1st Ed. $19.95

legal care for your software
Attorneys Daniel Remer & Stephen Elias
If you write programs you intend to sell, or work for a software house that pays you for programming, you should buy this book. If you are a freelance programmer doing software development, you should buy this book.—Interface
This step-by-step guide for computer software writers covers copyright laws, trade secret protection, contracts, license agreements, trademarks, patents and more.
National 3rd Ed. $29.95

patent it yourself
Attorney David Pressman
You've invented something, or you're working on it, or you're planning to start...Patent It Yourself offers help in evaluating patentability, marketability and the protective documentation you should have. If you file your own patent application using this book, you can save from $1500 to $3500.
National 2nd Ed. $29.95

nolo

SELF-HELP LAW BOOKS & SOFTWARE

ORDER FORM

Quantity	Title	Unit Price	Total

Sales Tax (CA residents only):

7%	Alameda, Contra Costa, San Diego, San Mateo & Santa Clara counties
6 1/2%	Fresno, Inyo, LA, Sacramento, San Benito, San Francisco & Santa Cruz counties
6%	All others

Subtotal _____

Sales Tax _____

TOTAL_____

Method of Payment:

☐ Check enclosed

☐ VISA   ☐ Mastercard

Acct # _____ Exp._____

Signature _____

Phone ( ) _____

Mail to:

**NOLO PRESS
950 Parker Street
Berkeley CA 94710**

Ship to:

Name_____

Address _____

_____

**For faster service, use your credit card and
our toll-free numbers:**

Monday-Friday 8-5 Pacific Time

US		1-800-992-6656
CA	(outside 415 area)	1-800-445-6656
	(inside 415 area)	1-415-549-1976
General Information		**1-415-549-1976**

Prices subject to change

Please allow 1-2 weeks for delivery

Delivery is by UPS; no P.O. boxes, please

ORDER DIRECT AND WE PAY POSTAGE & HANDLING!

One Year Free!

Nolo Press wants you to have top quality and up-to-date information. The ***Nolo News***, our "Access to Law" quarterly newspaper, contains an update section which will keep you abreast of any changes in the material in **How to Write a Business Plan** that will be of interest to you. You'll find interesting articles on a number of legal topics, book reviews and our ever-popular lawyer joke column.

Send in the registration card below and receive FREE a one-year subscription to the ***Nolo News*** (normally $9.00).

Your subscription will begin with the first quarterly issue published after we receive your card.

- -

NOLO PRESS
How to Write a Business Plan Registration Card

We would like to hear from you. Please let us know if the book met your needs. Fill out and return this card for a FREE one-year subscription to the *Nolo News*. In addition, we'll notify you when we publish a new edition of **How to Write a Business Plan.** (This offer is good in the U.S.only)

Name _____

Address_____

City _____ State _____ Zip_____

Your occupation_____

Did you use information from this book to start up a small business? ____Yes, ____No

Did you find the information in the book helpful?

(extremely helpful) 1   2   3   4   5 (not at all)

Where did you hear about the book?

Have you used other Nolo books?____Yes, ____No

Where did you buy the book?_____

Suggestions for improvement:_____

_____

_____

_____

_____

_____

_____

_____

_____

_____

_____

_____

▲

[Nolo books are]..."written in plain language, free of legal mumbo jumbo, and spiced with witty personal observations."

—ASSOCIATED PRESS

▲

"Well-produced and slickly written, the [Nolo] books are designed to take the mystery out of seemingly involved procedures, carefully avoiding legalese and leading the reader step-by-step through such everyday legal problems as filling out forms, making up contracts, and even how to behave in court."

—SAN FRANCISCO EXAMINER

▲

"...Nolo publications...guide people simply through the how, when, where and why of law."

—WASHINGTON POST

▲

"Increasingly, people who are not lawyers are performing tasks usually regarded as legal work... And consumers, using books like Nolo's, do routine legal work themselves."

—NEW YORK TIMES

▲

"...All of [Nolo's] books are easy-to-understand, are updated regularly, provide pull-out forms...and are often quite moving in their sense of compassion for the struggles of the lay reader."

—SAN FRANCISCO CHRONICLE

- -

Affix
25¢
Stamp

NOLO PRESS
950 Parker St.
Berkeley, CA 94710